€ 48,-

Documentation:
F. HIRAUX
*Centre de Recherches
sur la Communication en Histoire*

Translation:
Dr. E.J.L. BACON

Photography:
Th. DAVID and J.-J. ROUSSEAU

Design:
L. VAN DEN EEDE

D. 1984/703/6

©1984 by Fonds Mercator, Antwerp

No part of this book may be reproduced in any form by print, photoprint, microfilm or any other means without written permission from the publisher.

Printed in Belgium.

ISBN 90 6153 131 4/CIP

Frontispiece:

Portrait of Georg Gisze. Painted on wood in London in 1532 by Hans Holbein the Younger (1497-1543).
Berlin, Staatliche Museum, Gemäldegalerie.

This painting was the first order placed with Holbein by one of the merchants established in London. He did so as a demonstration of Holbein's talent. Many of the Stalhof merchants subsequently commissioned him.
Georg Gisze, the twelfth or thirteenth of a family of Cologne merchants transferred to Danzig, was born on April 2, 1497; he died in February 1562.
The Giszes had a room and warehouse in the London Stalhof.
Above the name of the model, G. Gisze, is his motto: NULLA SINE MERORE VOLUPTAS *(there is no joy without sorrow).*
On the white paper top left:
Didukiovi. Imagine Georgii Gysenii Ista refert vultus qua cernis imago Georgi Sic oculos vivos sic habet ille genas. Anno aetatis suae XXXIII. Anno Dom(ini) 1532.

"This picture that you see reproduces the features of the visage of Georg Gisze. And his eyes are really thus and so are his cheeks."
On the letter he is holding in his hand: Dem erszamen Jergen Gisze to Lunden in Engelant mynen broder to handen *(to the eminent Georg Gisze in London, England, to be handed over by my brother).*
The table is covered with an ornamental, richly decorated Anatolian table cover, a splendid example of this kind of knotted carpet which is so often found in Holbein's works and which is sometimes called 'Holbein carpet'.
Pens, scissors, an inkpot, a seal, a ring, a clock and a box containing coins are spread about the table which is lighted by carnations, rosemary and basil in a Venetian vase.
On the walls: keys, rings, a seal, a pair of goldsmith's scales and a precious string box.

EUROPE OF THE NORTH SEA AND THE BALTIC

Albert d'Haenens

EUROPE OF THE NORTH SEA AND THE BALTIC
The World of the Hanse

Preface by
ETIENNE DAVIGNON

FONDS MERCATOR

A REFERENCE TO ORIGINAL MEMORIES OF EUROPE

Faced with the challenges experienced by European unification, it is indispensable to be able to refer to original memories so as better to situate what it is proposed to undertake and the acquirements on which reasons to hope are founded.

This book about the Hanse comes out just at the right time. I strongly recommend it both to men of culture and to men of action.

Since its origin, Europe owes its vitality to its different poles and contrary constituents. This work reveals the economic, social and cultural part played by the North Sea and the Baltic from the 12th to the 16th centuries; it invites our reflection on the influence the northern part of our continent had on the rest of it.

The men, merchants from the North, appear. Privileging their own means, commercial traffic and the market-place, rather than violence and the battlefield, they animated the circulation of goods between East and West, North and South, from the 12th century onwards. Their practices engendered a culture and vision of the world which still today mark the urban scene, from Bruges to Danzig, from Bergen to Lisbon.

Professor d'Haenens and an international team of eminent historians familiarize us with the dynamism of that culture which respects differences and the realism of a concept which valorizes surpluses by bringing them into commercial traffic.

They tell us, discreetly but steadily, that European cultural patrimony is remarkably rich. It is as well to emphasize that, as the 21st century approaches, so that Europe may live better, learn from history and, profiting by that experience, at last develop fully.

ETIENNE DAVIGNON
Vice-President
of the Commission
of the European Communities

CONTENTS

The Hanse: a way of managing surpluses	A. d'Haenens	11

STRUCTURES AND MEN

The Baltic towns

Structure and spatialization of surpluses and margins: the town	A. d'Haenens	15
The topographical evolution of the Baltic Hanseatic towns	H. Stoob	51

The Merchants 63

Intermediaries	A. d'Haenens	65
Employers	J. Ellermeyer	93
Men of power	J. Ellermeyer	105

PRACTICES: HANSEATIC TRADE

Buying and selling 119

Commercial techniques	R. Sprandel	121
Hanseatic merchandise	F. Lerner	131

Organizing maritime traffic 147

Harbour activities	K. Slaski	149
The Hanse ships	K. Slaski	157

Managing the Hanse business houses 173

The Oosterlingenhuis in Bruges	J.-P. Sosson	175
The Peterhof in Novgorod	J. Blankoff	183
The Stalhof in London	A. d'Haenens	189
The Tyskebryggen in Bergen	A. d'Haenens	197
The Oosters Huis in Antwerp	J. Van Roey	207

Dealing with Hanse partners 217

The Hanse and the Rhine	Ph. Dollinger	219
The Hanse and France	S. Abraham-Thisse	229
The Hanse and England	A. Lewis	241
The Hanse and Italy	G. Rossetti	249
The Hanse and Poland	H. Samsonowicz	259
The Hanse and the Russian world	N. Angermann	267
Mapping the Hanse	K. Friedland	273

A DAILY ENVIRONMENT: THE TOWN

Constructors of urban realities 279

Lubeck	A. d'Haenens	281
Luneburg	A. d'Haenens	311
Bremen	A. d'Haenens	335
Goslar	A. d'Haenens	343
Stralsund	A. d'Haenens	353
Torun	A. d'Haenens	365
Danzig	A. d'Haenens	375

LONG-LASTING DYNAMISM

The flow of surpluses to the East 389

When the Hanse was strong	Ph. Dollinger	391
The slow process of disintegration	H. Van der Wee	405
The Hanse and Marxist historiography	K. Fritze	415

THE WORLD OF THE HANSE TODAY	A. d'Haenens	419
INDICES		421

The Hanse, a Way of Managing Surpluses

It is a law of life that any change springs from surplus or margin, and that was how it was in Europe. It began its change and expansion in the 11th century when the surpluses with which it was to swell itself committed it to going beyond its limits.

It was in the margins that medieval Europe managed its surpluses: in hamlets, remote spots, the margins of original tribal communities. In towns, rurality margins. In the regions East of the Elbe, margins to be conquered from an overflowing West.

It set about it in its own way. Clearing land, colonizations, urban foundations, trade and artisanry: western ways of managing surpluses.

The Hanseatic happening can be seen as a manifestation of that management. The history of the Hanse has fascinated me for twenty-five years.

This book attempts to express that fascination and the result of its exploration. It is the fruit of a convergence of intellectual, affective and material investments and competences, without which it could not have existed.

Research by my internationally known learned colleagues, and their contributions, form the essential part, as does the confidence and friendship of a publisher who, so that culture may be a living thing, agreed to take all the risks. The enthusiasm, devotion and intelligence of an associate at the Communication in History Research Centre at Louvain-la-Neuve. The go-ahead attitude of a photographer who has always been involved in our Centre's adventures. The patience and art of a maker-up who combines technique with intuition and sensitivity.

To them and to all the craftsmen who worked on this magnificent object of book-learning, I dedicate this element of our Western memory. May it enable us better to glimpse the call of the 21st century.

Louvain-la-Neuve. Whitsun 1984.

ALBERT D'HAENENS
*Professor at Louvain University,
Director of the 'Centre de Recherches
sur la communication en Histoire'.*

Structures and Men

The Baltic Towns

The town was the nodal element of the Hanseatic world.
The merchants lived in it and it was from the town that the networks through which surpluses circulated were managed. It concentrated, to despatch or distribute. It attracted overflows and turned them into profits.
The towns in the Baltic space were almost all new ones; their final structures did not go back beyond the 12th century and colonization.
They were not the product of a progressive, organic genesis, but the effect of systematic, rational wills which caused them to rise from virtually nothing. There were princely decisions and clever promotional campaigns to attract surpluses from the West. Stadtluft macht frei!. Town air makes one free!
East of the Elbe, the urban phenomenon was something new, a social and cultural transfer in virgin soil of urban tradition, the programmed transposition of a Western founder system: the first product to be imported, and the most important.
The Baltic towns were like Cistercian spaces, they were concentrated and organized around an empty space: here the marketplace and there the cloisters. There were similar functional constructions around this quadrilateral: the burghers' church corresponded to the conventional one, the Town Hall to the capitular room, the covered markets and warehouses to the store-cupboards. One and the same enclosure, both real and symbolic, whilst all the traffic converged on the centre.
There were not only space analogies. For one as for the other, there was the same concern with a common statutory model. Like Citeaux, Lubeck, taking pattern from Soest, acted as a patron, an institutional and administrative prototype. Just as the General Chapters of the Order were held in Citeaux, so the annual conventions of the Hanse (Hansetag) were held in Lubeck.
These analogies cannot be over-emphasized. Cistercian monasteries and Baltic towns both proceeded with organizational imagination, worked with identical logic and a common go-ahead spirit. Abbeys, towns, manifestations, structured space projections, surpluses and marginality as managed by the West. [A. d'H.]

ALBERT D'HAENENS

Structure and Spatialization of Surpluses and Margins: The Town

Like other towns in the Middle Ages, those on the Baltic were marginal. They spread along the shores and frontiers, for they lived on and by surpluses. From the West they digested overflows; in the margins they managed its surpluses.
All the towns revolved around the same structure.
Their centre was an area of availability, a place for meeting, a space for commercial traffic. It was an unfilled, empty space, propitious for social projection and invention. The communal church, the Town Hall, the covered market and the houses of guilds and corporations were grafted on to it.
The periphery of the town was enclosed by monumental surrounding walls, solid and visible, serving as skin, clothing and armour for the enormous urban body. The gates let in and regulated the rhythm of supplies. The walls were there to be seen and touched, inside and out. The men and women of the town, uprooted, having broken away from their previous identifying landmarks, needed to be explicit about their new territories and their freshly constituted spaces; the surrounding wall reassured them by cutting them off from the country and the outer world.
The houses were situated between the market-place and the surrounding wall. The older ones were of stone, the new, Flemish-pattern housing estates were of brick. They were arranged in draught-board style, on long, narrow plots parsimoniously cut out for the pioneer immigrants.

1. Abraham welcomed by Melchisedech.
A retable by Hans Bornemann of Hamburg between 1444 and 1447.
From the Premonstrant Abbey in Heiligenthal, abolished at the Reformation.
Now in St. Nicholas, Luneburg.

2. The town of Luneburg before 1450.
Part of the picture by Hans Bornemann.

The countryside is so detailed and precise that it enabled the painting to be situated between 1444 and 1447.
This realistic document also has an emblematic and fanciful dimension.
Beginning in the 15th century, the inhabitants of western towns were clearly aware of the space to which they belonged; the image by which they identified that space is both precise and symbolic. Urban mentality was then capable of rationalizing and looking objectively at its actual symbols, its own image.

THE BALTIC TOWNS

3. Market day in Antwerp (at the Meir and Meirbrug) at the end of the 16th century. Anonymous painting from the Antwerp school.
Brussels, Musées Royaux des Beaux Arts.

It was then that brick houses were built. Groups of buyers. An abundant variety of goods; peasants with their wares were most numerous.
What originally (in the 11th and 12th centuries) was peripheral and uninhabitable, has become central and active. Axis and dynamics of space and urban evolution, features of the change in the original space under effects and efforts of all kinds.

THE MAIN SQUARE

The empty central space served as the market-place, where the urban community got their supplies. Whereas in the monastic space it was available for relations with God (vertical axis), in the town it was filled with social practices (horizontal axis), commercial traffic and valorization.

In big towns there were often several markets: for cattle, hay, cereals, meat, wood and coal, fish, salt, wine, etc.

Every week, on specified days, tradesmen, craftsmen and peasants came there to sell their wares on fixed sites grouped by professional and corporative affinities.

The ground on which the butchers and others had their stalls was owned by the families of the founders of the town, to whom the stall-holders paid rent for their site.

At a later date the town arranged the ground floor of its Town Hall as a covered market, mainly for cloth, and cellars which brought it a good income.

4. Couple of peasants at the market.
An engraving by Albert Dürer (Nuremberg 1471-1528), 1519.
Nuremberg, Germanisches Nationalmuseum.

Like all the people from the country who came to the market in town, they brought the surplus of what they cultivated at home: milk, eggs, poultry, for sale to the townsfolk.
The man has an outer garment in a poor state. On the other hand the leather of his high boots seems good and strong. There has been no stinginess as regards the raw material. Rightly so, for his boots are very important to him for his work.

5. Lubeck market at the beginning of the 14th century.
According to Westermann's atlas.

A. Notre-Dame church. B. Cemetery. C. Market. D. Pillory. E. Balance. F. Market for coals. G. Market for hay. H. Merchants' street. J. Butchers' street.

1. Gunsmiths. 2. Butchers. 3. Bakers. 4. Belt-makers. 5. Money changers. 6. Shoemakers. 7. Grocers. 8. Needle makers. 9. Felt-makers. 10. Herringmongers. 11. Haberdashers. 12. Coiners. 13. Goldsmiths. 14. Roast viands caterers. 15. Saddle-makers. 16. Cloth cutters. 17. Tanners. Around 1300 there were 250 stalls and light material shops on Lubeck market.

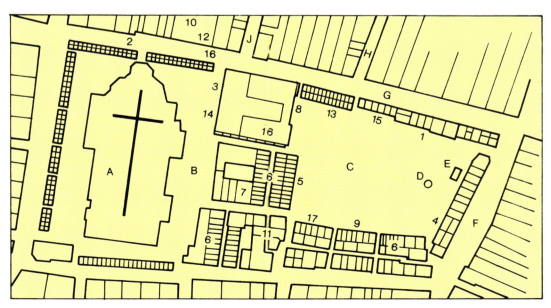

THE BALTIC TOWNS

A theatre

The main square was the town's theatre, for everyone and for all sorts of reasons and games (and gaming).

A theatre for the people, a space where there was life and where celebrations for the people took place, on market days or when the annual fair came. It was, too, a space for anger and grumbling on days of insurrection.

It was also a theatre for the patriciate and the bourgeoisie, who showed off in their order and organization. In a closed space visible to everyone, their components and those who embodied them could be counted. Their roles and social behaviour could be weighed up, appreciated and also criticized.

Processions and shows were organized on the occasion of celebrations marking the most important moments of the liturgical and civil year, such as the beginning of Lent, Easter and Christmas.

The shows, which were supposed to reconstitute biblical and evangelical scenes, were the opportunity to practise criticism which could regulate urban social life.

On the main square of Wismar in 1464 an *Osterspiel* (Easter play) represented the Resurrection and the Descent into Hell, localizing them in the Baltic region. This provided the opportunity for vigorous, social satire: the baker was suspected of selling hollow loaves, the shoemaker of using poor quality leather, the brewer of watering down his beer.

6. Mardi gras (Shrove Tuesday) on Nuremberg market in 1539.
Anonymous water colour on paper; early 17th century.
Nuremberg, Germanisches Nationalmuseum.

It was customary for the sons of patrician families to celebrate the beginning of Lent blithely. Here, they deride the Protestant preacher Andrew Osiander, sitting in a boat representing Hell. The carnival ended badly. Fighting broke out in front of the house of the austere moralizer. The Reformation put a stop to that kind of merry-making.

STRUCTURE AND SPATIALIZATION

A stage

7. Wedding procession on Bremen market, early 17th century.
Anonymus painting dating from the 1620's. Bremen, Landesmuseum.

On the left: the Schütting, the house of the merchants' guild, rebuilt in 1537-39 by the Antwerp architect Jan den Buscheneer. On the right: the Town Hall which has just been rebuilt (1595-1616). The procession is passing between the Rathaus and the Roland, sculptured by the Parler studio and, here again, marvellously polychromatic.

The market-place was also the scene of authority and power.

As the urban community asserted its autonomy and power, it tended to exercise justice on the market-place and to regulate corporative organization there.

The market, weights and measures and food regulations, together with punishments, progressively came under its control, at the expense of the lord of the place.

Justice was rendered on the main square. Offences were punished there in public, except for the death sentence. Market justice, as in Luneburg, was exercised under the archways of the Town Hall. Nearby stood the pillory (*Pranger, Kaak, Stock, Schandstein, Schandpfahl, Schandkorb*) and the Roland attesting to that power of which they were the permanent instrument and symbol.

A centre The main square was still and especially a multi-purpose centre, the very heart of the urban body.

From the start, the founders divided the central space in half: the town church and cemetery on one side, the covered market, Town Hall and open market on the other, in a significant and fecund proximity and tension. The cases of Lubeck, Bremen and Stralsund were examples of that.

Religious centres, liturgical spaces. Relations with the Beyond: with God and the ancestors, take place there.

Administrative centres, writing spaces. Relations with Here Below, with Authority and property, are settled and decided there.

A business centre, spaces for the settlement of accounts, often peaceful, sometimes violent. There are discussions and agreement with partners: merchants and craftsmen, other towns, seigniorial and princely territorial authorities.

This economic and social centre, remarkably articulate and active, was a veritable social core.

The church and the Town Hall were there like two muscle organs regulating the social, vital flux of the urban body.

The main square: a spatialized, monumentalized, spectacular expression of the go-ahead spirit, autonomy and self-management of a medieval city.

8. The market seen from a craftsman's window.
Part of the right panel of the retable called the Merode, painted circa 1425-1428 by Robert Campin.
New York, Metropolitan Museum of Art.

9. Houses giving on to Bremen market. Part of an anonymous 17th century painting, see illustration 7.

THE BALTIC TOWNS

THE TOWN HALL

10. Wroclaw Town Hall. East façade.

Erected, for the most part, in the last quarter of the 15th century. It is undoubtedly the most finished public building of the Middle Ages within the Eastern borders.

Situated on one side of the rectangular main square, the Town Hall (*domus civium*) was the most representative civil edifice. Originally it was a modest construction built on to the covered market. Growing bigger with the expansion of the town, it progressively became the administrative centre of the community and the scene of fashionable performances.

STRUCTURE AND SPATIALIZATION

Over the cellars where the wine was stored, the ground floor served as a covered market and a court. On the first floor were the meeting rooms which were later used for dances.

Of the stone era, the oldest (circa 1240) Town Hall still in existence is at Dortmund; the most elegant are at Münster and Brunswick. Of the brick era, Lubeck Town Hall was the model, except in the Teutonic East where, as in Torun, the quadrilateral type surmounted by a belfry developed.

11. Façade of Stralsund Town Hall.

12-13. Portico of the Marktgericht, ground floor of Luneburg Town Hall.

The frescos inside are by Daniel Frese who, in 1603, represented there the theme of real justice, incarnated by Christ, Daniel and Solomon.
This space was called the Niedergericht, *as opposed to the* Gerichtslaube, *the courtroom situated on the first floor.*

14-15. An urban court sitting in Volkach in 1504.
Volkach Stadtarchiv.

The court is set up. The twelve councillors have just met on the market at the place where justice is to be done. The judge arrives, bearing the staff of justice, wearing his sword and accompanied by the Sergeant.

He now takes his seat: the judge is the second person top left (judex). It is a case of theft. The objects produced in evidence lie on the ground in the middle of the quadrilateral. On the right: soldiers. On the left, the sergeant who, parchment in hand, calls the plaintiffs. One of them comes forward, bareheaded.

THE BALTIC TOWNS

A comfortable complex   On the ground floor: the covered market and courtroom.
On the first floor: the council chamber (*Rat*), of quadrilateral structure, 18.5 metres long in Luneburg, 45 metres long in Aix-la-Chapelle, with a flat or vaulted ceiling. The participants sat face to face around an empty space, as was the custom in monastic communities.

But little furniture: chests, benches and tables; a few cupboards. The walls were richly decorated from floor to ceiling and sculptured woodwork abounded.

Everywhere were symbolic references – painted, written or sculptured – to divine and earthly justice and to the Last Judgment. First of all they were in biblical and evangelical terms, then as from the Renaissance, in mythological and historical ones, with valiant knights and chivalrous models omnipresent.

The comfort and luxury were on a scale with that of the daily life of the councillors who sat there. The spacious rooms were just extensions of the privileged social classes who came there to look after their power.

16. The courtroom – *Gerichtslaube* – in Luneburg Town Hall.

Urban justice was dispensed in this room, built in the 14th century. The court sat around the quadrilateral bounded by benches (Ratstuhl).

17. The councillors bench (*Ratstuhl*) of Luneburg Town Hall.

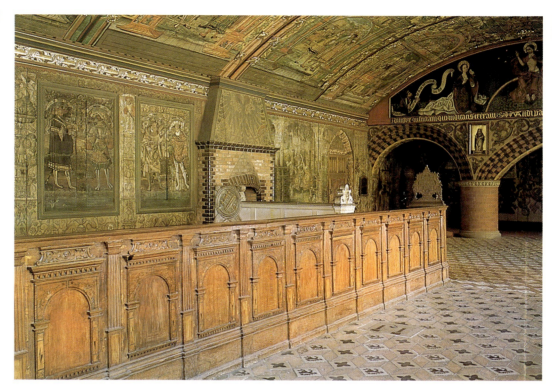

18. A trial in the Lubeck court in 1625. Part of a painting by Hans Heinssen. Lubeck. St-Annen-Museum.

19-24. Part of the decoration of Luneburg Town Hall court room.
These paintings, which date back to 1529, are attributed to Marten Jasten.

THE BALTIC TOWNS

A Council

The *Rat* was made up of 12, 24 or sometimes 36 members which the Latin texts called *consules*. They were appointed for life, though they continued to look after their own businesses. Two, or four of them were, in turn, named *proconsules* or burgomasters.

It was virtually a closed shop through co-opting in families which owed their wealth to foreign trade and did not live by manual work: generations of merchants, rich landowners, shipowners and a few big farmers.

In Hanseatic towns, urban policy was in the hands of Hanseatic merchants, whereas elsewhere the craftsmen had their say. In North Germany, and more particularly in Hanseatic maritime towns, craftsmen nowhere succeeded in obtaining real political influence. The urban patriciate owed that advantageous situation to its vitality and its ability to cope with changing economic realities.

The *Rat* was the sovereign authority and government of the town. It dealt with taxes, customs duties, public safety, civil servants, defence, money, justice and city legislation.

The offices were generally given out in pairs, in turn. There were councillors for finance, public works, the chancellery, money, the harbour, customs, windmills and the police.

25. The former Council Chamber (now the Peace Chamber) in Munster Town Hall.

The woodwork is from the early 16th century and from 1577.
The Burgomaster's seat, the cupboards in which the minutes of meetings were kept, and the crucifix (1540) still remain.
On the wall: 16 portraits of delegates to the Congress which was held there in 1648.

A body of civil servants   At their disposal they had a borough secretary and chancellery employees. A clerk of the court. Highly skilled master craftsmen for money, brick-works, the cellar; a master mason, a master blacksmith, a master joiner. Sergeants: from the port, the gates and the market, for the night watch. Employees: weights and scales. Workmen and menials of all sorts: servants, messengers, stable lads and carriers.
There was also the town doctor, the town schoolmaster and the chemist who, like the miller, was not a town employee but worked by tender or lease.

26. Approach to the Council Chamber (*Grosse Ratsstube*) In Luneburg Town Hall.

The urban community did not generally intervene. The Council called upon it only exceptionally. Normally it confined itself to making its provisions known by public proclamations or *Bürgersprache*, comparable to the *Morgensprache* of the Hanseatic business houses: *Bursprake* in Bremen, *Willkür* in Danzig, *Sentenzbogen* in Münster, *Kirchenruf*, after Sunday mass at the town church.

The Council's income came from fines, rates and taxes. There was the *Schoss*, an annual borough tax; in Rostock it amounted to 0.5 per cent of one's income, in Wismar 0.25 per cent. Taxes for defence: Cologne in 1379, the year of the peace, spent 82 per cent of its income on its militia and diplomatic negotiations. There was the *Wall- und Grabengeld*, a tax for fortifications, and the *Hafenkollekte*, a maritime town harbour tax. Then there were excise duties, and indirect taxation on consumer goods.

27. The secret debate room in Luneburg Town Hall dates from 1491.

It was there that burgomasters were elected (Burgermeisterkörkammer). Access was confidential.
In the bay: the four burgomasters in office in 1491.
The fireplace, table, wall cupboards and ceiling are of the period.

STRUCTURE AND SPATIALIZATION

The Chancellery, with its officials and employees, saw to the day-to-day management of the Council's affairs... and produced file upon file.
"Initially, urban chancelleries, like those of the princes, were kept by clerks. Their work, materialized in municipal registers kept since the 13th century, met the needs of the burghers as owners and merchants.
"The entry of sums due in a book possessing probative value opened the field to credit, near enough simultaneously in Hamburg, Lubeck, Luneburg, Stralsund and Riga. That period, the last quarter of the 13th century, marks the oldest vestige of the accounts of a Lubeck merchant, the precursor of account books which, throughout the Hanseatic period, were kept very haphazardly." [Pierre Jeannin]

28. The archives room (*Altes Archiv*) of Luneburg Town Hall, 1521.

29. The grand staircase leading to the state room (*Fürstensaal*) in Luneburg Town Hall dates from 1568.

30-31. The state room (Fürstensaal and/or Dantzhaus) in Luneburg Town Hall.

It is 34 metres long and 10 metres wide, and was built in the 15th century. The top part of the walls is decorated with Daniel Frese frescos (1607); they represent members of the House of Brunswick – Luneburg (from Otto the Child to Ernest II).
Its chandeliers, mounted in 1500-1502 by Hinrick Reymers, are remarkable, especially the one on which the Virgin figures.

STRUCTURE AND SPATIALIZATION

32. One of the upstairs rooms in Bremen Town Hall.

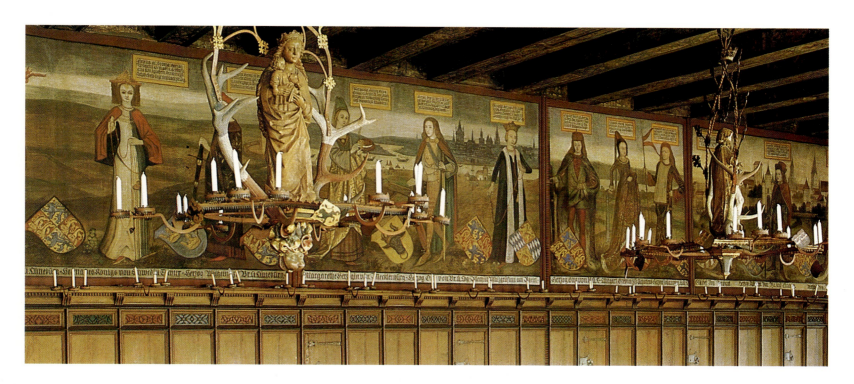

THE BALTIC TOWNS

COVERED MARKET

Originally, the Town Hall was only an annex to the covered market, but it ended up by supplanting it and reducing it to a part of its ground floor. Covered markets were built elsewhere than in the immediate surroundings of the main square, for instance, in the relatively close neighbourhood. The same applied to cereal and salt warehouses.

The richest corporations took the initiative. The stalls and their places became hereditary, though in principle selling or storage spaces were allocated annually by drawing lots, within the corporation.

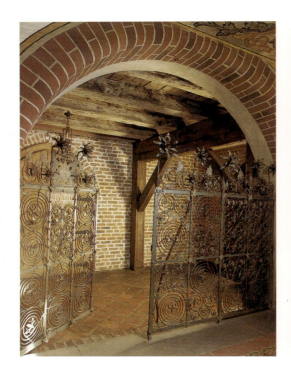
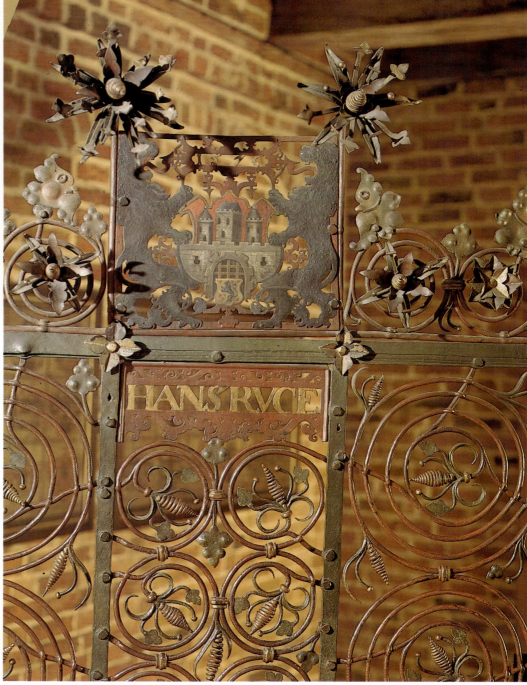

33-34. Grille, forged in 1576 by Hans Ruge, leading from the entrance hall of Luneburg Town Hall to the cloth room (Gewandhaus) situated under the *Fürstensaal*.

THE CORPORATION HOUSES

There were still houses of guilds and craftsmen around the main square or in its immediate vicinity. The following still subsist as significant examples: the *Artushof* in Danzig, the *House of the Captains* in Lubeck, the *Grosse Gilde* in Reval and the *Schütting* in Bremen.

The statutory annual meetings were held there, when the statutes were read and the Doyen (*Oldermann*) was elected. There were also festive occasions in the form of banquets, on the patron saint's day or when some important event was to be celebrated.

The members met there daily, usually in the morning, to make inquiries or simply to be together in their house where an atmosphere of welcome and safety reigned.

They clubbed together to assist needy members or for a mass and prayers for the souls of the deceased.

The building housed emblems, the dearest souvenirs, refined tools, mock-ups, strange and exotic objects brought back from some voyage or another.

Differences of opinion were arbitrated on. Sometimes a counter-power was constituted, contesting the power of the *Rat* opposite.

35. The Schütting, in Bremen.
Part of an anonymous painting, early 17th century.
Bremen, Landesmuseum.

36. The house of the merchants' corporation (Schütting, from schossen, to advance money) in Bremen.

It was Jan den Buschener, from Antwerp, who built it in 1537-1539. The big dormer window, decorated with a Hanseatic ship, is by Lüder von Bentheim (1594).
Theophilus W. Frese introduced a baroque note into it in 1756.
The portrait (Otto Gildemeister) and the window decoration are of a later date.

THE BALTIC TOWNS

THE COUNCIL CHURCH

Opposite the Town Hall and closely associated with it was the Council church whose spire broke the immured horizon. The church animated projects, rendered risks bearable, calmed fears and galvanized hopes, by rendering the Beyond familiar.

Everyone participated actively in its construction. Councillors and guild doyens formed part of the church council. Craftsmen and corporations paid up handsomely. Men and women helped the labourers. According to the Stralsund chronicler, "the poor worked during the daytime; the rich, at night."

Patricians and burghers wanted it to be more imposing than the cathedral, thereby removing from the bishop and the king the monumental symbol of the powers which they had arrogated to themselves. The high spire was to affirm the freedom of patricians and burghers and have their power recognized.

The churches of ancient Germany, West of the Elbe, were pre-Hanseatic, Romanesque and of stone. Those in the colonization zone, to the East, were Gothic and of brick; they date from between the middle of the 13th century and the middle of the 16th century.

37. *Sermon in a church in the 16th century.*
A wood-engraving by Georg Pencz (1500-1550). 1529.
Vienna. Graphische Sammlung Albertina.

38. *St. Luke retable.*
Painted in Lubeck, circa 1484, by Hermen Rode (deceased 1504).
Lubeck, St-Annen-Museum.

THE BALTIC TOWNS

The Council church was where the urban assembly met in prayer. It would be dedicated to Notre-Dame, the mother of God, or to Peter, Nicholas or James, the patron saints of fishermen and seamen, merchants and travellers.
It was also where the urban management meeting was held. It was the meeting room of the Council at its most decisive moments, and it was also where the dearest objects, archives, relics and ornaments were kept.
The pantheon of the patriciate, the epitome of the sanctuaries of merchants and craftsmen, the refuge of the poor and sinners.
Spacious inside, modest outside, a space of interiority, centred on its opulent, sculptured retables.

39. Worship of the saints.
Bruges, Groeninge Museum.

The Bruges burghers worshipped St. Ursula. The nun far left is probably the donor of the retable of which this panel is the eighth and last.
The polyptych, recounting the legend of Saint Ursula, was painted in Bruges before 1483, whereas the reliquary painted by Hans Memling was not then finished (1489).

STRUCTURE AND SPATIALIZATION

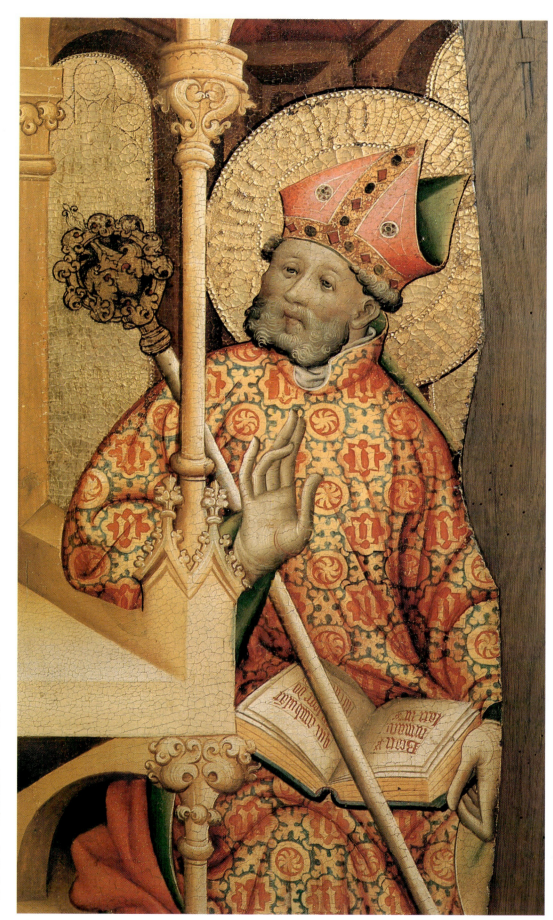

40. Saint Nicholas, the patron saint of merchants and seamen.
Part of a retable from Notre-Dame church in Lubeck, made before 1410 by a craftsman trained in Westphalia.
Lubeck, St-Annen-Museum.

St. Nicholas was popular in the West and the East, particularly in the Baltic regions, as is proved by the large number of churches dedicated to him in North German coastal towns.
Seamen evoked the Bishop of Myre, with the hope that he would come to their aid by calming rough seas and lead their ships back to port. He was also supposed to protect treasure placed in his custody from thieves.

41

THE BALTIC TOWNS

THE HARBOUR

Most towns were situated on waterways that were navigable by the small craft of the time.

The sea ports themselves were in reality only river harbours situated near the sea. They operated for better for worse, through toil and sweat, scantily assisted by crane and wheelbarrow.

These harbours were hardly integrated in the urban topography. They often remained outside of fortifications and gave the impression of being on the fringe of the town; the street network was not well-ordered in relation to the harbour installations.

Boats tied up to bollards, for which a due had to be paid (*Pfahlgeld*). Berths were divided up by nation, type of boat, size of boat and, mainly, by the nature of the cargo carried.

41. Wismar, circa 1627.
Schwerin Staatliches Museum.

STRUCTURE AND SPATIALIZATION

There were virtually no quays, except in Hamburg. Cranes were rare. So there was a rush for them and utilization was limited to a day or two. After that, ships had to drop anchor elsewhere and, in order to continue unloading, hire local craft.
Harbour personnel included harbour-masters who had taken the oath and were responsible for applying harbour regulations, allocating places to boats and collecting the dues.
Harbour workmen did the unloading, weighing or measuring of goods and, where necessary, the repairing of cargoes. They did not really need any particular skills or means other than physical ones. They simply had to turn up at the place of work and, if engaged, pay a due to the town and the corporation.

42. Wismar. The old port.

THE BALTIC TOWNS

43. Crane in the port of Bruges in 1479.
Part of the triptych of the Mystic Marriage of
Saint Catherine, by Hans Memling. 1479.
Bruges, Sint-Janshospitaal.

STRUCTURE AND SPATIALIZATION

44. Crane in the port of Antwerp.
Part of a hand-coloured wood-engraving, taken from Loeflichen Sanck, published in Antwerp by Jan de Gheet in 1515.
Hamburg, Staats- und Universitätsbibliothek, cod. 40, in scrin.

In port, seamen were strictly forbidden to release ballast and refuse into the water. Widening work on rivers, specially near the mouth, was undertaken in the 15th century.

45

THE BALTIC TOWNS

STORAGE

From the cellar to the loft, merchants' houses included storage space. The very structure of Hanseatic town houses, based on the Saxon farm model, lent itself particularly well to that end: from the street or from the *Diele*, goods were hoisted up to the granaries. The cereal areas were arranged (*Bodenraüme*) so that drying out and maintenance could be done regularly, for both excessive humidity and excessive heat had to be avoided. But in towns where cereals and salt were collected for overseas exportation, family storage facilities were soon to prove inadequate.

45. Warehouse in Luneburg.

It is the Alte Kaufhaus, *called the* Herringhaus *until the 15th century (herrings were the trading article 'par excellence' for Luneburg).*
Façade, 1741-1745, after a project by Haesler, the Stadtbaumeister.

In Lubeck and Danzig, in particular, dozens of warehouses were built, unaccompanied by any living accommodation. Such warehouses were needed, too, for foreign merchants, as an urban policy concerned with animating markets was developed in their respect.

Kaufhaus, Kornhaus, Spiker. Granarium, annonarium, domus frumenti. Warehouses for merchants from elsewhere and for the wholesale trade of the town's merchants. They were imposing brick buildings, six to eight floors high, near ports and ramparts, cf. the grain elevators of today.

The compulsory depositing of goods that were imported or in transit, the imposed use of the town's weights and measures, plus handling and guarding by municipal personnel, made it easy for the town to control trade and collect dues and taxes.

46. Warehouses in Bergen.
Recently reconstructed after being burned down in 1955.

THE BALTIC TOWNS

THE URBAN TISSUE

From Cologne to Magdeburg and in most Westphalian and Saxon towns, houses were made of stone.

In maritime regions, from Bremen to Riga, they were brick-built and their facades were patterned on Flemish models. A universe of terra cotta and symmetry, will and system, the monotony of which was broken by the use of decorative elements and colour variations.

Draught-board spaces, as encountered in all new worlds. Narrow lots which pushed upwards to obtain maximum storage space.

URBAN POPULATION IN THE HANSE WORLD

Bremen	circa 1400	17,000
Cologne	15th century	30,000
Danzig	circa 1500	20,000
Goslar	15th century	10,000
Hamburg	15th century	16,000
Lubeck	circa 1450	25,000
Luneburg	15th century	10,000
Reval	15th century	6,000
Riga	15th century	8,000
Rostock	1410	14,000
Stralsund	2nd half of 14th century	10,000

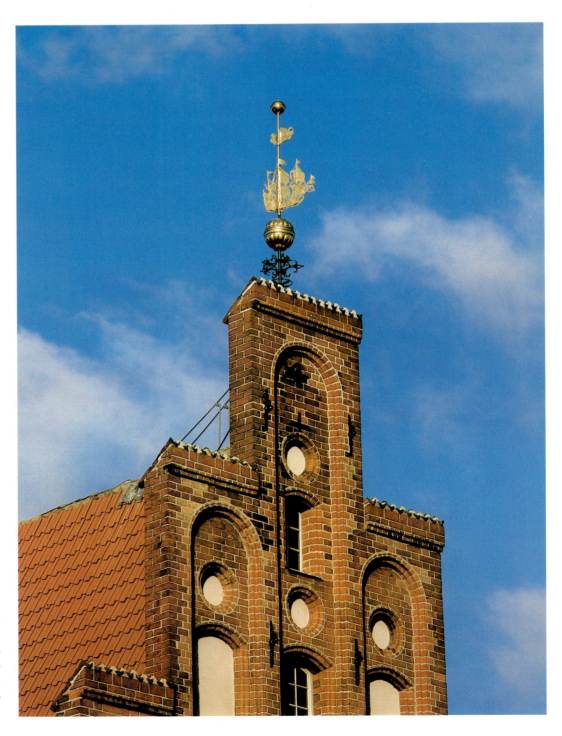

47-48. The house of the captains' guild in Lubeck (1535).

It has been kept intact until our times. The confraternity of captains, placed under the patronage of Saint Anne, and the confraternity of Saint Nicholas, made it an alms-house for 'poor seamen'.

BIBLIOGRAPHY

B. FISCHER, *Hanse-Städte. Geschichte und Kultur*, Köln, 1981.
H. PLANITZ, *Die deutsche Stadt im Mittelalter*, Wien und Köln, 1980.
W. SCHILD, *Alte Gerichtsbarkeit*, Münich, 1980.
H. HÜBLER, *Das Bürgerhaus in Lübeck*, Tübingen, 1968.
P. JOHANSEN, *Die Kaufmannkirsche in Oostseegebiet*, in *Studi in honore di Armando Sapori*, Milano, 1957, p. 312-325.
N. ZASKE, *Mittelalterliche Plastik und Malerei in Hansestädten. Zur hansischen Mentalität in der bildenden Kunst*, in Hansische Studien, VII, 1984.
M. BOGUCKA, *Das alte Danzig. Alltagsleben vom 15. bis 17 Jahrhundert*, Leipzig, 1980.

HEINZ STOOB

The Topographical Evolution of the Baltic Hanseatic Towns

For the Baltic Sea regions, the end of the upper Middle Ages marked a fascinating extension of major European trade. With the Hanse making great strides, a phenomenon was developing which stemmed initially from economic and social history and led, in the early 14th century, to the formation of coastal towns all round the North Sea and the Baltic, including mid-Sweden and Southern Finland.

49. Lubeck, seen from the air.

In the foreground the Holstentor; on its right the facades of the salt warehouses.
One or other of the gates. Church towers.
The rational, elegant facades of grand residences, impressive lofts/granaries.
Medieval Lubeck is encumbered with constructions which were built in recent decades and which blur what was prototypic of urban and harbour space in the Middle Ages town.

50. A 15th century conurbation.
A wood-engraving by Michael Wolgemut and his studio, illustrating a chronicle (*Das Buch der Chronicken*), published in Nuremberg in 1493. Nuremberg Germanisches Nationalmuseum. Acting as a frame for the sermons of the flute player of Niklashausen in 1476.

The engraving gives an idea of what the foundations of German colonizers in the Eastern countries must have been. A communal space bounded by fencing in the form of a palisade of branches, broken by a gateway. Cob houses with thatched roofs; a stone church.

51

THE BALTIC TOWNS

THE URBAN PHENOMENON IN HANSEATIC SPACE

In addition to the towns grouped around Lubeck, which the Hanse were later to call the 'Wendish district' because of its proximity to the Slav colonisation territories east of the Elbe, all the important coastal places on the Baltic Sea were to develop.

Among the 'Wendish' towns behind Lubeck, and leaving Hamburg and Luneburg aside, there were Wismar, Rostock and Stralsund, Baltic ports and – from time to time – Greifswald and Anklam.

Mention should also be made of the other principal Baltic towns. First of all those which were, at that time, under Danish domination: Schleswig, Aarhus and Odense, Roskilde, Copenhagen and Hälsingborg, Lund and Malmö.

In Sweden: Kalmar, Linköping, Nyköping and Stockholm, as well as Visby on Gotland island, of particular importance.

In Finland: Turku (Abo) and Vyborg (Viipuri).

In the Baltic countries: Narva and Reval, Pernau and Riga; more inland, on navigable rivers, towns which were not sea ports: Fellin, Dorpat (Tartu) and Wenden.

In Prussia: Memel and Königsberg, Elbing and Danzig, Culm and Torun. In Eastern Pomerania: Kolberg and Kammin, but more especially Stettin.

51. Urban dynamics up to about 1330.

The Baltic Sea, according to Adam of Bremen.

Ostarsalt, for the Vikings.

Ostsee, for the Hanseatic merchants, because for them it is the sea by which they go to the east.

Town founded before 1190 ■
                            1230 ◆
                            1250 ●
                            1290 ▲
                            1330 ✱

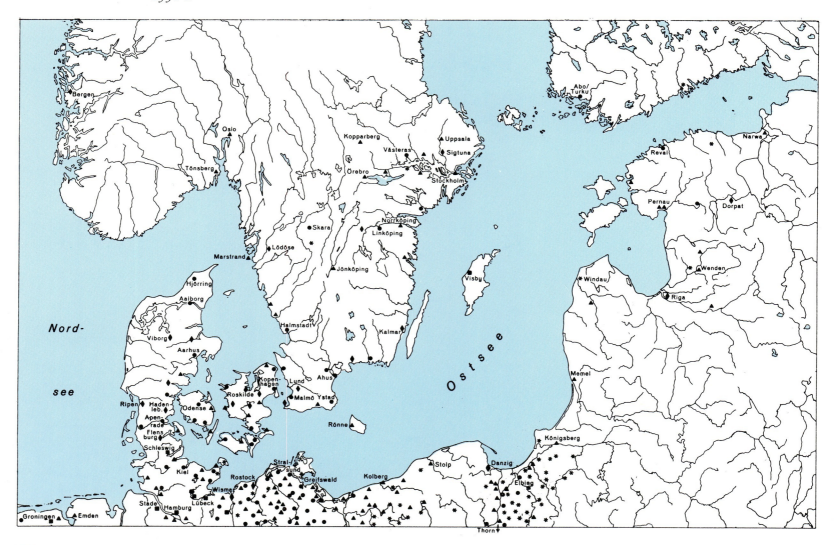

THE TOPOGRAPHICAL EVOLUTION

What all these towns had in common was contact with a rich hinterland, rapidly developing sea traffic, and harbour facilities that were very modern for the time. In addition, they built with bricks, in a manner previously unknown in those parts.

The more or less regular network of their streets arranged around the market, and their solid defence system articulated around the thick walls of the town, determined a typical urban mid-European structure which in most cases developed very quickly.

Town life, especially on the market place and in the port, was right away motley and cosmopolitan. The big merchants from Lower Germany and Holland set the tone: those who operated the export trade, those who possessed ships, all those who, as far as the Flemish coast, formed the centre of middle-class life in the North-West of Europe, continually developing the profitable trade routes.

The Hanse which was being formed did not take in all the towns on the Scandinavian coasts, with the exception of Visby, which was made a special case. On the other hand, the other towns of the Baltic ring keenly felt that they belonged to the association.

To realise the topography of all these towns, some concrete examples must be taken.

52. Brick urban architecture. Part of a 15th century miniature evoking the foundation of Venice and illustrating La Fleur des Histoires by Jean Mansel.
Brussels, Royal Library, ms. 9231, fol. 118.

THE PRUSSIAN TOWNS

Königsberg   The cadastral register shows organization around several centres.

Except in the very first days, the struggle against local populations played but little part in the choice of the merchant site. On the other hand, force, power and presence between the Teutonic Order, master of Prussia, and Lubeck, the driving force of the Hanse, were determinant.

The first establishment, not far from the mouth of the Pregolia, failed in 1242 because of the refusal by the Order to accept Lubeck law as the new one in place of its own, the Culm Charter. In 1255 the Teutonic Knights built a merchant nucleus of a town around Saint Nicholas' church beside their citadel on the Pregolia. But in 1262-1265 the Prussians conquered the place and destroyed it entirely. Urban life picked up later, situated between the fortress and the river. The Grand Master granted a charter in 1286.

The space was small – 11.6 ha – occupied by the fortress and the market. Therefore, the Torun weavers who came and settled shortly afterwards, occupied Löbenicht on the East side of the old town. They obtained an urban charter for their new town.

With Saint Barbara's church, the Town Hall built before the eastern walls of the old town, and its own coat of arms since 1416, Löbenicht was an independent town covering 7.3 ha. It possessed a hospital and a large abbey for women. Its high defensive walls, with four gates, backed on to those of the old town, on the banks of the Pregolia, with the communal mill.

In 1237 a third town, of 9 ha, was founded on an island in the middle of the river, opposite the old town: the Kneiphof, a Germanized old Prussian name, also called New Königsberg, and endowed, like the Old Town and Löbenicht, with a town charter. The new town had its own fortifications, with five gates. In 1330 it received the chapter of the cathedral, which was also the town's official church.

The three Königsberg towns each had their own relations with the Hanse, but they possessed a joint concession (Vitte) at the herring fair. From 1389 to 1422 the Burgomaster of the Old Town of Königsberg acted as Provost of the Hanse. With its extensive suburbs, Königsberg had 8,000 to 10,000 inhabitants in 1450, which made the town one of the principal cities in the possession of the Teutonic Order, after Danzig, with Torun and Elbing. The Grand Master lived in Königsberg from 1457.

The capital of the Prussian duchy in 1525, the town continued to develop; by 1544 it had its university. In 1626-1627 a surrounding wall with bastions joined up all the districts and suburbs of the three towns in a 382 ha citadel, but administrative unity of the towns was not achieved until 1724, by an edict of the Prussian administration.

53. Koeningsberg. Evolution of urban space. Map prepared by the *Kuratorium für vergleichende Städtgeschichte* of Munster University. Dir. Prof. Dr. Heinz Stoob.

THE TOPOGRAPHICAL EVOLUTION

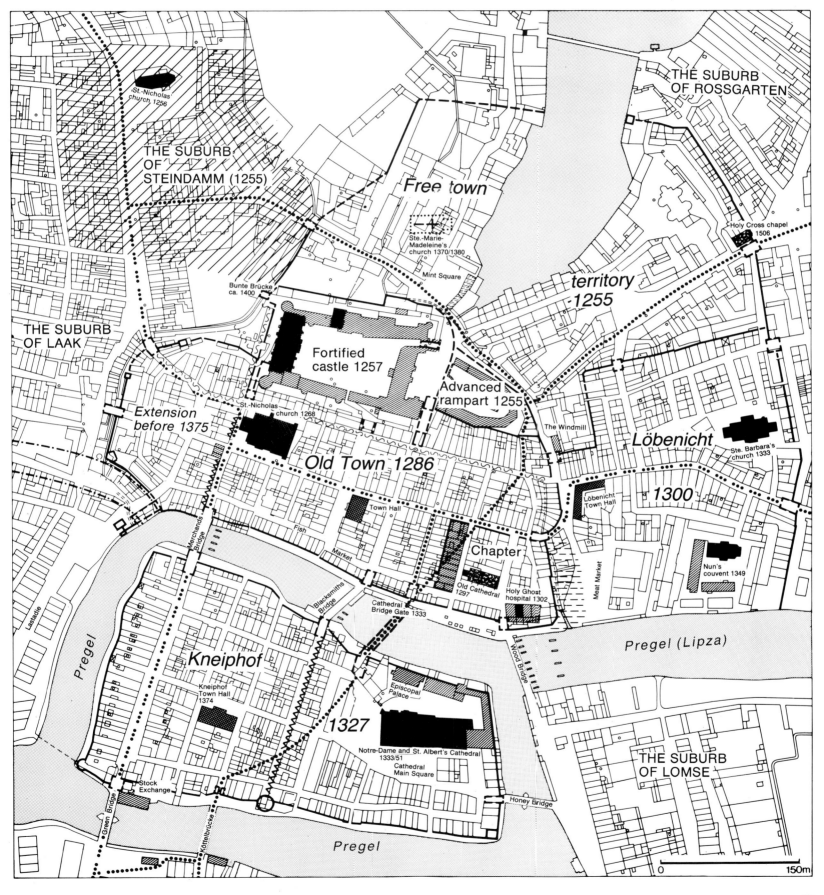

Elbing

The situation of Elbing at the mouth of the eastern arm of the Vistula was quite different. Elbing was the principal point of passage, between Frische 'Haff and the Drausensee, of the east-west trade routes which availed themselves of the Weichsel delta. In agreement with the Grand Master Hermann von Salza, the colonists arriving from Lubeck in 1237 entered into a defence agreement with the fortress of the Order, founded on Lubeck law. In 1246 the Teutons granted them an urban charter. In 1238 the parish church of St. Nicholas was joined by the church of Notre-Dame, founded by the Dominicans to the north-west of the town, and then, in 1242, by the Hospice of the Holy Ghost, situated between the town and the citadel. It became the general hospice of the Order in 1291, after the fall of Akkon. In 1256, Saint James' parish church was built, to the west of the town, and Saint George's leper hospital was situated outside of the walls, to the north-east. The town was enlarged in the 14th century by an independent district on Speicher island, but it had no church. It was connected to the old town by a gate, the *Schmiedetor*. However, in 1335-1337 the Teutons preferred to install a square town quite separate from the old one, surrounded by a moat for its defence and possessing its own parish church: the church of the Three Wise Men.

54. Elbing.
After W. Kalinowski, in P. Lavedan and J. Hugueney. *Townplanning in the Middle Ages*, plate CIX.

Danzig

Danzig, the principal Prussian port on the mouth of a river, was quite complex topographically.

The residence of a prince and an important international market of pre-Hanseatic times, it was initially situated around Saint Catherine's church, still called 'matrona loci', about 1271. To the south of that first centre, a commercial district developed around Saint Nicholas' church which most probably dates from the 1200's and was subsequently taken over by the Dominicans. Shortly after 1220 what was called the Rechstadt was erected. with Notre-Dame church and Town Hall; it became the real heart of the town.

The 'Old Town', to the north of the St. Catherine district, did not develop significantly around Saint Bartholomew until the 15th century, when the Order acquired the Duchy of Pomerania Minor and built a fortress on a loop of the river downstream from the city. But there was also, near the Vistula, the *Jungstadt* (Young Town) with its own privilege; then, built circa 1340 around St. John's church was the *Neustadt* or New Town, between the seat of the Order and the Rechstadt; lastly, from 1360, the 'Suburb' (*Vorstadt*) with its church of St. Peter and St. Paul, as well as the Speicherinsel, a churchless district. All these districts had their own particular personality.

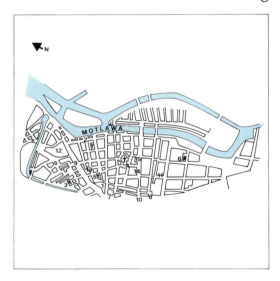

55. Danzig.
After H. Planitz, *Die deutsche Stadt*, p. 212.

1. Dominican monastery (1227)
2. St. Jean (before 1353)
3. St. Catherine (circa 1150)
4. Notre-Dame (circa 1240)
5. St. Nicholas (1190)
6. St. Peter and St. Paul (14th c.)
7. Breites Tor
8. Fischertor
9. Haustor
10. Hoher Turm
11. Ketterhagen Tor
12. Castle
13. Market (1178)
14. Langer Markt (after 1124)
15. Town Hall (1378).

THE TOPOGRAPHICAL EVOLUTION

Torun　In Torun, too, two towns developed on the banks of a river. The Old Town was finally situated near an Order fortress erected in 1231. In 1233 it enjoyed urban status and in 1239 the Franciscan monastery of Notre-Dame was added to the parish church of St. John.

From the landing-stages, five gates opened on to side streets which led to the city centre.

In 1250 the Teutons built a fortress and in 1264 granted an urban charter for a new town of about 12 ha, with a church, a Town-Hall and defensive walls encircling a free zone. At the same time the Old Town received permission to enlarge itself 16 ha to the north. Although an outer defensive wall was built around both towns in the 14th century, they remained independent of each other.

In 1454 the Old Town destroyed the Order's castle and annexed the New Town which had remained faithful to the Teutons.

Torun was to suffer much more than Elbing from the economic decline that followed the war between the Order and Poland.

56. Torun.
After M. and E. Gasiorowsky, *Torun*, Warsaw, 1974, p. 28.

1. *Market*
2. *Town Hall*
3. *Notre-Dame church*
4. *St. Jean church.*

TOWNS IN THE LUBECK ORBIT

To the topographical evolution of the Prussian towns belonging to the Hanse can be opposed that of the towns which revolved around Lubeck.

Wismar　The port is mentioned for the first time in 1211 in an imperial deed. The oldest part, near the port, is the Saint Nicholas district, most probably built between 1190 and 1203, beside the Grube, a place that was still navigable at that time, where the Aa left Lake Schwerin.

Beside the east-west orientated oval of the Saint Nicholas district a much bigger complex was built after 1220, the Marienstadt, with squares at right angles for the market, a parish church and, a little to one side, two convents, one Dominican and the other Franciscan, as well as a Hospice of the Holy Ghost.

The *burgenses* of Marienstadt are first mentioned in 1229. In 1237 there was some question of the construction *omnium ecclesiarum ibidem accrescentium*, and around 1250 the New Town in an arc curving to the west was added to the old districts, with its parish church initially consecrated jointly to Saint Martin and Saint George.

The total area of the town thus attained the not inconsiderable figure of 58 ha.

57. Wismar.
After H. Planitz. *Die deutsche Stadt*, p. 162.

1. *Dominican monastery (1292)*
2. *Franciscan monastery (1252)*
3. *St. George (1250)*
4. *Notre-Dame (1266)*
5. *St. Nicholas (1260)*
6. *Lübisches Tor (1284)*
7. *Mecklenburgertor (1272)*
8. *Poelertor (after 1250)*
9. *Alt-Wismar Tor (1278)*
10. *Market*
11. *Town Hall*

THE BALTIC TOWNS

Rostock

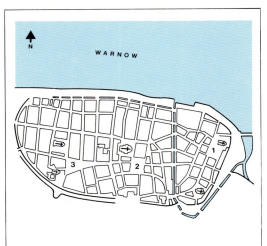

58. Rostock.
After P. Lavedan and J. Hugueney. Town-planning in the Middle Ages, plate cx.

1. Altstadt
2. Mittelstadt
3. Neustadt.

Rostock evolved similarly, with a linear development along the river landing-stages.

The first town centre was to the east, on the site of a former Wendish establishment with a church consecrated to Saint Clement; it probably developed around Saint Nicholas' church, prior to 1203. This site was the arrival point of a trading route from the south.

Rostock became bigger with Saint Peter's quarter and the Old Market and, a little apart, the Franciscan St. Catherine's convent which dates from circa 1240. The district gives the impression of having been built to a quite definite plan. The waters of the Grube bounded this first 18 ha town to the west.

A Marienstadt, much more extensive, began to be built in 1230 or even before, for two *plebani* of two districts of the town were named in 1231, and Notre-Dame church was mentioned for the first time in 1232. The *novum forum*, later the *forum medium*, appeared in 1258. It was a winding way, the middle part of which was called the *Faule Grube* after the waterway running through it.

In 1252, sources mention the parish of St. John beside St. Peter and Notre-Dame; the third district, more to the west, was developed before 1250 and it was in 1260 that the first documentary traces appeared on the gates of the fortified enceinte.

Stralsund and Greifswald

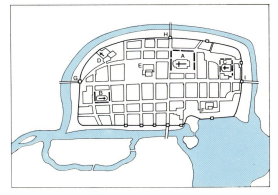

59. Greifswald.
17th century engraving.

A. St. Nicholas
B. Notre-Dame
C. St. Jacques
D. The Grey Sisters
E. Town Hall
F. Fette Tor
G. Windmill Gate
H. Butchers Gate.

Although smaller, Stralsund and Greifswald, the two neighbouring towns of Rostock, nevertheless developed in a similar manner. Both were set in three parts. St. Nicholas' church in the oldest district of the Old Town was later joined by St. Peter's church, since disappeared; then the Notre-Dame and St. James districts enlarged the town.

The wall surrounding Stralsund, begun in 1271, had three gates in the Saint Nicholas district and three gates in the Saint James district, giving on to the port landing-stages. Six gates in the Greifswald wall, which dated from 1264, opened up to ships. It was at that time that the lord decreed the merger of the three towns: *unum sit forum, unus advocatus et idem ius*.

With areas of 48 and 47 ha respectively, Stralsund and Greifswald remained far behind Rostock.

Anklam was even smaller: the most easterly of the Hanse Wendish towns was founded in 1243 with an area of 15 ha first of all, then of 25. Yet in the course of its development a St. Nicholas church was built and then a Notre-Dame church, whilst four gates to the north led to landing-stages on the Peene.

THE TOPOGRAPHICAL EVOLUTION

Lubeck

60. Lubeck.
After H. Planitz, *Die deutsche Stadt*, p. 141.

1. Cathedral
2. St. Gilles
3. St. Jacques
4. Notre-Dame (1170)
5. St. Peter (1170)
6. Burgtor
7. Holstentor
8. Hüxter Tor
9. Mühlentor
10. Castle
11. Market
12. Town Hall.

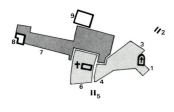

61. Genesis of Lubeck.
After Luce Petri, *Epoques médiévales*, p. 288.

1. Cathedral
2. Bridge
3. First establishment founded in 1143 by Adolphus of Holstein
4. Market
5. Port
6. First suburb founded in 1158 by Henry the Lion
7. 13th century extension
8. Castle
9. St. Jean Abbey.

Like the Prussian ports, the Hanse Wendish ports had a number of cores of development, centred around port activities, but they very quickly changed into one sole town, directed by one sole council. That can be read in a number of features of their topography, their organic growth, the identical list of their patron saints and the rapid construction of a wall surrounding all the districts. The roots of these similar evolutions are to be found in Lubeck.

There was probably an establishment around a market before 1138, the year in which the fortified hamlet of Alt-Lubeck which was situated upstream was definitively destroyed. That establishment would have been to the south, between Mühlentor and Klingenberg (the former salt market). Three roads led to the port. Count Adolphus II of Holstein turned this site into a town, but that was almost entirely destroyed a few years later in 1147 and 1157. Henry the Lion rebuilt it munificently on a bigger scale and in a fixed topographical form. The Franciscan St. Catherine's cloister, which did not then exist, was subsequently linked with it.

On the paths leading down to the Trave landing-stages, we find the word *Grube* eight times; as in Wismar and Rostock, it indicates the presence of a river arm.

Early in the 13th century the wish was expressed to have systematic planning into the suburbs of the fortifications to the north of the hill, where the Dominican convent is now situated.

Unless we are mistaken, for it is a very controversial point, the patron saints followed the same pattern here as in the other Wendish towns: the parish church of St. Nicholas with a sort of annex devoted to St. Peter, then Notre-Dame, which gradually became the town centre; and lastly, to the north, St. James. But in Lubeck in 1227-1229 the Saint Gilles parish church was built as well as monasteries of the mendicant orders, whilst the St. John monastery (of Benedictines, then of Cistercians) on the Wakenitz existed since 1177.

The setting up of the council around 1200 and the building of the surrounding wall after 1225 were a matter for the whole town.

In 1181 the town was placed under the protection of the emperor. The privileges of 1226 which designate it as locus imperii and *civitas... ad dominum imperiale specialiter pertinens* rendered it definitively independent of the neighbouring princes who quarrelled over its territory. That independence preserved the town from internal strife such as that which tore apart the Hanseatic towns of Prussia or Mecklenburg and Pomerania.

THE BALTIC TOWNS

Visby   Visby grew in the years 1161-1189. Until then the principal establishment of Gotland had remained under the influence of Schleswig, but the influence of Lubeck gradually made itself felt, by numerous merchants from Westphalia and Lower Saxony settling in the town.
Between the two old districts, one to the south around St. Peter, the other to the north around St. Clement and St. Olaf, and behind the Standgatan which marked the boundaries of the landing-stages, a whole network of streets sprang up. There were two parallel (Mallangatan, Saint Hans-Gatan) and numerous side streets called Gränd here but corresponding to the Gruben of Lubeck.

62. Visby.

The town had twelve churches. Notre-Dame church, begun in 1190, had hardly been consecrated in 1225 than it had to be enlarged – evidence of the vitality of the urban entity at that time. Lubeck heartily disliked its competitor and succeeded in 1293 in bringing it into subjection. That was the end of the go-ahead trading spirit of Visby.

Subsequently the 'Main Market Square' with the Franciscan St. Carine monastery were added to the new town centre. Perhaps the Saint Nicholas parish church taken over – as in Danzig – by the Dominicans, was first that of the German merchants before they built their Notre-Dame church between 1190 and 1225, the date of its consecration.

The rapid growth of the Hanseatic ports is in itself an important characteristic, since it suffices to distinguish them not only from the towns of the continent but, generally speaking, from all the towns of mid-Europe which were built in the 12th and 13th centuries.

The appearance of multiple parishes going together with the autonomy of the different districts – with the very significant exception, in Lubeck and Visby, of the oldest middle-class communities – makes it possible to draw conclusions about the phases of development and the causes and circumstances of subsequent unification.

The names of patron saints make it possible to understand certain relationships and interdependencies.

Lastly, the appearance of the port indicates the principal relations, in the form given them by Hanseatic history.

BIBLIOGRAPHY

P. JOHANSEN, *Umrisse und Aufgaben der hansischen Siedlungsgeschichte und Kartographie,* in *Hans. Gesch. Blätter* 731955.
W. HUBASCH, *Köningsberg,* in H. STOOB (Hg.), *Deutscher Städteatlas* II/1979.
E. CARSTENN, *Geschichte der Hansestadt Elbing,* Elbing, 1937.
ZBIERSKI, *Archaelogy on spatial changes in Gdansk,* in *Acta Polon, Hist.,* 34/1976.
K. BLASCKHE, *Nikolaikirchen und Stadtenstehung im pommerschen Raum,* in *Greifswald-Stralsunder Jahrbuch* 9/1970-71.
B. AM ENDE, *Studien zur Verfassungsgeschichte Lübecks im 12, und 13, Jh.,* Lübeck, 1975.

The Merchants

63. Hermann Wedich (1503-1560).
Portrait by Hans Holbein (1497-1544)
Signed H.H. on the cover of the book.
Distemper painting on wood.
New York, Metropolitan Museum.

Wedich, here, was 29 years old: Anno 1532.
AETATIS. SUAE. 29.
On the edge of the book: the shortened name of the model: HER. WED.
On the sheet of paper: Veritas odiu(m) parit (Terence Adria, v. 22). On his signet-ring: the family coat of arms.
After having been a merchant in the Stalhof, Wedich was a senator in Cologne and a councillor in Niederich.

It was the merchant who animated the Hanseatic world.
Through him, surpluses became goods. He turned empty spaces into market-places, basements into cellars and lofts into granaries.
Initially he accompanied his cargoes and was personally involved in commercial traffic networks. Later, he became sedentary, doing more in writing, working more without being personally present, keeping more at a distance.
His social position was ambiguous, uncomfortable and gratifying all at the same time. Uncomfortable at being an intermediary, dealing in things which he neither produced nor consumed. The discomfort, too, of plying his trade elsewhere; where he traded he was a foreigner, whether as a seller or a buyer.
But he had, of course, the profit resulting from his work, the satisfaction of increasing the value of something which, without him, would have had less value. There was, too, the pleasure and pungency of negotiating. The merchant negotiated with others, elsewhere. He revealed the peaceful virtuality of the foreigner whom he had previously known only by his warlike behaviour.
To the changing West, he offered an alternative, a new sociability: give up aggressive premeditation and replace it with other intentions, use negotiation instead of violence, competition instead of armed combat.
He undertook, in his way, to cope with ancestral fears. He saw to continuation, by having numerous progeny. He ensured solidarity through guilds, and by his invocations came to terms with celestial power. So, drawing upon continuously and deliberately acquired serenity, he succeeded in mastering uncertainties linked with what is unknown; anguish engendered by what is outside direct ascendancy, uneasiness stemming from deferred issues. [A. d'H.]

ALBERT D'HAENENS

Intermediaries

The merchant set all sorts of surpluses in movement. He was therefore an intermediary depending upon those he served.

His qualities were a real capacity to listen, observe and value, a sense of timeliness, a certain taste for risk. In short, the science of dealing, which he could practise only with empiricism and intuition.

But he also had to be enterprising. To be able to move cargoes around he had to organize and master his traffic networks. He had to get his cash in and invest it unceasingly. Boldness and prudence had to go hand in hand, and that is only within the power of wise, well-balanced men.

64. A merchant discussing business in his warehouse. Circa 1440.
Flemish miniature illustrating a French translation of the *Decameron*.
Paris, Arsenal Library, ms. 5070, fol. 314 recto.

65. A Nuremberg merchant's scales.
1497. Nuremberg, Germanisches Nationalmuseum.

In the Middle Ages a merchant had two specific tools of his profession, which he always carried with him: a sword to defend himself against attackers, and scales to weigh the money or precious metal he received in exchange for his goods.

THE MERCHANTS

COMMERCIAL TRAFFIC

The Hanseatic carried on commercial traffic between East and West.
"When a treaty with the Prince of Smolensk was signed in Livonia in 1229, four merchants from Riga and three from Gotland affixed their seals thereto as witnesses, as did colleagues from Bremen (one), Lubeck (two), Soest (two), Munster (two), Dortmund (two) and Groningen (two). Having firm access to the Baltic and Nordic markets, the Esterlins (or Osterlins) enjoyed the best conditions for supplying England and Flanders and being good clients in both countries.
The safety of persons and goods and the customs duty reductions granted by Western sovereigns (Henry III of England in 1237, the Countess of Flanders in 1252) were symmetrical with the advantages obtained in the East. The Hanseatic intermediary was favoured on both sides." [Pierre Jeannin].
Before 1250 the Hanseatic coveted his goods. He sought out products where there were surpluses and sold them at a good price where they were rare.

66. The ship comes home.
15th century miniature illustrating an Apocalypse manuscript.
Oxford, The Bodleian. Ms. Douce, 401, fol. 55 verso.

Watching the proceeds coming in for what he had entrusted to the sea: a mood, tension, risks for the merchant.

Then he became sedentary, through the increasingly general adoption of writing in business matters. He had delegation, representation and abstraction techniques which enabled him to manage and traffic from his business house. He entrusted his cargoes to middlemen and to captains of ships and lived more and more in a state of withdrawal, through bills of exchange, business letters and his accounts books.

He could now be here, there and everywhere, as he no longer needed to accompany his goods. His business expanded.

He counted on several markets, on diversified products and on several types of business.

In addition, he set up inter-city relationship networks. "The sons of a big family spread around, the branches to which they gave birth when they succeeded in other cities intercrossed in the following generations by migration in the same or the opposite direction. This extreme mobility favoured the homogeneity of merchant circles in the Hanseatic world." [Pierre Jeannin].

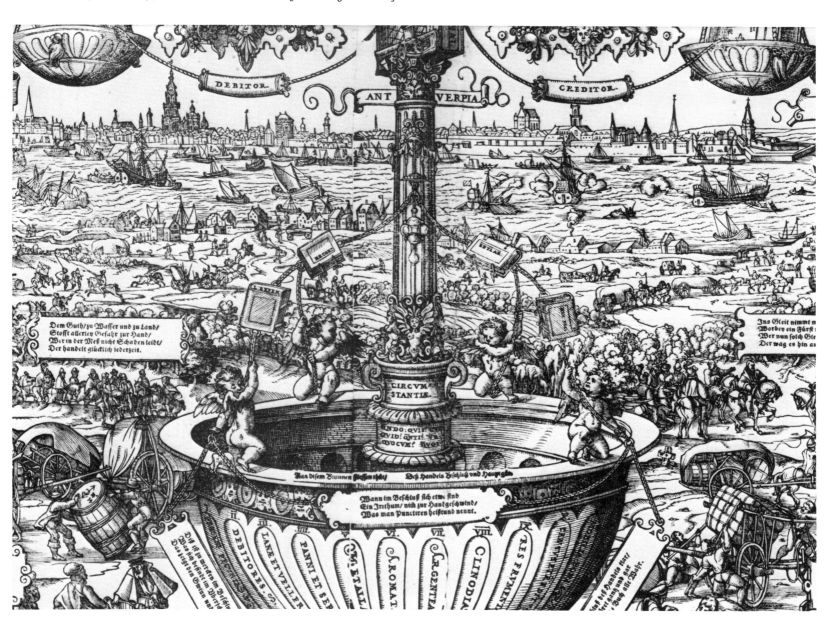

67. The port of Antwerp.
Part of an engraving devoted to the *Allégorie du Commerce* by Jost Amann. 1585. Brussels, Royal Library, Print-room.

THE MERCHANTS

68. Letter from Bruges to Torun on the tampering with furs – February 16, 1446. Toruń, Archivum Miasto Torunia 1667.

"Admirably and ornamentally written by the Elders of the Bruges business house, this letter informs the town of Torun, following a complaint by Bruges furriers and squirrel-fur dealers passed on by the Burgomaster and Town Council, that an Osterlin named Pierre de Roede or Bokel has developed a process which changes the shade of valuable furs (sables, martens and beavers); they had been convinced on seeing the deplorable result after steeping and they enclose with the letter a sample of the said raw fur; it seems that the said master and another Osterlin, Hinrick van Steene, have gone to Ostland and even to Russia to teach this article to other companions (furriers). Please spread this information, the purpose of which is to avoid the ruin of merchants, the more so as this Roede is probably in Torun at this moment."

The sample attached to the bottom of the document is the oldest example of medieval fur which is precisely dated (February 16, 1446).

"Medieval excavations seem, at best, to have reached only the débris of fur confirming, but without further precise details, the use of furs in some parts of the costume; it is possible that fabulous furs (ermine from the crown of Scotland, sable from the sapka of the great princes of Moscow and then the Czars) or more humble furs (kept in the acid soil of peat-bogs) go back to the Middle Ages, but proof is thin and it is difficult to imagine that a skin could last more than half a millenium.

On the other hand, there is no doubt about this sample forwarded and explicitly mentioned in the letter." [Robert Delort]

69. Exchanges between a Hanseatic merchant and Russian trappers at the Novgorod business house.
Part of the sculptured scenes decorating the stalls of the Novgorodfahrer of St. Nicholas' church in Stralsund. 15th century.

INTERMEDIARIES

THE MERCHANTS

WORKING FROM HIS OFFICE

In the 13th century the merchant began directing his affairs from his office. Occasionally he undertook a journey, when it was a matter of a big deal, but normally he worked at home, with a few clerks or apprentices, leaving it to a clerk or shipowner to carry his cargoes bearing his trade mark.

In his study he wrote his correspondence which he addressed to associates in other Hanseatic towns or business houses abroad. He kept his accounts books, often by a rule-of-thumb method, contenting himself with copying out separate memos from time to time.

70. The instruments of credit of a Stalhof merchant in the 16th century.
Part of the portrait of Georg Gisze painted by Hans Memling in 1532.
Berlin, Staatliche Museen Preussischer Kulturbesitz.

The business register, scales and seal can be seen.

In future, the merchant and his heirs had to be educated and know how to read and write; his city council arranged that.

It opened primary schools, despite opposition from the ecclesiastical authorities – the bishop or the chapter – which until then had a scholastic monopoly. It also instituted municipal account books: the debts book (*Schuldbuch*) in Hamburg in 1270; landed property book in Lubeck in 1277, Riga in 1286, Stralsund in 1288 and Luneburg in 1290. In the 14th and 15th centuries a decisive factor in the development of credit and trade was the entry by merchants of their sums due and contracts in registers.

71. The commercial instruments of a Stalhof merchant in the 16th century.
Part of a portrait of Georg Gisze painted by Hans Holbein in 1532.
Berlin, Staatliche Museen Preussischer Kulturbesitz.

In Georg Gisze's business house, bills of exchange along the wall. On one of them: Dem erszamen vorsichtigen hern Gisze to Lunden in Englant kome diessen briff. *(This letter has to be taken to London, to the honorable and sagacious lord Gisze.)*

ASSOCIATION

The merchant formed associations in order to cope with fears and perils, multiply means and cumulate efficiencies.

He set up guilds and companies with the regulars of a certain route or country, depending on common interests, traffic and trade, business trips.

There was the company of merchants who went to the southern part of the Scandinavian peninsula, the *Schonenfahrer*: in Lubeck already before 1365, in Hamburg and Rostock. The *Flandrenfahrer* company: in Lubeck, in Hamburg, with 84 members, in 1376, and the company of merchants who went to England and Spain; in Riga, Reval, Bergen, Novgorod and Stockholm. A merchant could simultaneously belong to several of these companies whose activities embraced a whole range of social functions: mutual assistance, conviviality at meetings and banquets, religious practices.

Each company had its chapel. Its members clubbed together to provide it with a painted or sculptured retable; they could celebrate mass and other divine services there. They placed votive offerings and tombstones there, to the memory of the richest and most imposing.

In the 13th century there were guilds in Bremen and Goslar; in the 14th, in Stettin and Riga. One of the best known was the *Artushof*, Arthur's court, in Danzig. From the end of the 14th century it welcomed ocean-going merchants, foreigners and shipowners.

Its regulations showed a care to ensure the good reputation of the group, maintain decent behaviour and avoid waste. "It was forbidden, under penalty of a fine and even debarment, to throw crockery at someone's head, play around with knives, play games for money, put something in the next man's glass to get him drunk, and to utter calumnies. The number of dishes served, as well as the number of entertainers, was strictly limited; wine was reserved for guests. The latter were required to leave the dining-room at 10 p.m. when the 'beer bell' sounded." [Philippe Dollinger].

72. An armed attack on a merchant convoy.
Part of an engraving devoted to the *Allégorie du commerce* by Jost Amann. 1585.
Brussels, Royal Library, Print-room.

73. The dangers of being a merchant. Painted on wood in 1511 by Paul Lautensack the Elder for the merchant Stefan Praun. Nuremberg Germanisches Nationalmuseum.

The merchant Stefan Praun (1478-1532) traded with Italy, where he twice nearly came to death: on Lake Garda, where he just escaped being shipwrecked, and on the road, where he was attacked by Venetian mercenaries. He survived on both occasions, thanks to the protection of the Virgin.
Here, Mary has just given birth, in the presence of Joseph. The Virgin in labour was the subject of particular devotion in several German regions.

THE MERCHANTS

74. The Guild House (*Artushof*) in Torun. Pen and ink drawing by G. Fr. Steiner. Circa 1730.
Berlin. Archiv für Kunst und Geschichte.

Built in 1385. Razed to the ground in 1802.
Prussian town merchant guilds readily referred to iconography and the symbolics of King Arthur and the Round Table.

INTERMEDIARIES

75. The *Oosterlingenhuis* in Bruges.
Pen and ink drawing (1602), dedicated to the Burgomaster of Cologne, Johann Hardenrath (deceased 1603), on the occasion of his visit to the Hanseatic houses of Bruges and Antwerp.
Cologne, Historisches Archiv.

Here the Hanseatic business house is seen from the north-west.

75

THE MERCHANTS

PRAYER

The merchant, by nature, had an uneasy soul. His accounting conscience rendered him open to all sorts of guilty feelings. The risks he took disturbed his serenity. He extricated himself by intense, active piety in which pilgrimages, votive manifestations, legacies and pious gifts played a large part. Before embarking on a voyage he saw to it that his temporal and spiritual affairs were in order. He made his will. He provided for donations for the salvation of his soul should he lose his life during the crossing.

76. Saint Nicholas, the patron saint of seamen.
Polychrome wood. Circa 1500.
Lubeck, St-Annen-Museum.

77. Saint Anne, patron saint of seamen.
Polychrome wood. Circa 1430.
Lubeck, St-Annen-Museum.

He assiduously attended sanctuaries, especially those dedicated to the Virgin. Mainly at Aix-la-Chapelle, but also Rome, Compostelle and Einsiedeln.

In 1508, when he was twenty-one years old, Franz Wessel, who was later to become the burgomaster of Stralsund, made a pilgrimage to Saint-Jacques. He reported it in his chronicle. The ship on which he embarked was carrying a hundred and fifty pilgrims "not counting women and girls". It called at "nearly fifty ports in Norway, Scotland, Flanders, England and France". On his return to Stralsund he was welcomed with joy by his parents, "for he was an only son and they felt sure that he had perished at sea or elsewhere".

78. Hanse merchant and his wife praying. Painting attributed to Master of the Altar Halepagen, Buxthude. Painted in Hamburg or Bremen circa 1500.
Bremen, Ludwig-Roselius-Sammlung.

The anonymous couple are painted on the volet of a retable. They figure there as donors. Serene and grave, typical representatives of the Hanseatic middle class.

THE MERCHANTS

79. Nativity of the Virgin.
The work of Master of the life of Mary, a painter-black and white artist of Cologne, 1463 to 1480. Representing the most eminent of the Cologne school in the second half of the 15th century, he possibly served his apprenticeship in Flanders.
Munich, Alte Pinakothek.

When the child appears in a middle-class home in the 15th century.

80. Virgin and Child.
Painting by Petrus Christus (approx. 1410-1472); active in Bruges from 1444 to 1472. Painted on oak.
Kansas City, William Rockhill Nelson Gallery of Art and Atklins Museum of Fine Arts. Acc. No. 6551.

The theme of Virgin and Child in the bed chamber was very often treated by 15th century Flemish painters. Christus' painting brings us into one of those middle-class homes which were the framework of everyday childhood and adolescence of merchants' children.

Following pages:

81-82. A Hanseatic merchant family: the Brömse of Lubeck.
Volets of a retable situated in the oldest chapel (15th century) on the south side of St. Jacques' church in Lubeck. Vers 1515.

The central part of the retable, a sandstone relief, represents the crucifixion.
On the left, Heinrich Brömse (deceased 1502) who was burgomaster of Lubeck, with his six sons, one of whom was a councillor, one an Aeltermann of the Stalhof in London and one a Novgorodfahrer.
Their patron saints: Bartholomew and George.
On the right: Heinrich's wife, Elizabeth Westfal, and their five daughters.
Their patron saints: Anne and Barbara.

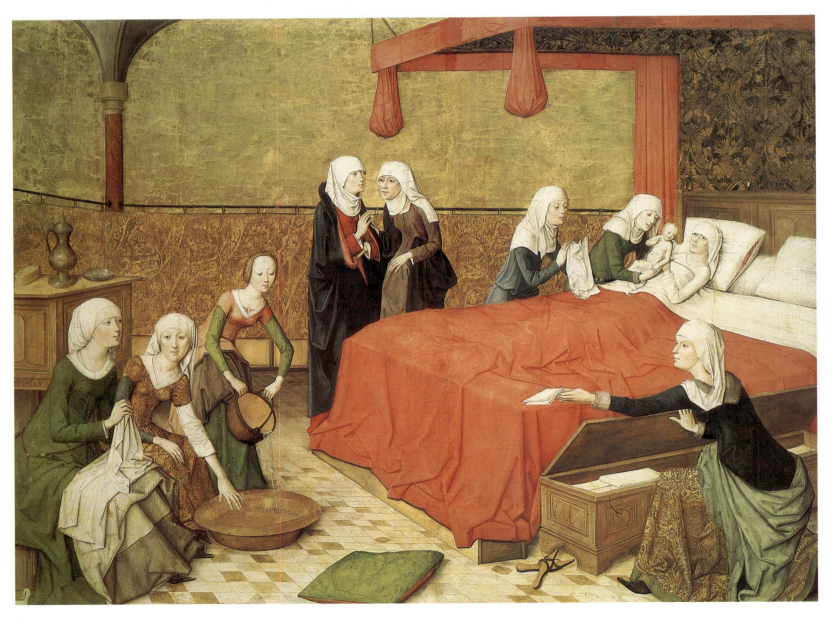

78

83. Members of the Holy Blood Confraternity in Bruges.
Bruges, the Chapel of the Holy Blood.

Painting (1556) which Peter Pourbus (1523-1584) was commissioned to paint by the Confraternity of the Holy Blood for the chancel of the Holy Blood chapel in Bruges.
The 32 members of the Confraternity are shown on two wooden panels (16 per panel). Those in the front row are kneeling; only the heads of the others are visible.
Here, the left-hand panel.
Front, centre, wearing a gold chain: the Provost of the Confraternity, Loys Thiery.
At the back: Paschier de Pape, the Confraternity clerk, holding a document.

84. A votive painting by Cord Middelborch (deceased 1572), in the Nikolaikirche, Stralsund.

85. Interior of St. Jean's church near the market (*Am Sande*), Luneburg.

TO BE RICH

Rich merchants formed part of the urban patriciate, as did persons of independent means, whose fortune, incidentally, had often originally come from trade.

At the end of the 14th century, the fortunes of the richest people in Hamburg exceeded 5,000 Lubeck marks. Those of the comfortably-off upper middle class ranged from 2,000 to 5,000, those of the middle class from 600 to 2,000, and the lower middle class from 150 to 600.

That classification was peculiar to Hamburg; obviously it cannot be extended to all the other towns. Everyone had his own activities. The amount of big fortunes was lower in the less flourishing towns, whereas the middle class tended to differ more greatly.

In the early 16th century, the biggest fortunes exceeded 40,000 marks, particularly that of Johann Bussmann, the richest Lubeck merchant. They were much smaller than those of the big Central Germany merchants. That of the Fuggers, for instance, was estimated at 375,000 Lubeck marks in 1511. That of the Welsers, in 1515, at 486,000. That of Claus Stalburg, of Frankfort, in 1515, at 82,500 marks.

THE MERCHANTS

87. Goslar *Bergkanne*.
Vermeil aiguière. Nuremberg 1477.
Goslar, Town Hall collection.

On the lid: scenes of work in the region's mines, rich in silver, lead and copper deposits.
On the belly: scenes with angel musicians.

86. Lubeck Town Hall court-room in 1625.
Painting by Hans Heinssen.
Lubeck, St-Annen-Museum.

In the background, on a table on the right: the 'pots of wine'.

INSPIRING CONFIDENCE

A merchant made a point of inspiring confidence by his attitudes, behaviour, measured, respectable gestures and deeds, weighed words, attentive listening and worthy presence.

By his carefully chosen clothing, too. Fur was the sign of luxury and elegance: as edging, lining, and headgear: beaver, otter, fox, squirrel, which he dealt with in enormous quantities – thousands of skins.

By his house, household, life style and numerous progeny.

Bourgeois by his commercial and financial activities, a rich merchant was inclined to adopt the usages and references of the nobility, of the aristocracy, for his way of life. He surrounded himself with knightly symbols, valiant figures. They were mythically represented on the walls of rooms in the Town Hall, on the facades of guild houses, in his manuscripts, on his furniture and on his table service.

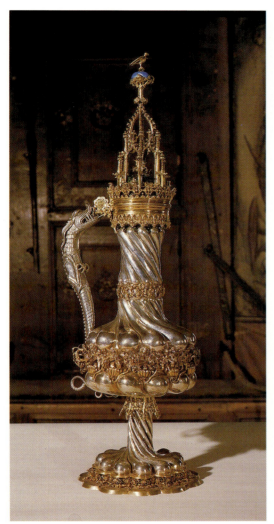

THE MERCHANTS

TO BE EMINENT

In his town the Hanseatic was a person of distinction. He formed part of the dominant social class. He invested the dignity of his rank, dignity which stemmed from his authority and power.

He was careful, therefore, to play a prestige role in urban and ecclesiastical events. He organized festivities in the Town Hall and on the main square and paid for most of the entertainment out of his own pocket.

Especially from the beginning of the 16th century he took care to be seen about and commissioned his portrait to be painted. So Hans Holbein painted about a dozen portraits of Stalhof Hanseatics from 1532 onwards.

He wants to be present, when he is away on business in London or elsewhere, and after his absence for ever, his death, he wants to remind his successors of the weight and importance of what he undertook for business.

88. The burgomaster Johann Springintgut (deceased 1455) and the city secretary (*Stadtschreiber*), Marquardus Mildehöved. Late 15th century. Painting on wood. From Luneburg Town Hall.
Luneburg, Museum für das Fustentum.

At the persons' feet: their coats of arms by which they are identified.
The burgomaster's soul goes to Heaven. It leaves a body which has been imprisoned for twelve weeks in the damp cellars of the town prison, situated under the biggest tower of the Luneburg ramparts (Am Graalwall).
Springintgut was one of the victims of the war of the prelates (Luneburger Preielatenkrieg). Contemporary literature was much concerned about his fate.
After Springintgut's death, Mildehöved became secretary of the town of Hamburg. He married Windel Kruse, the daughter of a Luneburg patrician, in 1459.

89. Portrait of a Lubeck merchant, Hans Sonnenschein, 1534.
By Hans Kemmer (1495-1561) who settled in Lubeck around 1522.
Lubeck, St-Annen-Museum.

THE MERCHANTS

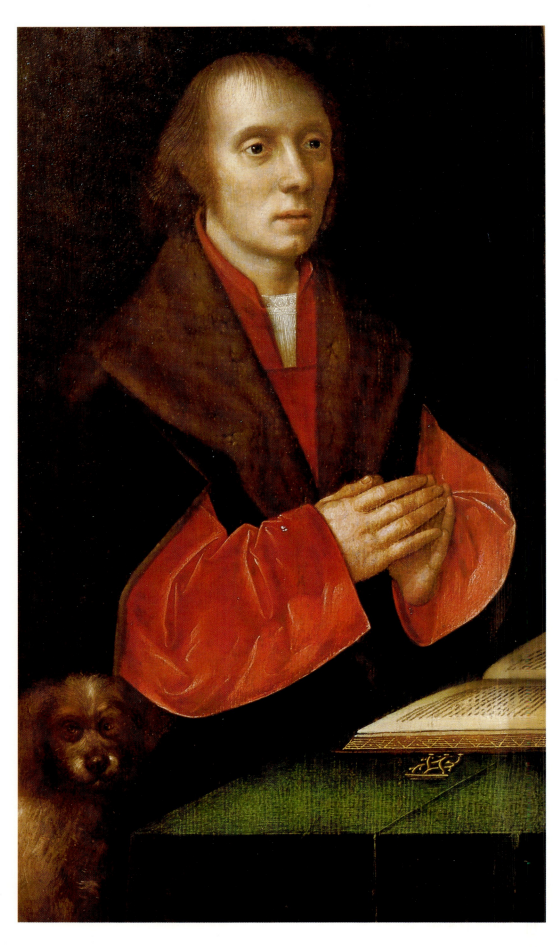

90-91 A merchant and his wife in 1520.
Volets of a retable painted by Jacob von Utrecht.
Lubeck, St-Annen-Museum.

INTERMEDIARIES

THE MERCHANTS

STATUTES OF THE DANZIG ARTUSHOF CIRCA 1390.

Firstly, the four men elected pursuant to custom to preside over the Court will co-opt the four eldest who frequent it; to those eight the Council will add four of its members from among those who frequent it. Those twelve will administer the Court with the best of will and will regulate everything concerning it. If they do not manage to do so, the matter will be brought before the Council and the community; what they decide will be enforceable. Decisions concerning the Court must be made in the morning, before lunch.

92. A guild meal in the 16th century.
Pen and ink tinted drawing, 1522.
Project by Hans Holbein the Younger for a stained glass window for the Stalhof Guildhall in London.
New York.
After Paul Ganz, *Die Handzeichnungen Hans Holbein* d.j., xix z.

INTERMEDIARIES

The Court will be open on Sundays and on feast-days after lunch, and on weekdays at the hour of evensong. When the beer bell rings, everyone must part company; only the four Elders and their guests may remain to drink. Anyone staying longer shall buy a barrel of beer for the company. Entertainers must leave at the same time as the others. There may not be more than two couples, to be paid one pfennig and a half. (Then follow the rules about the number of menservants and their wages, the lighting, and the drinks and food offered to the guests).

No one may invite guests to the Court before making sure that they are worthy to be admitted and are not likely to cause injury to anyone. Should such prove not to be the case, the guarantor of the guest will be responsible and will pay a fine of half a last of beer. No one is admitted to the Court unless he possesses assets of at least 20 marks. Tradesmen may not enter, whoever they may be. Nor may those who retail beer or those who have worked for a wage during the preceding year.

The Court is forbidden to all those who cannot assist a man in his rights or who marry a woman of bad reputation. Also excluded are those who have knowingly travelled to prohibited regions or have shipped goods there, until such time as they have purged their wrong and have furnished the Elder with an attestation of respectability equal to the honourable character they possessed before they contravened the law.

If anyone is accused, on this head or any other, of having transgressed the rules of the Court and of having fraudulently violated those rules, he shall pay a fine of two marks, to be shared equally between the Town and the Court, and he shall remain debarred from the Court until he has paid. [P. Simson]

93. A meal at the van Liere's in Antwerp, 1524.
Utrecht, Centraal Museum.

In the centre of the picture, the coats of arms of the van Liere family. At the head of the table is Arnold van Liere, lord of Santhoven and Woldesele, successively councillor and burgomaster of the town of Antwerp between 1500 and 1529, the doyen of the Guild of St. Luke and owner of the van Liere mansion built for him in 1516.

JURGEN ELLERMEYER
Professor at Hamburg University

Employers

The merchant was not only a businessman, he was sometimes, and even often, an employer.
He needed a labour force for handling work in the port and warehouses, as well as for goods traffic on land and sea, so he kept an eye on immigration from the country, wage and price trends, etc.
Workmen uprooted from the country only to fall into the snares of the town, needed work in order to survive; they sought employers.
Having engaged them, the merchant usually looked after their upkeep and that of their families. Sometimes he found them lodgings and helped them.
In this way the merchant employer became responsible for the social security and assistance of the most deprived. He competed with ecclesiastical institutions, traditionally caritative, by founding hospitals, and with the town by building low-priced housing.
In this sphere the Hanseatics were sometimes pioneers, for instance by founding the Holy Ghost hospital in Lubeck in the 13th century. [A. d'H.]

94. Employers and workmen on the market place.
15th century miniature.
Paris, National Library, Ms. French 288, fol. 198.

95. Mobs on the quay in Antwerp in the 15th century.
Part of a painting representing the port of Antwerp, painted between 1518 and 1540.
Antwerp, Nationaal Scheepvaartmuseum.

ENGAGING WORKERS

In Luneburg An agreement with the lord (second half of 13th century), then pressure by the owners and in particular by the clergy, checked salt-works extension; at the end of the 16th century they were simply kept running, without being enlarged.

Increased production capacity was not obtained by taking on more workers, but by technical improvements.

Commercial traffic remained limited because of the preponderance of Hamburg.

The downturn in the economic situation caused groups to close ranks.

The Slavs (Wends) were systematically excluded. Discriminatory measures were written into commercial law (for shopkeepers in 1350) and into burghers' rights (exclusion in 1409). Behind those barriers lay the authority of the Council, which upheld the security of the middle classes and its own interests.

In the late 15th century, membership of the guilds was deliberately restricted by fixing the maximum number of members, recruitment from father to son and complicating the terms of admission.

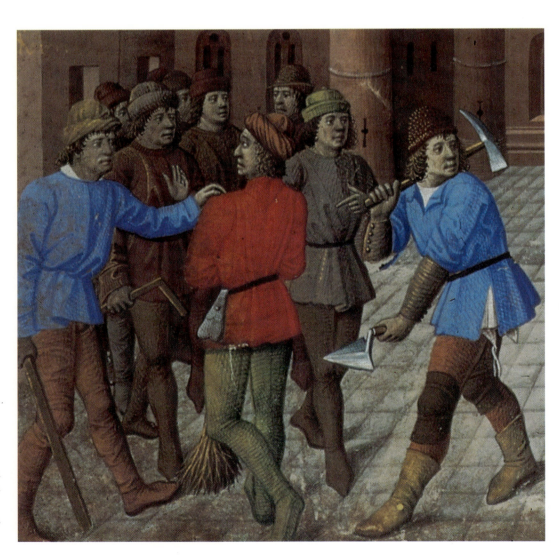

96. A team of building workers. Part of a French miniature illustrating Les faits et dis des Romains et autres gens, circa 1475. London, British Museum, Ms. Harl. 4375, fol. 123 recto.

Jobs were lost, or in any case no new ones were created, and wages came down.

The upper classes and the Council took care to "feed according to their rank" the intermediate classes of society who, as has been seen, had a stabilizing influence; that was all right as long as those intermediate classes did not constitute obstacles to the upper classes carrying out their economic undertakings. They endeavoured to keep well away from the town those who could not enter the corporations, or to engage them for unskilled jobs in trade, shipping or manufactures. There were nevertheless undesirable arrivals.

Luneburg had less 'need' of the poor than Hamburg, even for its defence which, in any case, would not have stood up for long in the face of a serious military threat.

Limitation, both natural and deliberate, of economic possibilities other than salt, which the salt-works owners solidly controlled, helped to contain the demographic growth of Luneburg at the end of the Middle Ages and the beginning of the modern epoch (10,000 to 14,000 inhabitants).

With less growth, there were fewer food and lodging problems. It was for that reason that for centuries Luneburg gave the impression of being 'a rich town'.

97. A team of carpenters at work. 14th century miniature illustrating the *Poltillaue Nicolae de Lira*.
Arras, Municipal Library, ms. 2.

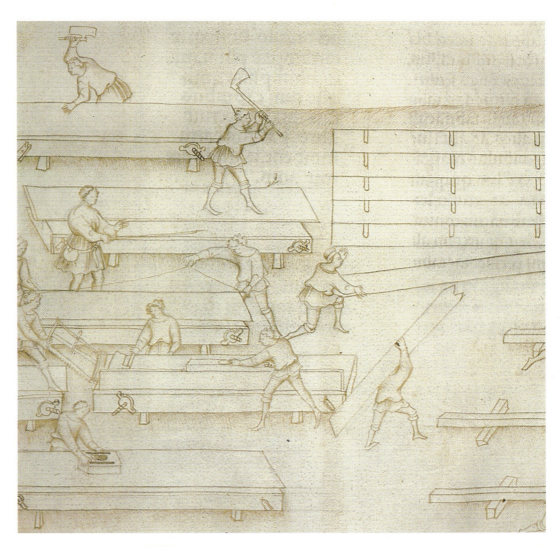

In Hamburg In a town like Hamburg, economic activity seemed much more dependent on the commercial economic conditions.

Favoured by its geographical situation and strengthened around 1600 by the contribution of foreign partners, trade developed and brought numerous ancillary or parallel activities in its wake. It accentuated the decline of some (brewing) and encouraged the development of others (dyeing, sugar refining, printed cotton goods).

To be able to defend itself, especially in view of the progress made in artillery, Hamburg moved up into the heights. At the beginning of the Thirty Years War a big new town was created, surrounded by fortifications. These defence efforts were shared with a few other Hanse towns that had remained powerful.

This new town enabled Hamburg to develop well beyond the limits of the Hanse, which could no longer contribute much to it, apart from the jealousy of the inhabitants of Luneburg and Lubeck, who had – but this was not the first point of disagreement – taken offence because Hamburg had welcomed the Merchant Adventurers in 1567 and definitively in 1611.

In the new Post-Hanseatic town, growth problems arose in the same terms as before. Hamburg was a town that was essentially turned towards trade in which, a psychological advantage, no one felt excluded from that sector of activity: neither the burghers (until the law made a distinction between 'small' and 'big' burghers), nor the seamen who, in accordance with general usage, were allowed a part of the cargo carried.

Under such conditions, an economic slump or difficulty in maritime communications could have very heavy consequences: unemployment among seamen and in different economic sectors, the exporting and processing of imported raw materials, difficulties for everyone, from grocers to dock hands, financial losses for money-lenders and sleeping partners, reduced customs and fiscal income, and therefore a shortage of money in the coffers of the town just when it was being increasingly solicited to back up trade (diplomatic and military interventions, facilities offered to outside 'capitalists') or to cover even more urgent social needs in such a period (assistance for the poor, distribution of bread.)

The losses suffered by landowners and industrialists caused them to react briskly to the installation of new forms of industrial activity, manufactures, and the extension of the town and the real estate market. Up to a point, they hampered each other and also slowed the merchants' wish for expansion as well as that of those who, as the town developed, were financially concerned in strides being made by new districts and new suburbs. When a period of prosperity returned, new inhabitants were attracted, some wealthy, others not, the cost of living, rents in particular, increased, and finally the numbers of the poor increased in proportions such that enlightened minds felt obliged to act (the Institution of Public Assistance in 1788), which did not manage to change things very much.

FEEDING THE PEOPLE

The town authorities were vigilant as regards corn procurement and cereal prices, by foresight as much as by political interest. The cereal procurement policy of the town of Cologne was generally considered as a success. The organization was suitable and, after the years of famine 1437-1439, the town possessed a big silo, employed four master cerealists and watched the market evolution attentively. All that was done in relatively good understanding with the lords of surrounding territories, and so that policy could, up to a point, benefit the region too.

The most serious problems arose in towns that were more concerned with the grain trade than Cologne.

In competition regarding basic foodstuffs, the merchants stuck at nothing. It is reported that on several occasions the inhabitants of Lubeck destroyed parts of the town of Stralsund in 1238 and 1277 in order to get their hands on Pomeranian cereals and, in 1249, to appropriate herring fishing areas around Rügen.

Within the scope of their more limited possibilities, the Luneburg and Magdeburg merchants also sought to set up monopolies, and the attitude of Hamburg towards rival towns and peasants is well-known.

The first action to limit grain was the establishment of tolls, but in Hamburg in the 15th century that no longer sufficed. As from about 1359, rich private persons were obliged to constitute reserve stocks and the towns did the same thing later on (1445). The Council promised to limit exports and see that public reserves were constituted. On the Reformation it undertook that the administration of the 'Caisse de Dieu' should hold a certain quantity of goods available for the poor. It was only after the great constitutional, financial and foodstuffs crisis of 1556 that the first regulation concerning corn provided for the purchase of cereals by the town authorities.

At the beginning of the 17th century and – even after the belated construction in 1660/1661 of a big new corn-exchange – again at the beginning of the 18th century, the burghers were bound to elect delegates entrusted with those problems. As from that date flour was ground for the poor at the expense of the town and sold cheaply, but persons who had no right to it also benefited.

All that was necessary although in the Middle Ages they tried to fight rising prices by a buying policy and, at the latest as from the Reformation, it was recognized that the poor had certain pre-emption rights over cereal imports made by the rich, and on the wholesale sales carried out by bakers, brewers and merchants within the town.

ACCOMMODATION

Initially, this sector was more or less favourable. In Hanse towns, especially in those founded recently, the disappearance of seigniorial rights made it possible to constitute a land tax which was quite favourable for economic development. The restrictions and stringencies imposed by the authorities for purposes of common interest (enlargement of the town, protection of existing houses, possibly also anti-speculation landed property measures), were considered – and still are today – as beneficent incitements, resulting from a higher property right exercised by the town. But it was not long before that property began to be excessively concentrated in the hands of a limited number of burghers.

With the arrival of new populations in a town bounded by its ramparts, it was not possible to reserve the benefit of legal protection for landed property owners alone. The latter were privileged in that they were granted additional political rights – in Hamburg that applied till the 20th century.

The numerous housing locations which created dependence relationships is explained not only by the lack of building ground and the increased size of the buildings, but also by the large amount of freedom which quickly became a feature of a real estate market concentrated in a few hands. Such an accumulation was to be found in Cologne in the 12th century. It concerned dwellings, shops, industrial premises, revenue-earning houses, cellars and lofts. Loans on landed property, which were highly developed in Hanse towns, facilitated the purchase of real estate. That was further found in Bremen in the 19th century in a form peculiar to 'Germanic law', to such a point that it contributed to the birth of a particular lengthwise style of building, on which modern architecture is still patterned. The general overhead expenses represented a weight a part of which landlords attempted to have borne by the tenants. Differences concerning modes of habitation and housing possibilities, the existence and extent or, on the contrary, the non-existence of landed property became so accentuated in Hanse towns that, in the late Middle Ages, they were officially recognized and expressed by obligations to be complied with (taxes, the constitution of reserves of corn or arms dumps) or by rights granted (grazing rights, capacity to give evidence in court, possibility of brewing beer), which not only reflects social stratifications but also constitutes them.

There was never a housing policy taking into account the large number of insanitary dwellings (in particular damp cellars in Hamburg and some Baltic towns), nor was there a lack of cheap offers. Lodging in alms-houses was quite often rented, i.e. it benefited those who were able to pay. However, in the second half of the 14th century, in Lubeck in particular, rich burghers made it a point of honour to provide some small form of lodging without charge. Much stress has been laid on the exemplary nature of these 'resting-places' of one or two floors in corridors and courtyards, but only a small fraction of potentially profitable lettable accommodation was changed in this way into 'resting-places for the poor' or, more rarely, into 'cellars for the poor'.

ASSISTANCE

The term 'social assistance' covered widely differing realities: aid provided by the patriciate in various fields, administration in its neutral, general sense but also with all its positive connotations (rendering difficult situations bearable) and negative ones (administering want instead of abolishing it); lastly, charity – limited and individualized in terms of the situations and persons concerned – but also able to go further than organizations.

The criteria according to which the town authorities granted their assistance, which was indispensable as a supplement to that given by the Church and private persons, stemmed rather from a concern for mercantile rationality than from humanist preoccupations, though these were not foreign to town administrations. The noble educational ideal developed by the humanists was turned into a principle of general prevention as expressed in the regulations governing beggars in the town of Nuremberg in the 14th and 15th centuries, as well as in imperial police regulations as from 1530.

That means to say that the Hanse towns gave no particular impetus in this sphere. They kept moderately to the broad outlines of reforming ideas about the poor (against excessive distribution of alms; against an influx of foreign beggars to the town), evolving prudently, faced with the tasks to be accomplished, between 'general prevention' and the modern concept of 'existential assistance'.

These beneficent measures arose from a certain landed property and real estate condition which was itself largely dependent on trade.

98. Dormitory in the Holy Ghost hospital in Lubeck. The alcoves date from the 18th century.

99. The Holy Ghost hospital in Lubeck.
Built in 1280 for the elderly and the sick.

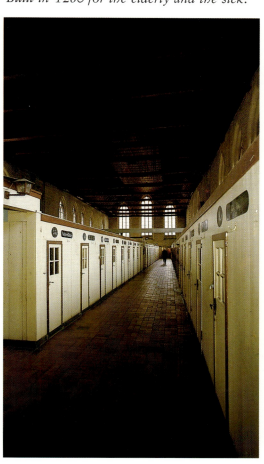

THE MERCHANTS

When Lubeck trade was still greater than that of Hamburg and the population ratio of the two towns was about three to one (around 1300, about 15,000 to 5000), the price of ground-plots was up to twice as high in Lubeck as it was in Hamburg, and housing costs were situated in the same proportion. In the early 16th century when Lubeck had about 25,000 inhabitants and Hamburg only 15,000, but with greater long term commercial assets, the level of prices in Hamburg on the real estate market had caught up with that of Lubeck. Prices depended principally on trading possibilities and the resultant utilization of the land. Then the economic attraction of Lubeck and its population figure had hardly changed till the early 19th century and so housing problems had evolved but little. Unlike Hamburg, Lubeck still offered the idyllic but deceptive image of those dwellings in courtyards and corridors, partly conserved.

Merchant foundations dating back to the 15th or 16th century and intended for habitation are to be found in Hamburg. But the 'regulation on the plague' drafted by Blökel, the town doctor, in 1597, and which was quite ineffective, tells us about the utter misery of the dwellings which the sumptuous new 17th century town did not abolish and which, during the 'golden age of trade' in

100. Retable in the Holy Ghost hospital in Lubeck.
Polychrome wood. Early 16th century.

In the centre, four scenes: the Holy Family, the Adoration of the Three Wise Men, Saint Ursula and her companions, the Ten Thousand Virgins.
On either side: four statues of saints.

the 1790's, took forms such that the Council was forced to intervene. The middle classes were also affected. The evidence of another doctor, Rambach, in 1801, and the expulsion of the destitute by the French in 1813-1814, show how little weight all that carried when up against the interests of capital.

The social assistance regulations strengthened the classes of society to whom they applied, as well as the general moral principles on which they were based. Before the Reformation, but even more because of it, it was not considered sufficient for the 'receivers' to guarantee, actively or passively, the salvation of the soul of the 'givers' and to recognize their pre-eminence; they were also expected to undertake to work and become skilled. Reintegrating them in the labour circuit seemed to be the most profitable thing for everyone. Nothing in the field of assistance for the poor and sick measured up to the economic dynamism and autonomy of the dominant classes when the Hanse was at its strongest.

An alms-house for needy seamen was opened in Hamburg in 1556. An orphanage was built in Lubeck after the famine and plague of 1546 and 1548, and one in Cologne in 1602. The orphanage in Hamburg (1604) was the

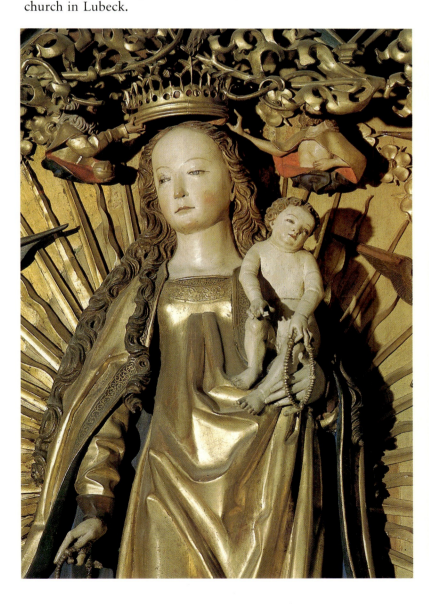

101-102. The Virgin with mantle. Polychrome wood. Retable, first quarter of the 16th century, in the portal of the Holy Ghost church in Lubeck.

THE MERCHANTS

result of activity by Dutch immigrants and a copy of what was being done in the Netherlands. A pest-house for the plague-stricken was built in 1606, after being called for by the reformer Bugenhagen. In 1622 a work shop for prisoners sentenced to hard labour was built on the model of similar institutions founded in Amsterdam in 1595-1597.

On the initiative of the Church a similar work shop was started in Cologne in 1636 but was quickly closed down. In 1697 there was a municipal alms-house for the poor where work was compulsory. In 1763 a convict prison for habitual beggars was built. Luneburg and Cologne at the end of the Middle Ages, and Hamburg and Lubeck at the beginning of the Modern Epoch, did nothing really glorious as regards tolerance towards Jews. Generally speaking, those who were different or most deprived were rejected or kept under close watch, rather than assisted. Hamburg, on the other hand, offered possibilities.

103. Dyers. 15th century Flemish miniature.
British Museum, Royal Ma. 15, E III, fol. 264.

AND SOCIAL PROGRESS?

A lot of credit must be given to the Hanse in a number of fields: civil law, criminal law, legal procedure, maritime law, protection of borough property, general policing, organization of industrial activity in towns, assistance for the destitute. But it is also worth while reflecting on the effect that a measure could have on one class or another of society.

Progress was largely due to the political autonomy that the Hanse towns endeavoured to preserve. At the beginning of the Modern Epoch that autonomy gave way to a development policy on the scale of several regions. The imperial towns fell behind in administrative organization compared with the other towns.

In Cologne, a town which kept itself to itself, the developing territorial authorities imposed all sorts of restrictions which limited trade outlets and consequently industrial progress, whilst increasing the number of poor people.

In Luneburg and in towns like Lubeck, favoured by the existence of a hinterland and maritime outlets, and to a lesser extent in Hamburg, autonomy which withdrew within itself led to sclerosis of the former holders of economic power, and indeed to inactivity approaching the peace of cemeteries.

Measures, even limited ones, concerning administration or public assistance "contributed to educating our people so that they could reach a higher degree of culture"; yet it could be seen that in towns just as in territorial seigniories "the socialization process was accompanied by a power appropriation process" generally to the profit of the holders of economic wealth.

Social order in Hanse towns was more the result of a 'regulation' than of 'dictatorial obedience', but there were various means of having "the ideal of order and discipline" respected in order to defend "the indispensable trade, soul and prosperity of the town". (Hamburg in the event, but all the others too.)

In the Middle Ages, not to follow those lines meant being poor, but it also implied that the person was a 'baddy'. Whilst in the 17th century the Hamburg authorities evoked "the ship on which everything was embarked", the time was long past when the ordinary seaman had any say in matters. In slump times, to obtain "agreement between those who command and those who obey", the Council, all-powerful since the Hanse period, sometimes evoked the prosperity of Sparta. But there was a big difference between the economic and political organization of the Greek 'model' and the Hanse towns – which was just as well for the regions on which those towns left their mark.

JURGEN ELLERMEYER
Professor at Hamburg University

Men of Power

Economic power and wealth lead to social power.
A successful merchant finished up, sooner or later, with a seat on the Council and played an active part in city management, so he became a man of power.
He could then have his say regarding urban laws and institutions, possibly making them more favourable for his personal undertakings and projects. This was to the detriment of the territorial prince and at the expense of social groups subordinate to him.
To have acceded to economic and social power in the daily confrontation with concrete realities, without having recourse to violence, but by negotiation, made the Hanseatic in power a reasonable and moderate man.
[A. d'H.]

104. Sitting of the city court in Lucerne. 1513.
Miniature ornamenting the Luzerner Chronik by Diebold Schilling the Younger (1460 – between 1517 and 1522).
Lucerne. Korporationsgemeinde der Stadt Luzern.

105. Roland, polychrome, Bremen.
Part of an anonymus painting in the 1620's.
Bremen, Landesmuseum.

In 1404 it replaced a wooden statue which Archbishop Adalbert's menservants had burned in 1366.
It was surmounted by a canopy in 1513 and flanked by an escutcheon bearing the imperial eagle and the inscription:
Vryheit do ik ju pjenbar
de Karl und mennich vorst vorwar
desser stede ghegeven hat
des danked gode is min radt.
It was the symbol of urban justice and freedom.
When Berlin lost its autonomy in 1448, its Roland was pulled down and thrown into the Spree.

URBAN MERCHANTS AND PRIVILEGES

The rich merchants fiercely defended their hard-won privileges, which they said were evident and natural — as the heredity of fiefs had become — a vital though intangible necessity, acquired by work and merit.

The economic policy of the town, in the community sense, but in which private interests inevitably mingled, was meant to assure management and be prospective. It was in fact complex and difficult. The privileged had to be protected, whilst initiative had to be left open, if only to allow the most powerful merchants to make still bigger profits.

The mechanism was more or less as follows: in exchange for a privilege, it was first necessary to have something to offer; the more one received, the more one was liable to lose; if one did not want to stop at that point, the best thing to do was to calculate and define the terms of agreement oneself. Consequently, privileges, a means of regulating competition, encouraged expansion.

The privileges granted the big merchants accentuated the social difference in the urban community, right up to an extreme polarization which was the character of Hanse towns known 'for their wealth'.

The merchants dominated production and therefore the craftsmen, industrial quarters and surrounding countryside.

The Hanse formed opposition to foreign countries and lords, though they were not, at least at first, really hostile to it. It was also a creation of big towns against smaller ones, yet the latter, because of certain advantages, sought to enter the association, against neighbouring regions and non-trading populations, which could also find advantages in belonging to the Hanse. The big merchants changed towns; they extended their business relations to several metropolises. In short, they did not consider such and such a town by itself, but the organization of the Hanse itself as the instrument of their activity.

However, it happened that the Hanse became of less interest in the eyes of merchants, for a while and then definitively, e.g.:

a) when privileges acquired abroad could neither be retained nor enlarged;

b) when the trading positions of a town considered separately seemed solidly established and it appeared more advantageous to go it alone;

c) when neighbouring regions surrounded themselves with barriers or advanced by leaps and bounds;

d) when the council of merchants had been able to establish its autonomy and authority sufficiently, possibly by opening up a little to the middle classes;

c) when the little towns lost too much, with the big ones benefiting.

The Hanse, as can be seen, was an instrument rather than an imprescriptible commitment.

In Lubeck Lubeck very quickly had its council, dominated by merchants.

Its rapid emancipation stemmed from its enormous geo-economic assets in North East Europe. The town had everything necessary to become the turn-table of sea trade in the North and the Baltic; it was also the base for expansion to the East.

Many political personages interested themselves in its development: the Count of Holstein, the Duke of Saxony, the King of Denmark and the Emperor. Their interests, whether convergent or divergent, were always those of the merchants. Locally, there was no powerful sovereign as in Cologne for instance, where struggles between the archbishop and the merchants were long and bitter and involved craftsmen.

The merchants were able to organize themselves to strengthen their legitimacy when faced with the authority of the count, then of the duke, and with the feudal competition of the Guelphs and Staufers. The count increased his power in Hamburg, but Lubeck became imperial (1181), then a Holstein possession and finally, through its economic weight, a free city of the Empire. Lubeck owed a lot to Henry the Lion in the great strides it made so quickly and the exceptional economic dimensions it attained. The duke granted Lubeck merchants rights over the lands of which he was the master, thus enlarging the town's hinterland. He acted as a mediator between the Germans and the Gotland merchants and rendered commercial traffic possible between Germany and Sweden, as well as opening up that country to German emigrants and capital. He declared war and destroyed Bardowick which had at one time been favoured by its nearness to Luneburg.

Lubeck was the first German town to have the right to mint money (1266). It created the joint definition of coinage fineness in 1255 and that, most probably, was the beginning of the Wends monetary union which was extremely important for the Hanse.

Lubeck often used its arms and negotiated with the Emperor as well as, in the 16th century, with the King of Denmark.

It was able to enter into any agreements it needed such as one with Hamburg in 1242 guaranteeing transport and legal protection, and another one by which it obtained corporative rights in England in 1267/1282. Then there was the decision in 1293 by the councils of the North German Hanseatic towns to recognize Lubeck as the supreme juridical body for the Novgorod business houses, in the place of Visby which had been so important up to then.

To that dominant position abroad corresponded a strengthening of power at home: regular taxation was very soon established (the land tax no doubt goes back to 1226), a city due was defined thirty years before that of Hamburg (1240; in both towns in replacement of an older Latin code); the Council's decisive influence in organizing justice; a more than favourable regulation for the election of the Council, alleged to be due to Henry the Lion; a town school subject to purely formal control by the Church, but in fact already serving the objectives of the merchants (1262); lastly the Council itself, which was important because of all the administrative regulations it produced, and which, in order to be able to accomplish all its tasks, created at the end of the 13th century five 'offices', as they were later called, which it entrusted to its members.

THE MERCHANTS

108

In Hamburg The new town was founded in the late 13th century. The lords granted customs facilities to the Elbe hinterland merchants so that the town could become an important trading centre. Agreements simplified commercial traffic, with Luneburg for instance, and guaranteed trade with Lubeck and Bremen.

Whenever necessary, documents were falsified and arms used to eliminate competition from Stade which possessed mart rights and blocked access to the sea.

Protection by the Counts of Holstein usefully opposed the right of the former lord, the Archduke of Bremen who banked on Stade.

At the same time, it was in the interest of the Duke of Brunswick to help the Hamburg and Lubeck merchants to form a Hanse in England. They thus freed themselves from the powerful influence which Cologne exerted on German merchants in London.

The merchants then instituted a city due and in 1270 Hamburg became a free town.

In Luneburg Salt, to an enormous extent, and fish to a much lesser extent, asserted Luneburg's importance in the economy of the region, first of all, and in that of Hanseatic Europe later.

The manifest interest of salt spared the town early struggles between the lord and the urban community. Each party contributed to the development of the salt-works, the importation of the necessary timber and the setting up of export networks.

By the middle of the 12th century, the lords had eliminated rival salt-works by force (Oldesloe between Hamburg and Lubeck). In 1273 Luneburg received the salt monopoly for all the principality.

Towards the end of the 13th century the salt-works became the property of the town, although a large part of it had belonged to the local clergy.

The inhabitants of Luneburg sought first of all to come to agreements with other corporations (fiscal matters in 1263, currency agreement in 1293) and took advantage of dynastic conflicts to free themselves from the excessive influence of their duke. It was only later that they sought more solid backing in the Hanse and the leagues of Saxon towns.

In 1229 the town gave master salt-makers the right to vote. The owners of the salt-works dominated Luneburg Council. For a very long time the latter kept its institutional predominance, its social representativeness which was deliberately limited to one group, and its political and economic orientation, without there being any real opposition. Production increased threefold in the 13th century and a large part of it was exported from 1200 onwards.

In the 16th century, competition by bay-salt from Southern Europe appeared, but the quality of the Luneburg product and the weight of those who were behind it: the master salt-makers, members of the Council, Dukes of Brunswick-Luneburg, Lubeck investors and intermediaries who headed the Hanse, kept its place for it on the Hanse markets.

106. Part of the decoration painted on the cradle-vault of Luneburg Town Hall courtroom. Early 16th century.

THE MERCHANTS

MERCHANTS AND URBAN MANAGEMENT

By urban autonomy we mean a power such that the most powerful social class (and not necessarily all the social groups) had the means to guarantee the economic foundations of its power. The autonomy was the result of a process by which economic power managed to convert itself into political domination.

The economic basis of the autonomy was provided by distant trading, by exports and by profit made on commercial traffic in basic commodities, in addition to trading in luxury goods and especially in major consumer products – locally, in the neighbourhoods and by commercial traffic with distant countries. There was relative stability in goods traffic and gross income.

Improved lines of communication and progress in commercial techniques enabled merchants to lead a more sedentary life. At the same time, densification of the trading network made it necessary to set up in a safe central place from which an eye could be kept on everything and to which the greatest number of foreign merchants could be attracted; a place, too, where small related business activities and artisanry could develop.

It was necessary to facilitate joint transactions and regulate competition, to impose decisions in increasingly complicated matters, in short, to put an economic policy into practice.

The big merchants constituted a council or, in towns bound by Magdeburg law, a board of councillors.

Representatives of the nobility and other burghers also sat on the Council, though generally without their actually managing it.

The seats were often hereditary, although in a commercial town social divisions were less strict than elsewhere.

107. The Council Chamber (*Ratsherrenstube* or *Huldigungssaal*) of Goslar Town Hall.
The painted decoration dates from the 1520's.

Nevertheless, important political decisions belonged to a relatively small group of families, often allied by marriage and united by common interests. Even when those who wanted to sit on the Council were not explicitly required to possess a fortune of a certain amount (as they were in Bremen) or which came from a specified activity (as in Lubeck), the honorary nature of the office and sometimes the obligation in which Councillors found themselves to make a special financial contribution, favoured the transition from economic power to political domination; inhabitants without a fortune were virtually excluded. A fortune also guaranteed the qualities of responsibility and value in the work which it was the duty of the possessor to perform for the town. Since big fortunes had been made – and could still be made – through foreign trade, the export industry and the working of natural resources, the policy of those who, because of those activities, dominated the Council would naturally be aimed at protecting those sources of income.

The more a town or a town group possessed a profitable sector of activity, the more chance it had of making other profits. The diversity of commercial and artisanal activities in Nuremberg was greater than in Cologne.

When contemporaries said that Luneburg was a synonym of salt, they were speaking the truth: salt-works owners monopolized seats on the Council.

The Council presented itself as the defender of the general interest, as an instrument of a higher legitimacy. At the Reformation it saw itself as 'Obrigkeit', an authority proceeding from divine will.

In the early 15th century the full powers of the Council became a necessary condition if the town wanted to be a member of the Hanse.

108. The Grand Hall (*Oberen Halle*) of Bremen Town Hall.
Early 17th century woodwork.

MERCHANTS AND SOCIAL TENSIONS

Generally speaking, social disturbances were not very numerous and were not revolutionary in Hanse towns. They were nevertheless very important because of the underlying stakes and the history of the Hanse which they inflected. A remark on methodology: neither here nor elsewhere can social struggles be reduced to a simple, clear-cut pattern. It is extremely difficult, in trying to explain them, to base oneself on a classification of the population into classes or clearly defined groups. There were so many of them, the bounds are difficult to establish and were probably artificial, for interests were so mixed.

Men from the privileged classes took part in working-class revolts, for personal reasons that were quite different from their class interests: economic reasons which opposed them to their competitors, ambition, etc. In city struggles, there was no need for merchants to deal tactfully with their opponents, as they had to do when business brought them up against feudal lords; their reactions were therefore much more animated and the means employed were very hard.

Outside threats suspended social tensions, but the contrary also happened. Interest sometimes blinded certain groups to such a point that the freedom the town had acquired was threatened. Both the Emperor and Lords seized the opportunity to occupy land offered them by some party or the other in return for protection. It is very easy to approximate 14th and 15th century disturbances in Hanseatic towns as a whole to the victories which Denmark won against the Hanse.

The 14th and 15th century disturbances nevertheless had deep-lying reasons within the towns, between the big merchants who had the power and all the others who were kept at arm's length.

Another cause of problems and sometimes of conflicts was migration from the countryside to the town.

On the one hand, the high death rate in towns rendered that influx of population necessary; people from the country were welcomed for the cheap labour they represented, and as lodgers or soldiers, etc.

On the other hand, depending on the economic situation and the interests of each group, they became undesirable competitors. They were blamed for rising prices; they were considered as a burden upon charitable institutions and as dubious persons, and their flight from the countryside aggravated tension with the lord from whose authority they had fled.

Hanseatic Diets took matters in hand if they became too general. At the beginning of the 15th century those meetings endeavoured to work out a joint strategy to contain or repress opposition.

Disturbances increased after 1370, especially in Lubeck. It was decreed that any town in which the Council was changed, even partly, by force, would be thrown out of the Hanse and the leaders would be liable to the death penalty.

Such decisions certainly carried weight, but it is difficult to ascertain their final impact. It can at least be inferred that disturbances which occurred after the adoption of those measures, in Hamburg for instance in 1410, 1457/58 and 1483, were heavy with revolt.

The Reformation crystallized all the discontent. Further revolts broke out. When no negotiation, no agreement, no reform appeared possible between the over-powerful merchants and the rest of the population, revolts broke out. Yet there were neither major massacres nor massive, spectacular arrests.

Eight burgomasters and councillors were executed during the 'big revolt' in Brunswick in 1374, but there was nothing of that sort when Hamburg artisans rose in rebellion in 1375 and those in Stade in 1376. The new Lubeck Council of 1408-1416 simply took a place left vacant by the departure of two thirds of the members of the former and much criticized Council.

The exasperation which gave rise to the revolts had all sorts of reasons: the intransigence of the Council, reactions to foreign enterprises which failed and caused increased unacceptable burdens, violation of burghers' rights, detraction from a group's privileges, abuse of power or errors in management, protests by certain groups which though wealthy saw themselves kept out of political decision-making or who held Council policy responsible for a decline in their economic situation.

There were also reasons peculiar to the life of the Hanse. The increase in outside political influence by the Hanse in the second half of the 14th century had consolidated and multiplied hopes of profit for the merchants. In a way, the middle classes, small tradesmen and craftsmen also benefited by that evolution, but none of them possessed instituted political influence, whereas the Councils strengthened theirs even more through the development of the Hanse in towns.

Different sectors of the population benefited to very varying degrees from the heyday of the Hanse.

The plague epidemics which became more frequent from the middle of the 14th century favoured a grouping of wealth among the survivors of the upper classes and enabled the rich to acquire landed property at a knock-down price and reap huge profits from the situation.

Silence, secrets, incomprehension and misunderstandings weighed heavily. It was not permitted to know the oath taken by councillors or the amount of tax paid by the rich – which is essential for the reputation of business houses.

Rumours, suspicion, defiance. Meeting-places and inns were watched by Councils. The feeling of belonging to the same town, the awareness of having the same history, counted for little.

The opposition endeavoured to provide itself with representative bodies, but no committee of that sort lasted very long.

A more general and more ambiguous policy was to get representatives of the opposition on to the Council. Admission was on a personal basis, and the composition of the Council was scarcely changed. The function of that gesture was finally to run down the opposition and reward those who had avoided violent confrontation with the Council.

Even a lasting consultative body such as the Hamburg Board of Elders, which was active (or sometimes somnolent, said the burghers) after the Reformation, was not above the temptation of paying more attention to the affairs of the Council or its own than to those of its mandators. Its members crowned their rise through the various bourgeois bodies by being admitted to the

Council. Belatedly, in 1695, the election of Elders by the bourgeois body was imposed, and they were ineligible for a seat on the Council, but in 1712 that "democratization" was cancelled. Generally speaking, the Hamburg authorities, under opposition pressure and through the force of technical imperatives resulting from the growth of the town, delegated a little responsibility. But for them it was a means of offering less chance of attack without losing a large part of their power. Perhaps they could even strengthen their real authority in that way, for discontent which could previously be expressed directly now had to "go through official channels" which always immobilized the stratifications of society even more.

Merchant republics were established and were very stable sociologically for a long time.

The determinant element, therefore, was not the existence of a middle class but the fact that, in the Middle Ages, by successive economic differentiations, the evolution of constitutions, and the acquisition of privileges, several intermediate classes developed. They consolidated situations by rendering them more bearable. That succeeded all the better in that each of those classes was more aware of its own value, its respectability and its superiority over those that social imagination placed below it, and forget its dependence. The craftsmen backed the big merchants against the 'impudent rabble' in Hamburg in the 18th century.

109. Portrait of Hermann Hilldebrandt Wedigh, a Cologne merchant in the London Stalhof, 1533. By Hans Holbein the Younger: ANNO 1533, AETATIS SUAE 39. Berlin, Staatliche Museum, Gemäldegalerie.

The model was identified by the seal-ring on the first finger of his left hand.

BIBLIOGRAPHY

U. BROSTHAUS, *Bürgerleben im 16 Jahrhundert. Die Autobiographie des Stralsunder Bürgermeisters Bartholomäus Sastrow als kulturgeschichtliche Quelle*, Köln und Wien, 1972 (*Forschungen und Quellen zur Kirchen- und Kulturgeschichte Ostdeutschlands*, II).

K. FRIEDLAND, *Lübeck, Typ einer Ostseestadt. Fragen und Feststellung zur prägenden Kraft neuer Gemeinschaftsformen*, in *Politik, Wirtschaft und Kunst des staufischen Lübecks*, Lubeck, 1976.

J. DIETER, *Geschichte des Hospitals. I. Westdeutschland von den Anfängen bis 1850*, Wiesbaden, 1966 (*Sudhoffs Archiv*, Beiheft 5).

W. EBEL, *Bursprake, Echteding, Eddach in den niederdeutschen Stadtrechten*, in *Rechtsgeschichtliches aus Niederdeutschland*, Göttingen, 1978, p. 175-194.

Practices: Hanseatic Trade

The Hanseatic was a commercial traffic man

His job was buying and selling, moving goods from where there were surpluses to where they were lacking. Surplus products that were hardly worth considering in one place were changed into products which, if not rare and precious, were in any case appreciated and profitable elsewhere, due quite simply to their displacement.
So the Hanseatic merchant lived by his flair, a first glance had to be as unerring as possible. That did not come to him solely through his intelligence, courage and toil, but rather through his practical knowledge of the places and networks in which he operated.
As business expanded, he had to master technical, commercial and accounting know-how and have greater means of circulation and transport.
Means of maritime transport were vital for the Hanseatic; he had to have ships, captains, seamen and ports. He needed relay stations, too, to enable him to be present permanently, through representation, at crucial places in his many networks and at the very heart of his far-off and often most profitable practices. The Hanse business houses, consulates before such things existed, extensions of the Baltic mould, make one think of Cistercian abbey priories. He also had to have partners in the different procurement regions which were at the same time points of sale. To observe the Hanse in its practice is to watch it sell and buy, organize maritime traffic, manage business houses and deal with its partners, not to mention being careful not to reduce a remarkably lively, complex and go-ahead association. [A. d'H.]

Buying and Selling

In the early days of the Hanse, the merchants themselves handled their goods traffic. They personally did the buying and selling in the field, with the expectation of big profits.

They went to sea, often in groups, at their own risk, with the danger of losing not only their cargoes but also their lives.

Then they progressively became more sedentary, managing through delegation and from their business houses. More business was done in writing, through agencies, in an increasingly mediate manner, entrusting to intermediaries the task of making their commitments potentially profitable.

So the sedentary merchant became a man of written dealings and accountancy, a city councillor, an administrator of the port and of whatever was necessary to be efficient and competitive in long distance trade. [A. d'H.]

110. Portrait of a merchant.
Painted by Jean Gossaert (circa 1478-1536).
Washington, National Gallery.

The merchant business house is now structured by its relation to absence. The Hanseatic has become sedentary; he no longer personally travels the exchange and circulation networks. He now does his business by mediation, counting on intermediaries and on networks from which he is directly absent. Therefore, the written word and documents are essential, indispensable and of priority importance for him.

The merchant's world is increasingly one of texts, paper, pen and ink, in short – of abstraction. The filing system and trade papers, trade bills, have become of primary importance in the merchant's business. Manifestly the latter again appears here as purely empiric.

111. Panic at sea.
Miniature end of 13th century.
Brussels, Royal Library, ms. 9543, fol. 88 verso.

A storm is raging. To avoid the ship sinking, the merchants throw their wares overboard – ceramics and bales.
In the early Hanseatic days, merchants risked their own skins to keep the commercial traffic networks going.

ROLF SPRANDEL
Professor at Wurzburg University

The commercial techniques

112. The *Allégorie du Commerce*, by Jost Amann (1539-1591) 1585 wood engraving signed twice I.A. 87.5 × 61 cm.
Brussels, Royal Library, Print-room.

"*Johann Neudörfer the Elder (Nuremberg 1497-1506), the author of books on accountancy and the founder of German calligraphy, taught ornamental writing and mathematics in Nuremberg. The biographer of artists in his birth-place, and a good sketcher, Neudörfer the Elder was interested in the history of art. He formed the project and texts of a vast 'allégorie du commerce' which Jost Amann engraved on wood in 1585, accompanied by German verses on accountancy composed by Kaspar Brinner (or Brunner), a Nuremberg arithmetic teacher. Jost Amann (Zurich 1539 - Nuremberg 1591), painter, an artist in glass and an engraver on copper and wood, arrived in Nuremberg around 1560 and became a burgher there in 1577. (...)*
The Allégorie du Commerce is a large six-wood engraving.
A five-line title surmounts the composition. Enframed by the coats of arms of European trading cities and pages of a journal, Mercury holds by a ring the central knife-edge of a pair of scales in the pans of which, equally balanced, are the debit and credit accounts. Under the scales, a fountain, the basin of which is ornamented with account-book headings, is surmounted by a Fortune holding a pair of wings and a tortoise, the emblem of the wealth which devolves upon the moderate.
Around the fountain lies the picturesque panorama of the Antwerp roadstead, seen from the Tête de Flandre. (...)
In an architectural setting enframed by allegories of Obligation and Freedom, the lower part of the engraving shows scenes invoking the activities and qualities of merchants. (...)
Numerous inscriptions facilitate comprehension of the Allegory." [Anne Rouzet].

113. Scales, 1537, from Hamburg. Nuremberg, Germanisches Nationalmuseum.

The Hanseatics were not the equal of the Italians or the Flemings as regards accountancy and fiduciary techniques. They were too rule-of-thumb for that and were not so accustomed to writing. The original world of the Hanse was in fact still impregnated with orality. Only immediate agreements were known, from man to man, agreements entered into by people who were close to one another and knew one another intimately, who themselves performed the essential part of their transactions side by side, including dangerous and laborious operations.

It took several generations for these merchants, men of empiricism and concrete action, to learn, master, explore and utilize the refined resources of information and writing based on absence and abstraction.

They therefore sent their assistants, heirs and successors to Bruges and Cologne to learn the rudiments of written business techniques. But willingness cannot change a turn of mind and a whole mental universe overnight, time is needed. They managed it, however, in the 16th century. But already, at the head of Central German merchants, the Fuggers had the commercial traffic and circulation networks well in hand, to be mastered only at the price of advanced accountancy and fiduciary techniques. [A. d'H.]

BEFORE THE HANSE

The Hanseatic commercial techniques and community forms continued structures and mental habits that had been established centuries before.

The emporia The foundation for the ancient structures was an association of merchants frequenting the same places and trading from their emporia. An emporium was a business house that was usually situated near a seigniorial citadel. It also included a small community of craftsmen.
The merchants had obtained the right to trade and, even better, they enjoyed various economic and juridical privileges. Religion played an important part. Travelling merchants had celebrated pagan forms of worship; later they were converted to Christianity.
Besides the structured business houses there also existed simple meeting-places, in the estuaries and on islands near the coasts. Travelling merchant communities met at regular intervals and on important dates. They did business together and with the peasants and fishermen of the neighbourhood. Travelling merchant communities were composed of merchants and armed seamen. They were bound by a solemn oath.
They elected 'elders' who had a number of powers, juridical in particular, and who were also responsible for the community within the Hanse and vis-à-vis others. Merchants pooled their interests on several occasions, in the full sense of the word: a common treasury, sharing profits and losses.
Travelling communities generally took the same routes. For long crossings on northern seas it was the custom to travel in summer; the winter was spent in an emporium.
When European merchant space became larger, when new towns were built or older cities took on greater commercial importance, the habit of travelling together remained. Special groups then formed among the merchants of a town, e.g. in Cologne or Hamburg, the community of the '*Englandfahrer*'.

Peasant trade The merchants were in constant trading relations with the peasants of their region. That trade represented an ancient complement, typically northern, to the trading by travelling merchant communities and, later, to the Hanse trade. For the peasants it was a seasonal activity when work on the land was slowing down, whilst it was a necessity when poor harvests rendered subsistence more problematical than ever.

THE HANSEATIC PERIOD

The history of the Hanse falls into three periods. The first saw the formation of the Hanse from communities of the Middle Ages, in the second half of the 12th century. The second period, that of maturity, extended to the middle of the 14th century, when the Hanse was at its height after its victory over Denmark. This second period was also a phase of commercial form development. The last period ran till the end of the 15th century; it was a time of increasingly bitter struggle against competition.

The first phase in the conquest of foreign markets

The first period was one of expansion. Little by little the Hanse conquered new markets. Its autonomy increased, although it was scarcely easy in commercial places as firmly structured as Bruges or London.

An important stage in this process was the abolition of the 'right of visitors' (*Gästerecht*) in Bruges in 1282. To achieve that, the German merchants had to boycott the town. Before that abolition, foreigners, Hanseatics or South Europeans, only had the right to trade with the Bruges burghers; now they were able to trade between themselves, which both favoured them and put the Bruges merchants on the sidelines.

The oldest forms of credit were internal to the communities, credits being guaranteed by them collectively. A document of 1165, defining the urban right of Medebach, a small Westphalian town which took part in the beginning of Hanseatic trade on the Baltic, stated, inter alia, that when a burgher of the town was travelling abroad he had no right to bring a fellow-countryman before a local court: he had to seek advice from fellow-countrymen present, forming a sort of arbitration tribunal, or else wait till he got back to his own country to settle his difference. As regards someone who entrusted one of his fellow-countrymen with money to be invested for their mutual benefit in trade with Denmark or Russia, he should not do so, went on the document, without two trustworthy witnesses being present.

Credit was not guaranteed in writing; the guarantee was a matter for the internal reputation of the community. It was probably the Western neighbours of the Hanse which gave it the habit of individualized credit relations. This change implied that magistrates or other official persons acted as guarantors, in one way or another, when a credit contract was entered into. Initially purely oral, this guarantee was subsequently confirmed in writing. The more important forms of commercial credit were participation credit and seller credit. It was supply which stimulated consumption and not the reverse. But the real driving force of the economy was commission commerce which sought credit locally and offered it abroad. Towards the end of this first phase there was a network of urban jurisdictions which guaranteed a credit. Bruges and London formed part of it; their courts ensured Hanse credit abroad.

The second phase: influence of Italian techniques The second Hanse period is marked by Italian influence on commerce and credit.

Exchange The registers of urban courts turned into debt ledgers and fulfilled notarial functions. To that were added the merchants' debt ledgers and the exchange which encouraged imports and exports and facilitated triangular traffic, e.g. between mid-Germany, Lubeck and Flanders.

The oldest bill of exchange we have found was drawn in Bruges in 1290 by Reinekinus Mornewech, a Lubecker trader and councillor, on the council of that city. It is kept in the Lubeck municipal archives. Two Hamburgers in Bruges handed Mornewech 150 marks sterling for the benefit of the town of Lubeck; the trader promised to pay them or their representatives, within fifteen days of their return to Hamburg, the corresponding value in Lubeck currency. Charges were to be borne by the debtor. Formally, that bill of exchange was a domiciled promissory note. But a note attached thereto requested Lubeck council to pay the bill of exchange, if possible in Hamburg. The 'reimbursement of expenses' clause enabled interest payment. These two Hamburg merchants were obviously specialized in exporting from Hamburg to Bruges.

Another note from Mornewech requested Johann d'Ypres, a Lubeck councillor, to repay the bearer a credit of 260 silver marks. He referred to an acknowledgment of debt signed by him and left in Bruges with the creditor's host. It was, in short, a way of reassuring the creditor in case he was not paid the sum he expected in Lubeck.

In a third document accompanying his letter, Mornewech wrote that the burghers of Herford, Magdeburg, Brunswick and Stendal had been fully paid, but that their debts with certain inhabitants of Ghent and Ypres, towards whom he was himself committed on behalf of the 'abovementioned burghers', remained unsettled.

It was in the interests of mid-Germany merchants to possess money in Flanders, because they exported to mid-Germany from there. They carried with them proofs of debt from Lubeck to which they had perhaps come one day, from their country of origin, with corn or timber. It is not impossible that Lubeck council may have acted as a bank for local buyers of these goods from mid-Germany.

The account book Another 'borrowing' from Italian commercial techniques played an even more important role for the Hanse than the bill of exchange: the account book. Its use spread at about the same time as that of the bill of exchange. In the early 15th century there was hardly a Hanseatic merchant of some importance who did not have his account book, the *Handlungsbuch*. The rare vestiges that have come to our notice of this copious accountancy were in relation with court proceedings, which shows that such private accounts could have proof value before the courts.

Take the example of books kept by Vicko von Geldersen, a Hamburg merchant, in the second half of the 14th century. The outer aspect of the book is representative of the level attained by the Hanseatics' accountancy. Entries were made simultaneously under several headings, which then enabled their rational filing. The reality is less sure; there are gaps, filled in later more or less arbitrarily. The language is a mixture of Latin and Low German. Merchants used both, the Latin relatively well.

There are also entries to be seen beside the entry by the merchant himself, so there must have been employees authorized to make entries in the transactions book. It can also be seen that not all the employees had an equally good knowledge of Latin.

Domestic credits It was principally credits granted by the merchant which were entered in the account book. Credits of all kinds: commercial, financial, maritime (participation in ships, with part of the profits made on the freight), local credits to artisans, house rents, etc.

Proofs of repayment were attached to some acknowledgements of debt in the book of the Hamburg merchant Von Geldersen. Scattered entries were coupled with others of the same nature, presumably to provide a conspectus.

Actually, there is no account book enabling the state of a merchant's business to be determined exactly. Nevertheless, these entries rendered the merchants precise and very important services. Without that accountancy, the Hanseatics would never have been able to multiply, as they did, their participations in trading companies. The book of the Veckinchusen brothers of Lubeck, in the early 15th century, reveals the multiplicity of forms and the complexity of a number of deals.

The shipping business *wedderlegginge*; *sendeve* commission company; *vulle mascopei* or 'integral company', mostly composed of members of the same family and in which the associates jointly engaged all their goods and chattels.

The most usual form was the *wedderlegginge* which implied a reciprocal contribution of funds: a merchant placed capital with another merchant and participated in some of the latter's business deals, pro rata to the amount placed.

Foreign credits Credit operations abroad remained but little developed, compared with what they were in the Hanseatic sphere itself. In that field, credit developed because of the intensification of relations between towns, including the form of veritable leagues.

In 1361 a port customs duty appeared, the proceeds being administered in common and spent in the war between the Hanse and Denmark. Bills of exchange were used to distribute those proceeds from the places where they were collected to those that were bearing the cost of the war.

The principal motivation of creditors was to find an investment. Rich merchants endeavoured in that way to make their surpluses profit-earning. For a time, that encouraged foreign credit.

After the collapse of the Italian firms Bardi and Peruzzi in 1339/40, the Hanse helped the English for about ten years to finance their war on the continent. In May 1340 the biggest loan – 4,400 Florence florins – was granted to the King against a long term mortgage of English customs resources. That kind of transaction shows that at the time the Hanse had very large assets available in Flanders as a result of its trade. These assets were used, between 1340 and 1370, to buy gold for Lubeck currency, at the average rate of 23,000 Florentine florins a year. Purchases were effected by means of bills of exchange drawn on Lubeck council. These purchases represented an attempt to link the Hanse monetarily with an overall European economic system. Gold coins minted in Lubeck, with a titre aligned on that of florins and ducats, would have been able to ensure monetary unification. Until then, the Hanse had used only silver money.

The Hanse put an end to that attempt in 1370, no doubt because its trade balance with Flanders began to show a deficit and the indispensable assets were no longer available. However that may be, the role played by the bill of exchange as an instrument of credit was a very important one for several decades.

115. The Holy Family.
Part of an engraving by Lucas Cranach the Elder (1472-1510).
Berlin, Staatliche Museen Preussischer Kulturbesitz, Kupferstichkabinett.

Learn to read, write and count. A father's constant concern as regards his sons, successors and staff. Initiate them into other languages and in particular the language of the business house or region with which he did business; initiate them, too, into commercial and banking techniques.

In the 15th century a young man was sent from Riga to Bergen to learn business.

In Lubeck and Cologne, merchants made provision in their wills for grants to enable young commercial factors to learn Russian and Esthonian.

In the 13th century there were schools in Hanseatic towns, and even earlier in Flemish and Meuse regions. H. Pirenne drew attention to an early 12th century text (the Vita Abundi*) stating that Abond's father sent his son to a collegial school in Huy to learn accountancy.*

As regards Italian towns, it would appear that virtually at no time was there a break in the practice of handwriting.

Forms of credit

Merchants sought investments for their money. That developed three main forms of credit: the purchase of seigniorial land in the country; public loans by cities; urban mortgage credit, i.e. the buying of mortgages. This last form was limited in volume by the real estate value. However, relatively, very much use was made of the mortgage market capacity. In the best years of the second half of the 14th century up to 20,000 Lubeck marks, i.e. about 25,000 Florentine florins, were handled on the Hamburg mortgage market. In the following century this figure was tripled and no doubt corresponded to the upper limit of what the real estate sector could support. In all, this type of credit had – by its nature – only a limited importance for trade. There also existed all sorts of consumer credits and small industrial credits intended for the weaker and lower-paid groups, so sealing dependence relations within the towns.

The third phase: the attempt at economic integration

During the third period in its history the Hanse again sought integration in the Italian and West European economic system. But this time it was the installation of Italian firms in Lubeck which marked this integration.

The driving force is to be found in the Hanse payments to Rome. Precious metals were too rare and the undertaking too risky for cash to be transited through Europe, so these payments had to be combined with deliveries of goods to the south.

Hanseatic payments to the pontifical curia are better known for the 14th than for the 15th century. According to collectors' archives, 5 to 10,000 florins in a few years transited the Hanseatic regions in Avignon where the Papacy was then installed.

114. A merchant's accounts.
Part of an engraving devoted to the *Allégorie du Commerce*, by Jost Amann. Circa 1585.
Brussels, Royal Library. The Print-room.

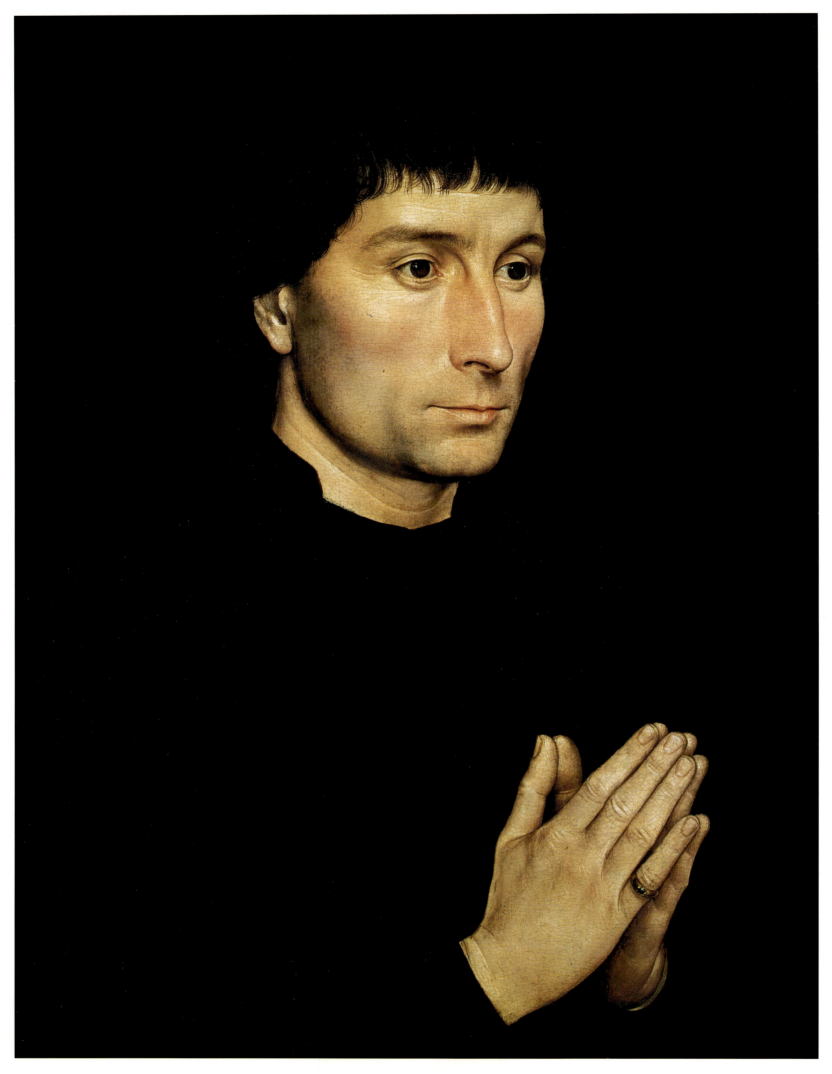

The Medicis had a subsidiary in Bruges. They left there for Lubeck at the beginning of the 15th century. Some Italians who founded their own firm (with the Medicis' money, it is true) acted as their correspondents. They were known in that capacity in Lubeck between 1405 and 1465. One of them, Gerard Bueri, married the daughter of a Lubeck burgomaster and acquired burgher rights in that city in 1428.

THE END OF THE HANSE: ITS REASONS

The reasons which explain this attempt at economic integration are also the ones which explain its failure. There was first of all the knowledge acquired by foreigners of Hanse domestic trade; that knowledge was inherent in the permeability of the Hanse vis-à-vis competitive economies and particularly those of England and Holland.

In 1417 the Hanseatic diet, by bringing in a 'visitor's right' (*Gästerecht*), attempted to limit the freedom of movement by foreigners on its own markets by forbidding them to trade between themselves or carry out any retail trade. But that measure – when it was actually applied – did nothing to reduce foreign presence.

The principal episode of the economic war conducted by the Hanse against the competition it was facing in its own zone of influence was the attempt to impose Bruges as a warehouse, whereas that city already had de facto predominance in the western trade of the Hanse. In 1442 the Hanseatic diet decreed that only cloth bought in Bruges could be sold in Hanseatic towns. That measure was supposed to paralyse Dutch trade; it did not work! Dutch expansion in the Baltic continued.

The permeability which the Hanse was incapable of remedying finished by coming to the end of its economic vitality, and the big Italian firms gradually turned away from the fading Hanseatic scene. Also, the balance of payments of the Hanse with Flanders and also with Italy undoubtedly showed a more frequent deficit. As regards credit, that favoured the development of inter-regional intermediaries.

One of the very important sectors of activity of the Medicis was to advance money for payment obligations to the south. At the same time the state of the balance of payments dissuaded foreign creditors from committing themselves long term.

It was no longer rare to hear of the bankruptcy of a firm that did business with Italy.

116. Tommaso Portinari (circa 1432-1501), Bruges agent of the Medicis.
Painted by Hans Memling.
New York, the Metropolitan Museum of Art, Benjamin Altman Bequest.

Portinari lived in Bruges from 1480 to 1497, in the Bladelin mansion where the Medici bank had been situated since 1466.
He was at first its managing director, and then an agent for his own account.

BIBLIOGRAPHY

K. PINZ, *Die Allegorie des Handels aus der Werkstatt des Jost Amann. Ein Holzschnitt von 1585*, in Scripta Mercaturae, I, 1974, p. 25-60.
F. IRSIGLER, *Hansekaufleute - Die Lübecker Veckinchusen und die Kölner Rinck*, in Hanse in Europa, Ausstellung des Kölnischen Stadtmuseums, Köln, 1973, p. 301-327.
H. SAMSONOWICZ, *Remarques sur la comptabilité commerciale dans les villes hanséatiques au XVe s.*, in Finances et comptabilités urbaines du XIVe au XVIIe siècles, Actes du Colloque de Blankenberge, Pro Civitate, Coll. hist., 7, 1964, p. 207-211.

FRANZ LERNER
Professor at Marburg University

Hanseatic Merchandise

The Hanse undertook to circulate the goods of regions between which it animated a vast network of commercial traffic. In that way it injected agricultural resources, ores and all kinds of industrial products into business from which it drew profit through its circulation activities.

From the North it carried butter, fish, meat, skins, iron and copper.

From the East: alum, furs, cereals, timber, honey, wax, ash, amber, copper, tar.

From the South: spices, figs, almonds, walnuts, oil, grapes, silk, copper.

From the West: beer, dyes, woad, wine, wool, salt, silver, tin, glass, ceramic, cloth, arms, metal tools.

In this vast circuit the quality of the products was a singular asset. Hanseatic products were superior to similar articles manufactured in the countries from which the raw materials came. There was fineness in their manufacture, strength, technical qualities, aesthetic attraction. The Hanse was able to re-export finished products to the very countries from which it had bought the semis.

In the vast, fertile plains of Northern Europe, trade was flourishing well before the Hanse was formed. [A. d'H.]

117. Arrival of wine in the port of Bruges early in the 16th century.
Miniature taken from a 'Bréviaire' attributed to Simon Bening, a miniaturist painter, born in Ghent, who entered the St. Jean and St. Luke corporation in Bruges in 1508.
Munich, Bayerisches Staatsbibliothek, Codex lat. 23.638, fol. 11 verso.

This illuminated design illustrating the month of October – the month of wine, in the calendars – signals the arrival of wine in a Nordic port.

A lighter, visible on the right of the crane, has just brought in the wine. It had been loaded aboard at Ecluse or Damme, outer harbours of Bruges, beyond which big ships could not navigate owing to the shallowness of the Reie.

The unloaded barrels are lined up on the paved quay. They are 'pipes' holding at least 450 litres each. One has just been broached in order to fill a sampling-tube; an assistant prepares to stop the flow with a spigot.

The merchant invites the client to taste the wine. The latter has no doubt been introduced by a third party, a broker. A carrier awaits the potential buyer's decision in order to remove the goods. A pot situated on the straw at the front of his sledge would seem to indicate that he expects to be paid in kind. A street can be seen in the background, beyond the canal bridge.

From the 15th century the wines of France – from Poitou, la Rochelle, Bordeaux and Orléans – as well as wines from Spain, Italy and Greece, went through Bruges.

118. Prices, in Prussian marks, are related to a common measure, the 'last'.
After W. Bönhke, *Der Binnenhandel des Deutschen Ordens in Preussen*, in *Hansische Geschichtsblätter*, vol. 80, 1962, pp 51-53.

ARTICLES SOLD IN PRUSSIA FOR THE TEUTONIC ORDER IN 1400

Saffron	7,040	Hungarian steel	21
Ginger	1,040	Trave salt	12.5
Pepper	640	Herrings	12
Wax	237.5	Flemish salt	8
French wine	109.5	Wismar beer	7.5
Rice	80	Flour	7.5
Steel	75	Wheat	7
Rhine wine	66	Rye	5.75
Oil	60	Barley	4.2
Honey	35	Ash	4.75
Butter	30		

BUYING AND SELLING

Pre-Hanseatic trade   In the spaces south of the Baltic Sea, agriculture and stock-breeding had been rich since ancient times and provided surpluses utilizable for commercial traffic.

Trade at first was mainly local. Very soon, however, there were goods of supra-regional importance: first of all, salt, which was as rare as it was indispensable for man and beast. There were other products, too, which were available on the borders of Eastern and mid-Europe, but which were sought far beyond those frontiers.

That was the case with amber, semi-transparent resin of the tertiary period, surrounded by the mysterious forces of static electricity. It was found on the shores of the Baltic; since prehistoric times it had been the subject of trade thousands of kilometres away.

Nomads on horseback hunted squirrels, ermine, foxes and bears in the steppes, for their furs.

The immense forests of Eastern Europe provided much sought-after wild honey.

The people of the East also traded in wax, potassium and potassium carbonate which was extracted from certain plants and flax. In exchange, they greatly desired to acquire quality craftsmen's wares, jewellery and liturgical objects, in addition to salt.

This trade had lasted for thousands of years and extended over vast territories. In the Middle Ages it gradually became concentrated in newly founded towns.

Dense in the regions of lower Germany, the urban tissue became more sparse as one penetrated the vast territories situated between the Oder and the Volga where the scattered population rendered the formation of centres of supra-regional importance superfluous. A few markets sufficed for exchanges.

The burghers of towns situated on the mouths of rivers in Northern Germany served the North Sea and Baltic Sea coasts with their ships.

Hardy traders penetrated the continent, taking their goods to local markets and transforming the old system of commerce into a flourishing inter-regional new one.

Their association gave them strength. Their relations with the markets of Northern Germany and their business experience ensured their superiority.

They were derisively called Hansen. This nickname, which was an allusion to the most common German Christian name Johann, of which Hans is an abbreviation, was taken up by them to designate their association as a community of interest.

Hanseatic commercial traffic   The volume of Hanseatic trade constantly increased as from the 12th century.

At the end of the Middle Ages, activity was very diversified. The Hanse merchants, seeking to utilize their carrying capacity to the maximum – their ships were not very big – and cutting out very costly overland transport as much as possible, were careful to see that their vessels never journeyed empty, whether outward or homeward bound. They constantly endeavoured to balance exports and imports, if not in value, at least in volume.

HANSEATIC MERCHANDISE

Their supremacy on the markets they frequented partly stemmed from that policy. They met demand and attended to supply in so far as they found a taker in the other direction. Because of this balance in its commercial traffic, the Hanse conquered a dominant position on markets, especially in the region of Eastern Europe around Nijni-Novgorod, enabling it to determine supply. The Hanse merchants bought only those goods for which a demand existed on the West European markets. Up to a point they sought to obtain (and succeeded for certain goods at least) a sort of monopoly.

Their competitors did not remain inactive, of course. The Dutch and English, and to a lesser extent the Danes and Swedes, also went to the Baltic at the beginning of the Renaissance to assert themselves on markets dominated until then by the Hanse. They succeeded so well that the latter finished by losing its role as an intermediary and succumbed to their competition.

But the habit of trade relations between the West and the North of Europe had now taken root. The imprint of the Hanse on trade between the East and the West, and with Scandanivia also, still remained after the three or four centuries of its existence.

Salt Salt was of particular importance in relations with Northern Europe.

The big development of herring fishing in the North and Baltic Sea and fishing-grounds on coasts warmed by the Gulf Stream, in particular from Norway to the Lofoten Islands, meant the consumption of large quantities of salt, indispensable for preserving fish. Besides, salted herring and dried cod were the foodstuffs for Lent and the days of fasting during which Christians were not allowed to eat meat, so the West could not manage without salt. The

119. The Old Market, Cologne.
Engraving by Johann Toussyn and Abraham Aubry. 1650.
Cologne, Stadtmuseum.

The market is organized in sectors, by products of the same type.

BUYING AND SELLING

Hanseatic merchants took charge of the marketing of these products in North-West Europe and even in Italy as regards cod. The salt came first of all from the Luneburg salt-works. To reduce carriage costs, the town of Lubeck constructed the Stecknitz canal linking the lower Elbe with the Baltic Sea. This connection was completed in 1398. From then on, salt was taken to Lubeck by waterway and then trans-shipped on to sea-going vessels. But the Luneburg salt-works could not by themselves meet Scandinavian demand for long. The Hanseatics went further afield, to Biscay, to find bay-salt for their clients in the North. In addition they supplied the fishermen with flour and with barrels in which to put their herrings. They also sold them tools and some de luxe products.

Cereals Since the German colonization, cereals abounded in the countries situated south of the Baltic.
Danzig became the port for exporting cereal surpluses from Poland; Königsberg for those from East Prussia which belonged to the Teutonic Order; Riga and Reval for grain from the Baltic countries.
Supply was so abundant that the Hanseatics sought new outlets. They found them in the busy regions of North-West Europe, in Flanders, Wallonia and Northern France.
At the Champagne fairs and markets as important as Bruges they purchased objects that were much sought after by their clients in Northern and Eastern Europe; cloth and quality products from metallurgical craftsmen. It was also the opportunity to dispose of over-abundant cereals in the Baltic ports, for in

120. Production capacity of two salt-works in Luneburg, 1200-1800.
After H. Witthoft, *Produktion, Handel... der Luneburger Saline 1200-1800*, 1978. Production capacity of the salt-works, volume of trade.

"It would be difficult to exaggerate the importance of the Hanse salt trade in the 14th and 15th centuries.
Requirements were considerable. According to kitchen accounts kept in the middle of the 15th century in Upper Saxony, the annual consumption per capita can be estimated at around fifteen kilos.
Salt provisions needed about a barrel of salt for four or five barrels of herrings or for ten barrels of butter.
Yet this precious commodity was almost entirely lacking in the East. The small salt content in the Baltic Sea did not make the salt-pans worth working. As regards rock-salt from the Luneburg mines, the only ones mentioned were the very small ones of Kolberg.
Since salt was heavy and low in price, and had to be carried long distances, it had necessarily to be transported by sea; so it was the ideal product for maritime trade.
Lastly, being taken to the East, it was the principal return freight for ships that had taken other heavy products to the West: cereals, timber, ash." [Ph. Dollinger].

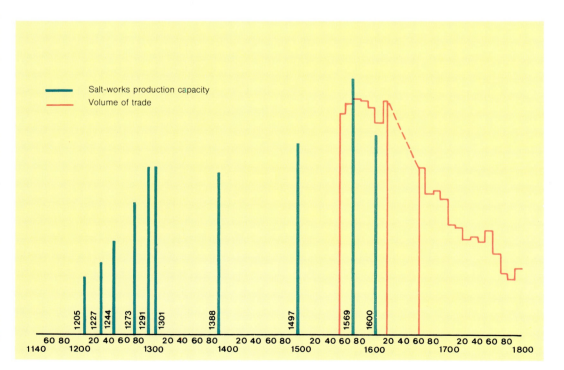

134

North-West Europe, in the towns but also very often in the country, local agricultural production was insufficient to feed a constantly growing population. Inadequate means of communication prevented that shortage from being made up for by supplies from the hinterland. By sea, on the other hand, the Hanseatic could meet the demand.

The importation of cereals from Eastern Europe became one of the pillars of Hanseatic trade in these rich, populated regions.

Northern Europe bought cereals from the Hanse in the form of flour. North-West Europe, on the other hand, took delivery of grain as loaded, without any intermediate operation, in the Baltic ports, as the North-West had enough windmills to grind the grain.

England also participated in the Hanseatic network for similar reasons: sheep breeding and the wool industry were developing more quickly than the island's agricultural production.

So the Hanse ended up by having almost a monopoly in the delivery of cereals to North-West Europe.

121. Exportation of cereals from Danzig. After N. Ellinger Bang, *Tabeller over Skibfart og Varetransport gennem öresund 1497-1660*, vol. 2, *Tabeller over Varetransporten* A (Table 4) 1933.

"Cereals, and rye in particular, were, with salt, the Hanseatic article in which there was the greatest expansion at the end of the Middle Ages. Unfortunately, the absence of valid figures before the middle of the 16th century makes it impossible to measure the traffic growth. Rye, barley and, secondarily, wheat, were grown everywhere. From the 13th century, the middle Elbe countries, Brandenburg and Mecklenburg, shipped these cereals to the Low Countries and Norway. But in the 14th and especially in the 15th, it was Prussia and Poland which became and remained the big cereal producers. Exported through Danzig to the whole of the West, demand never ceased to grow. Failing figures, the extent of cereal exports can clearly be seen from the political influence they ensured for the Hanse. We have seen that from the end of the 13th century, the pressing need for grain and flour placed Norway in close economic dependence on Wendish towns. Later, the scarcity and rising price of corn in Flanders enabled the Hanse on many occasions to reap substantial benefits. Lastly, at the modern epoch, it was France, Spain and even Italy which called for Hanseatic cereals. So corn exports were one of the most certain foundations of the community's power and even, in the 16th century, for its temporary revival."
[Ph. Dollinger].

EXPORTS OF CEREALS FROM DANZIG

Period	Total rye passing the Sund	Exports from Danzig			
		Rye	Wheat	Flour	Barley
1490–1492		8,473	128	95	
1562–1565	50,676	42,720	4,826	4,424	603
1566–1569	43,771	34,089	2,258	1,390	495
1574–1575	35,773	28,796	3,493	1,750	277
1576–1580	25,297	14,071	1,437	1,259	41
1581–1585	24,431	19,860	2,258	1,305	187
1586–1590	39,295	28,633	2,982	1,472	498
1591–1595	45,290	29,080	2,097	1,082	676
1596–1600	50,070	38,585	4,773	1,221	474
1601–1605	37,818	32,282	1,664	903	208
1606–1610	55,472	38,980	3,258	255	796
1611–1615	44,378	34,765	1,941	227	507
1616–1620	68,326	51,778	5,679	263	1,418
1621–1625	48,576	32,845	3,794	109	475
1626–1630	20,973	8,139	690	150	37
1631–1635	45,466	31,004	6,807	210	114
1636–1640	45,251	31,778	8,011	232	2,067
1641–1645	53,910	42,090	12,383	377	4,676
1646–1650	53,056	34,554	11,162	158	1,541
1651–1655	28,745	17,788	4,550	35	947

BUYING AND SELLING

Wine There was no viticulture worthy of the name in North-West Europe in the Middle Ages, but Cologne, with the Rhine and Moselle, was a very big wine market.

The Hanseatics supplied North-West Europe, Scandinavia and Eastern Europe, despite sometimes keen competition from the French and, as regards England, from the Gascons.

Wine was an article that was much sought after but it was considered a great luxury and was sold in small quantities.

That was not the case, however, for Rhine wine. In the first place the clergy used it for liturgical purposes, a regular and foreseeable market. Private consumption in Northern and Eastern Europe was also extensive. Wine was the drink of the burghers, comfortably off or very rich townsfolk.

Everywhere, in their own towns, but also in the herring markets of Schonen, Bergen, Königsberg, in the Baltic countries and even in Russia, the Hanse merchants did a wholesale trade in wine and, where they had acquired the necessary privileges, sold retail as well.

The wine trade ran up against a limiting factor, however: that of price. Throughout the Hanseatic sphere wine was and remained dear; it was not drunk every day.

Beer Contrary to mid- and Southern Europe, beer here was not only more ancient than wine, brought in by the Romans and over the Alps, it was also very much cheaper.

All the simple beers had one point in common: they were produced by superficial fermentation and had to be drunk as soon as they were produced; they could neither be kept nor transported.

122. Transporting wine.
Part of an engraving devoted to the *Allégorie du Commerce* by Jost Amann. 1585.
Brussels, Royal Library, Print-room.

HANSEATIC MERCHANDISE

It was in Northern Germany, in the cradle of the Hanse, that a new brewing process was developed in the Middle Ages; it did away with those two disadvantages. This new beer, with in-depth fermentation, was invented and marketed by the Hanseatic towns; it would keep for a long time and could be transported, even over long distances.

The Mumme of Brunswick, the Gose of Goslar, the beer of Einbeck or Paderborn, were very quickly considered as models of quality. They were distinguished from one another by differences in the taste.

These highly esteemed products enjoyed a European reputation. Even in essentially viticultural regions, including those of growths held in high repute, North German beer was considered a refined pleasure. When the Emperor visited Frankfort-on-Main, an Empire town surrounded by vineyards and the turn-table for Alsace and Rheingau wines, the City Council never failed to offer him a cask of Hanseatic beer. Like all the towns in the south, the city had a local beer industry, but it produced only superficially fermented beer, a drink for the lower classes, it would appear. In Augsburg, as in Munich, the art of in-depth fermentation was introduced only in the early 16th century.

124. Duty on Beer.
Part of a stained-glass window by the stained-glass artist Arnoult de la Pointe, for Tournai cathedral (right transept). Circa 1500.

123. Brewing operations.
Drawing, 1455, in the *Digestum Vetus* of the town of Kampen.
Kampen Stadsarchief.

So the Hanseatic towns had an advance of several centuries in this important branch of production. Without competition, beer was one of the pillars of its export trade. However, fully fermented beer, wherever it was sold, remained a dear, high quality product which was never an everyday drink. Light beers competed with it everywhere on local markets, and neither the production capacities nor the means of transport of the Hanse sufficed to obtain a monopoly for it. The tonnage available permitted only limited trade.

Manufactured products

The wet coopers, manufacturers of wooden casks and recipients, whose fortune was closely connected with the beer and wine trade, formed large corporations in the Hanseatic towns, bringing together numerous masters and companions. They exported their products, as did the craftsmen who worked metals in various ways, from gold and silver smiths to copper pot makers, Grapen.

Trade in maritime equipment: ropes, pitch, tar, was also flourishing, no less than the highly developed rope trade in the big North Sea and Baltic ports. These products were exported by the Hanse, but they represented the conversion of raw materials which were themselves imported. The wood worked by the coopers or the flax used in rope-works were not local raw materials. Neither was the timber used in building the patrician houses of the Hanseatic towns, or the magnificent stones ornamenting the facades. They were brought in by waterway, sometimes over long distances. Building timber, pitch and tar came from the forests of Eastern Europe. The Hanse merchants brought honey and wax from the forests of the vast plains of Poland and Northern Russia, to be sold on the markets of North-West and mid-Europe.

125-126. A large number of manufactured products were transported in tuns.
Part of an engraving devoted to the *Allégorie du Commerce* by Jost Amann. 1585.
Brussels, Royal Library, Print-room.

The engraver's initials are on the lids.

Metal and glass workers bought from the Hanseatics potassium extracted from ferns growing in those same forests. Iron and copper came from the Faluns mines.

These raw materials, often marketed in semi-finished form, formed the basis of a whole series of conversion industries in Hanse towns.

From wax, magnificent candles were made, to be used in churches and processions; with honey, specialists made gingerbread. Craftsmen in wood and metal furnished products of remarkable quality.

The volume of artisanal production in the Hanseatic towns was far from being able to meet the demand from markets which the Hanse had conquered. It was for that reason that it bought industrial products in Western and mid-Europe on a large scale and transported them over long distances. The wares had to be of good quality and relatively constant outlets existed for them in Scandinavia and Eastern Europe.

But it was not possible to pay for them with money – and even less with silver money as in the times of the Vikings, the thirst for precious metals by the industrialized countries was too great.

In the Northern and Eastern countries there was increasing interest in exchanging goods; production remained very much behind vis-à-vis demand in quantity and quality, despite the arrival of artisans from mid-Europe and especially from Germany in towns which began to develop under their influence.

On the other hand, in South-East Europe, Transylvania and Slovakia, the influx of these craftsmen made it possible to do without the importation of finished products.

In the exchange of goods, the iron industries played an important part. Arms of all sorts, but they were really of less account than small metal objects of everyday use (knives, scissors, needles, weights, etc.). Tools for peasants and masons, known for their quality, were export articles that were much in demand. The production centres were the iron mines and workshops of the Meuse. Dinant was famous for its brass and copper wares. The Hanseatics also bought in Lower Germany. The term 'brocante de Nuremberg' was used to denote a varied assortment including small mirrors.

The Hanseatic merchants took the risk of transporting goods as fragile as pottery by waggons and small boats. Rhenish pottery from Sieburg and Raeren was carried on the Rhine to Holland and then trans-shipped to Hanseatic vessels for Scandinavia and the Baltic countries.

In Bruges, the Hanse merchants obtained precious export goods from the Mediterranean regions and the Near East, through the intermediary of merchants in Lower Germany or directly from the Fondaco dei Tedeschi in Venice. Spices, silks, sugar-loaves, incense and alum formed part of the products they offered (in small quantities and not everywhere).

It is difficult to imagine the variety of products sold through their intermediary. Any demand for luxury products was readily listened to, and the network of their business relations enabled them to know where to get what was wanted.

BUYING AND SELLING

Textiles   Among exports from Western Europe, first place went to textiles of high value manufactured in Flanders and England. Woollen cloth in particular remained unequalled for a long time. It was of such quality that it was unbelievable that there could be anything better. Colours and styles were sufficiently diversified to be able to satisfy all tastes. The Hanse merchants increased their profits by importing wool, to Flanders in particular, where production was insufficient. But not to England, where locally produced products were still more greatly used and wool imports were forbidden.

Bruges cloth represented, in volume at least, the main part of what the Hanseatic merchants had to offer in North-West Germany. Norway was interested in linen sold by the Bergen business house.

Furthermore, the Hanseatics were present on certain local textile markets such as Ypres, but it is difficult to evaluate exactly the extent of that presence and its variations. There is some evidence that it was quite large.

Furs   Furs were either indispensable or a luxury. Through the Nijni-Novgorod business house the Hanse was able for several centuries to supply Western Europe with furs from small mammals captured in the Russian steppes and

127. Textiles, an essential article in Hanseatic traffic.
Miniature extracted from a manuscript comprising a translation by Nicolas Oresme of a work by Aristotle, 15th century.
Rouen, Municipal Library.

Here, wax candles, brushes, cloth, spices and hats are on offer.

Cloth was always by far the leading article in imports, both of German towns and in the Eastern countries. The Osterlins brought to Bruges furs, wax, tar, ash and cereals; from Bremen came greatly appreciated beer.

But if they brought these provisions from the East, they returned there as buyers, mainly of cloth produced in Ghent, Ypres, Tournai, Malines and, later, in Antwerp and Bergen-op-Zoom. Bruges set the fashion in clothes; the Hanseatics bought their suits in Bruges: Flemish materials of almost infinite variety, something to satisfy everybody.

This priority is explained by the extent of requirements, the variety of qualities and prices, and almost certain profits ranging from 15 to more than 30%.

In the 13th century and in the first half of the 14th century it was almost solely Flemish cloth that was negotiated by the Hanseatics. As from the 15th century, English and Dutch materials became of increasing importance.

HANSEATIC MERCHANDISE

forests: squirrels, martens, ermines, from which linings and trimmings were made. Fox, lynx and bear were furs that, on occasion, were much in demand.

When Russian and Polish furriers managed to get into the East German markets, at Posen, Frankfort-on-Oder and Wroclaw, it was the beginning of the end for the Hanse, the end of that commercial network that covered all Europe because it was capable of supplying anything.

Leipzig, at the end of the 17th century, inherited from the Hanse: its furs fair took the place that was left vacant.

128. Hieronimus Holzschuher.
Portrait by Albert Dürer (1471-1528). Oil on linden tree wood.
Berlin, Staatliche Museen Preussischer Kulturbesitz, Gemäldegalerie.

Right: the artist's monogram.
Left: HIERONYM[US] HOLTZSHUER. ANNO DO[MI]NI. 1526. Etatis.Sue. 57.
The Holzshuhers were an old patrician Nuremberg family; the oldest, Heinrich, is mentioned in 1288. They sat on the Town Council continuously from 1317 to 1806. Several of them became burgomasters and diplomats.
In 1498, Jerome (deceased 1529) married Dorothea Müntzer. He was a councillor from 1499 and burgomaster in 1509 and 1520. Goodness, intelligence and alert of eye, fine features, sensual mouth; wealth and importance, symbolic of furs.
"Men aspired to have furs as if it was a matter of their eternal salvation" wrote Adam, the Bremen professor (deceased 1081).
"The fur trade was commonly assumed to be the foundation of Hanseatic wealth. Yet its importance is not always shown in figures as clearly as might have been expected. In Lubeck trading in 1368 it came only in fifth place, after Swedish butter; perhaps there were exceptional circumstances. On the other hand it was outstanding in the affairs of some big merchants such as the Veckinchusens, and mention is made of ships carrying more than two hundred thousand furs with a value of several tens of thousands of marks."
[Ph. Dollinger].

HANSEATIC MERCHANDISE

129. Central panel of a Danzig triptych. Work by Hans Memling, painted in Bruges between 1466 and 1473 for Angelo di Jacopo Tani.
Danzig cathedral.

Christ-Judge is sitting on a rainbow surrounded by the twelve apostles with the Virgin and John the Baptist. Above, the four angels with the instruments of the Passion.
The figure of Christ is a tribute to Roger de la Pasture. Memling has in fact copied it from the Polyptych of Beaune; the figures of the Virgin and Saint John also partly recall that work.
The person kneeling on the pan of the balance of Saint Michael has the features of Tommaso Portinari whom Memling represented several times. It is strange, however, that the head of Portinari was added after the work had been finished by the artist, who had to cover the underlying head with a coat of bitumen and white-lead. Why this presence of the young 'superior' of Angelo Tani? Some have thought it an act of adulation by Tani with regard to his master; others have supposed that Portinari had paid for part of the work, or that he had bought it from Tani, subsequently asking Memling to paint his portrait on it. That hypothesis is hardly convincing, however.
This grand triptych has a curious history. Intended for a church in Florence, it had been embarked in Bruges on a ship belonging to Tommaso Portinari, Medici's agent. But the vessel, which was also loaded with materials, furs, spices and other highly-priced goods, was captured on April 27, 1473 off Gravelines by a Danzig corsair, Paul Bencke, who made a gift of the valuable triptych to the cathedral of his town, where it was placed on the altar of the Confraternity of St. George.

130. Central panel of the *Triptych of the Passion* by Hans Memling.
Dated 1491 on the gilded frame of the central panel.
A two-volet triptych, which was customary in Lubeck, but unusual in the Low Countries.
Lubeck, St-Annen-Museum.

The triptych was ordered by the brothers Heinrich and Adolf Greverade of Lubeck, for the altar of the chapel erected by them in 1493 in the Marienkirche. Adolf was a canon in Louvain when he died in 1501; Heinrich stayed in Bruges a number of times.

Objets d'art

To be transported, valuable objects were wrapped in linen cloth. There were liturgical objects, for which the demand fluctuated but was, on the whole, not inconsiderable. Gold and silver ware, bronzes, bells that were not too voluminous, but sometimes whole altars and stained glass windows were exported. The Hanse often acted as an intermediary between those who placed orders and the best craftsmen in North-West Europe.
Religious manuscripts, missals, psalm-books and the magnificent Flemish prayer-books were also supplied.

143

BUYING AND SELLING

131. Beer jugs.
London, Guildhall Museum.

'Gré au barbu' (Bartmann) *by Raeren.
It is decorated with the head of Gambrinus, medallions and an inscription:* Drinch ond est gots nite ferges *(Drink and do not forget God).*
Found in Bishopsgate, London, in the vicinity of the Stalhof.

HANSEATIC MERCHANDISE

132. Dagger of the Middle Ages.
London, Guildhall Museum.

Found at Brooks Wharf, London. It was especially in Thames Street that knives and daggers were found. They were imported in large quantities from the Rhenish Siegerland and Antwerp.

Beginning in the second half of the 15th century, the Hanseatic merchants supplied their clients in the north and east of Europe – in small numbers at first but in larger numbers later – with printed matter: incunabula, and especially xylographs of one sole sheet, calendars and slender publications of all sorts.

An outstanding feature: the variety of products

The variety of products imported and exported was an outstanding feature of Hanseatic trade. The balance of its commercial traffic formed the basis of its success. If only to utilize the carrying capacity of its ships and not have ships sailing empty, the Hanse had to begin in both directions. The industrialization of North-West Europe was possible only because the Hanse was not solely concerned with finding outlets, but was able to supply an abundance of raw materials and provisions, thereby playing an intermediary role between East and West.

BIBLIOGRAPHY

R. DELORT, *Le commerce des fourrures en Occident à la fin du moyen âge (vers 1300-1450)*, Rome, 1978, 2 vol.

M. MALOWISI, *L'approvisionnement des ports de la Baltique en produits forestiers pour les constructions navales, au XVe et XVIIe siècles*, in *Travaux du 3e Colloque international d'histoire maritime*, Paris, 1960, p. 25-40.

H. VAN WERVEKE, *Die Stellung des hansischen Kaufmanns dem flandrischen Tuchproduzenten gegenüber*, in *Mélanges H. Ammann*, Wiesbaden, 1965, p. 296-304.

M. LESNIKOV, *Lübeck als Handelsplatz für osteuropäische Waren im XV Jahrhundert*, in *Hansische Geschichtsblätter*, 78, 1960.

K. HOYER, *Das Bremer Brauereigewerbe*, in *Hansische Geschichtsblätter*, 1913.

Organizing maritime traffic

Anything concerning maritime traffic was essential for Hanseatic trade, which lived on long distances and maximum potential profitability.
Sea transport was imperative, for it could carry heavy loads, both outwards and homewards, without being exacting as regards energy, for the sea and wind cost nothing.
The Hanseatic merchant was therfore very careful about harbour organization and marine techniques. He frequently went down to the harbour to watch for the arrival of his ships unless, as in Bruges, he scanned the horizon from his patrician tower.
Watching his cargoes being loaded or unloaded, having a flair for a good piece of business, a temporary partnership or the purchase of a promising arrival of merchandise, buying, selling, engaging, keeping an eye on the proper running of the harbour, the turn-table of his ventures, formed an important part of his role as an intermediary. [A. d'H.]

133. The port of Hamburg.
Miniature illustrating the chapter *Van Schiprechte* of the *Book of Rights of the Town* (1497), fol. 106.
Hamburg Staatsarchiv.

134. Coasting and harbour navigation in the port of Antwerp.
Part of an engraving devoted to the *Allégorie du commerce* by Jost Amann. 1585.
Brussels, The Print-room.

ORGANIZING MARITIME TRAFFIC

135. The office of the manager of the port of Hamburg.
Part of a minature illustrating the chapter *Van Schiprechte* of the Book of *Rights of the Town* (1497), fol. 106.
Hamburg Staatsarchiv.

Harbour Activities

A crane that circles unceasingly. Businessmen. Workmen. Seamen. Strollers. The vigour of cargo handlers. Ceaseless waggon traffic. A mingling of passengers, animals and goods that smack of foreign parts.

Harbour activities. Here is the flow and re-flow of goods going to or coming from other shores, making or demolishing the precarious fortunes of the merchants concerned. It is they who engage the dockers, pay the ostlers, keep an eye on the installations and supervise the transfers of cargo. They have a stake in a good number of boats which risk being wrecked. Boats already ordered are being built there.

Heady risks, audacious measures. When the waiting and the voyage are over, there will perhaps be something left to ensure the future of the merchant's heirs. [A. d'H.]

136. Crane in the port of Hamburg.
Part of a miniature illustrating the chapter *Van Schiprechte* of the *Book of Rights of the Town* (1497), fol. 106.
Hamburg Staatsarchiv.

The dockers who handled the loading and unloading of cargo, formed corporations. One already existed in Danzig in 1468. Here, the merchants are supervising operations.

TRAFFIC IN THE PORT OF LUBECK

March 18, 1368 to March 10, 1369

Goods	Principal origin	Imports	Exports	Total
Cloth	Flanders	120.8	39.7	160.5
Fish	The southern part of the Scandinavian peninsula	64.7	6.1	70.8
Salt	Luneburg	—	61.6	61.6
Butter	Sweden	19.2	6.8	26
Skins, furs	Sweden, Livonia	13.3	3.7	17
Cereals	Prussia	13	0.8	13.8
Wax	Prussia, Livonia	7.2	5.8	13
Beer	Wendish towns	4.1	1.9	6
Copper	Sweden, Hungary	2.3	2.4	4.6
Iron	Sweden, Hungary	2.4	2.2	4.6
Oil	Flanders	2.7	1.5	4.2
Sundry foodstuffs	Livonia, North Germany	0.4	3	3.4
Deniers, silver		0.7	2	2.7
Wine	Rhineland	1.3	0.9	2.2
Linen cloth	Westphalia	0.2	1.1	1.3
Miscellaneous		39.9	16.6	56.5
Not distinguished		41	49	90

137. Securities in thousands of Lubeck marks.
After G. Lechner. *Die hansischen Pfundzollisten des Jahres 1368*, 1935, p. 53.

TRAFFIC IN THE PORT OF LUBECK

March 18, 1368 to March 10, 1369

Movement of 680 ships entering and leaving port

Sailing in	%	Source. Destination	Sailing out	%
289	33.7	Mecklenburg-Pomerania	386	42.3
250	28.8	The southern part of the Scandinavian peninsula	207	22.8
145	16.8	Prussia	183	20.1
96	11.2	Sweden	64	7
35	4.3	Livonia	43	4.7
28	3.2	Fehmarn	27	3
12	1.6	Bergen	—	—
3	0.4	Flanders	1	0.1
858	100		911	100

138. After G. Lechner, *Die hansischen Pfundzollisten des Jahres 1368*, 1935, p. 66.

HARBOUR ACTIVITIES

139-140. Handling goods in the 16th century.
Part of an engraving devoted to the *Allégorie du Commerce*, by Jost Amann. 1585.
Brussels, Royal Library, the Print-room.

141. The port of Stralsund.
Engraving taken from the *Cosmographia* by Sebastian Munster, which appeared in Bâle in 1550. Drawn by H.R.M. Deutsch (1525-1571).
Stralsund, Stadtarchiv.

Far right, in the axis of a street which, through a gate, gives on to the sea: the Town Hall.
Few ports possessed developed equipment, particularly well-fitted-out quays. The presence of the latter was therefore an important economic asset much publicized by towns.

142. Port activities, late 15th century.
Part of a miniature by Jean le Tavernier, of Oudenaarde, for the *Chronique et conquestes de Charlemagne*.
Brussels, Royal Library, ms. 9068, fol. 100 verso.

Wheelbarrows, sledges: human energy and animal energy had to supplement the rather sketchy harbour infrastructure.

151

SHIPBUILDING

Up to about the middle of the 15th century, Lubeck and Danzig were the principal shipbuilding centres of the Hanse. As from the end of the Middle Ages, they experienced keen competition from Bremen and Hamburg.

In Hanse towns, yards were grouped on municipal land *(Lastadie)* and were leased to builders, whilst remaining subject to control by the authorities. Later, in Danzig, around 1460, they formed their own corporations. In the late Middle Ages, ship-owners appeared who financed the building of ships. In 1421, for example, Johannes Kedin in Stralsund had three of the town's thirteen yards.

For some harbours, such as Lubeck, Stettin and Danzig, sources mention repair yards or Brabank (Bragebank, from braggen = to caulk). They were equipped with winches and pontoons for lifting the boats up.

Ships built in Hanseatic yards were renowned. Therefore regulations brought in by Hanse town councils in 1412 and the Prussian States in 1441 prohibited their sale to foreigners. However, shipowners eventually saw their interests prevail. In Danzig they obtained unrestricted right of sale in 1453. There was a decline in Hanseatic town shipyards in the 16th century, as they were overtaken by Dutch competition.

In the first half of the 17th century the average tonnage of a ship built in the Netherlands was 104 lasts, about 210 tonnes, whereas the average Hanseatic ship tonnage was no more than 97 lasts. In Danzig, the number of naval master carpenters fell from 130 in 1526 to 18 in 1611.

143. Timber quay in the port of Antwerp. 1515.
Part of a woodcut: *Antverpia Mercatorum Emporium.*
Antwerp, Prentenkabinet.

144-145. Shipyards.
Part of a miniature dating from the 1460's, illustrating the *First Punic War.*
Brussels, Royal Library, ms. 10770, fol. 41 verso.
16th century engraving.
After Gerds and Gehrke, *Und am Bug der Greif*, Rostock, 1979, p. 39.

146. A 'cogge' being repaired in port.
Part of a miniature from a 15th century manuscript containing an *Ancient History up to Caesar.*
Oxford, the Bodleian, Ms. Douce 353, fol. 31 recto.

ORGANIZING MARITIME TRAFFIC

MANAGING AND MAINTAINING A HARBOUR

Progress in shipbuilding brought about a technical revolution in the harbours.
Larger ships could no longer make fast directly, as shallow-draught craft could.
Changes in the 'cogge' and the howker led to changes in the harbours. New construction appeared: jetties, quays, landing-stages, equipped with bollards and warehouses.
A Stralsund harbour tariff in 1278 made mention of a tax to be paid for unloading ships by means of a crane *(Windegelt)*. Also, grain could be dried on payment of a fee *(Colegelt)*.
The big Danzig crane built before 1363 was replaced in about 1470 by the present brick structure.
Harbours were administered by civil servants appointed by the town municipalities.
In Danzig their salaries and harbour maintenance costs were covered by income from a tax introduced in 1341 on each commodity coming up the Vistula *(Pfahlgeld)*. The mooring master *(Pfahlmeister)* saw to it that the

147. Shipyard workers.
Anonymous painting from the Gouda school, 1565.
Gouda, Stedelijk Museum Het Catharina-Gasthuis.

Specialized artisans, hard workers. They paint on the port shipyards under uncomfortable conditions.
They have but few means: some tools but mainly a know-how passed down from generation to generation and utilized in a solidarity which animates people who, to survive, depend on their hands and their energy.

HARBOUR ACTIVITIES

boatmen discharged no ballast in the fairway. The wharf-master and his assistants supervised the condition of the quays and channels, regulated craft movements and designated the anchoring berths. Sworn inspectors, mentioned in sources in 1378, checked the quality of cargoes such as timber, ash, tar, hops, hemp, honey and wax.

The administration of other Hanseatic harbours did not differ appreciably from this model.

BIBLIOGRAPHY

K.-F. OLECHNOWITZ, *Der Schiffbau der hansischen Spätzeit. Untersuchungen zur Wirtschafts- und Sozialgeschichte des Hanse. Abhandlungen zur Handels- und Sozialgeschichte*, III, Weimar, 1960.

Op de rede. Het leven aan de waterkant in Europese havens, Catalogus van de tentoonstelling te Antwerpen van 14 juli tot 16 september 1973, Antwerpen 1973.

F. PRÜSER, *Die balge, Bremens mittelalterlichen Hafen*, in *Mélanges F. Rörig*, 1953, p. 477-488.

G. ASAERT, *Scheepvaart en havens*, in *Maritieme Geschiedenis der Nederlanden*, vol. I, Bussum, 1976, p. 180-205.

148. 15th century lighthouse. Part of the *Cosmographia* by Sebastian Münster.

149. Traffic in the port of Lubeck, 1552. Part of an engraving by Elias Diebel. Lubeck, St-Annen-Museum.

Prefiguration of a 20th century city port. A prototypic idea of what Western ports are today!

KASIMIERS SLASKI
Poznan History Institute

The Hanse Ships

A large part of the success of Hanseatic trade was due to its navigation techniques.

In the 12th century, trade with the North Sea and the Baltic Sea was effected in ships of less than 25 tonnes burden. They were, for instance, the howker (*holk*) used for traffic between the mouths of the Rhine and England; the 'cogge' (*cog*) from Friesland, a flat-bottomed boat used for coastal trade; and the boats of Scandinavians, Western Slavs, Russians and Esthonians.

As long as the cargoes were mainly luxury articles, small in volume, the above-mentioned ships were quite sufficient. But once commercial traffic between the Lower Rhine and Lower Saxony towns, on the one hand, and the Baltic region, on the other, began to increase in volume for mass-produced goods, the need was felt for other means of sea transport, more suitable for that new kind of trade. It is to the credit of the Saxon town merchants, especially those of Lubeck, a town which was founded in 1159, that the 'cogge' was adapted and developed to that end.

150. Loading a ship.
Miniature illustrating a manuscript of the *Trojan War* by Conrad von Würburg, circa 1440.
Nuremberg, Germanisches Nationalmuseum. Hs. 998.

151. A 'cogge'.
After a miniature taken from the *Dialogi* by Gregory the Great, representing Saint Paulin de Nole sailing to Africa.
Brussels, Albert I Royal Library, ms. 9916, fol. 61, recto.
13th century, had formed part of the St. Laurent abbey library, Liège.

Stem and stern are crowned with dragons' heads, in the manner of Scandinavian ships.

TYPES OF SHIPS AND THEIR FUNCTIONS

The 'cogge'   The principal Hanseatic ship of the 13th-14th century is fairly well-known, largely due to iconography and the discovery of a wreck in Bremen in 1962.

The 'cogge' differed substantially from its Fresian prototype. It had a keel, clinker-work, a mast step and Norse type masts, all adaptations that stemmed from the experience of Scandinavian and Slav shipyards.

The new 'cogge' retained its flat bottom although fitted with a keel. The stern-post was almost perpendicular; the stem-post was very little out of the vertical; the sides were much higher than those of Scandinavian and Slav ships. All these features increased the capacity of the 'cogge', an important matter for a merchant ship.

152. The fourth seal of the town of Lubeck.
Dates from 1280.
SIGILLUM BURGERSIUM DE LUBEKE.
Hamburg, Staatsarchiv.

THE HANSE SHIPS

153-156. Seals appended to a document sealing the alliance between Hanseatic towns. November 11, 1436. Lubeck, Stadtarchiv.

1. Kiel: SIGILLUM CIVIUM KILENSIUM.
2. SIGILLUM BURGERSIUM DE LUBEKE.
3. SIGILLUM WISMARIE CIVITATIS.
4. SIGILLUM CIVITATIS STRALESSUNDIS.

Emblematic dimension of a ship, conspicuously a 'cogge'. A Hanseatic town identified itself with that ship, recognizing in it a means of moving ahead and of survival; reasons for being proud, also, and showing itself to the best advantage vis-à-vis others.

159

157. A 'cogge' with a modern rudder. Seal of the town of Elbing, 1242.
SIGILLUM BURGENSIUM IN ELVIGGE.
Hamburg, Staatsarchiv.

The hinged rudder, fixed to the stern and actuated by a tiller, appeared for the first time on the seal of the town of Elbing, founded in 1237 within the context of the conquest of Prussia by the Teutonic Knights. This kind of rudder facilitated handling at sea, due to a better lever effect.
Bremerhaven, Deutsches Schiffahrtsmuseum.

Oak and elm were mainly used in building 'cogges'. The mast often consisted of one spruce trunk from the forests of Russia, Prussia or Poland. The planking, clinker-built, was fixed to the ribs with big, iron, curved-end nails. When the 'cogge' was built, crevices were caulked with tow and tar. To preserve the sides, a mixture of resin, sulphur and linseed oil was used. This oil, called 'harpoys', was referred to in 1252 in a tariff of the town of Damme.

'Cogges' differed from former types of ship by their massive construction. Pieces of planking found in Bergen were up to 5 cm thick; the traverse beams of the wreck found in Bremen were 40 × 40 cm thick. At the bottom of the 'cogge' was the keelson, a large beam with a mast step in which the foot of the mast was fixed. To protect the cargo against seawater, all the bottom of the ship was covered with a hanging-bridge or wooden grating. The hold was partitioned off in several compartments so that different kinds of cargo could be carried.

'Cogges' had a single mast 16 to 24 m high. The mast bore a horizontal yard fitted with a ring for hoisting or lowering it as required. The sail, of strong sail-cloth, was rectangular in shape. When the wind was favourable, the sail surface could be enlarged by two or even three *bonnets*, pieces of canvas which were attached to the lower edge of the sail. Paul Heinsius calculated that a 12.8 × 19.2 yard carried from 82 to 175 sq.m. of sail-cloth; 120 to 330 sq.m. when the *bonnets* were added. The bowsprit carried no sail but was used solely to facilitate the handling of the yard by means of a halyard joining the yard to the end of the bowsprit.

158. Building a 'cogge'.
Engraving taken from the *Peregrinatio in terram sanctam* by Bernard von Breydenbach. Printed in Mainz in 1483.

Shipyards did wonders with particularly modest means. Man had not yet delegated to mechanical techniques the know-how acquired from long familiarity with a natural material: wood.

THE HANSE SHIPS

At the beginning of the 13th century the 'cogge' had retained some of the earlier features such as, for instance, the oar-shaped rudder attached to the port side, or the dragon heads crowning the stem and stern after the fashion of Scandinavian ships. A very important innovation was the modern hinged rudder, fastened to the stern and moved by a tiller. It appeared for the first time in 1242, on the seal of the town of Elblag.

It is probable that from the beginning of the 13th century 'cogges' were built with decks over the whole of their length, for that would have been vital for carrying provisions that would have been adversely affected by dampness or salt water, such as flour, ash or some dress materials. The deck rested on several transversal beams, the ends of which jutted out over the planking.

In the second half of the 13th century, castles appeared on Hanseatic ships, like those of Southern and Western Europe. They consisted of scaffolding erected on the stem and stern and were used in the event of attack and also as look-out posts.

In the 14th century, if not earlier, crescent-shaped half-decks began to be placed at the stern and sometimes at the bow of the 'cogge'. Such a deck covering the poop of a ship fitted with a castle can be seen on the seal of the town of Damme (1309); similar scaffolding is visible above the stem.

During the 14th century these constructions ended up by being incorporated into the 'cogge' itself, forming a quarter-deck and forecastle that were elevated in relation to the main deck. The larger quarter-deck contained cabins for the ship's company or prominent people.

159. Wreck of a 'cogge'.
Bremerhaven, Deutsches Schiffahrtsmuseum.

In the port of Bremen in 1962 a 'cogge' was found which had sunk shortly after being completed, in a high tide, around 1380. The following are its characteristics:
Length: approx. 23.5 m.
Maximum breadth: approx. 7.5 m.
Draught: approx. 2 m.
Tonnage: approx. 120 t.
Crew: between 15 and 20 men.
Height to bulwark: approx. 4.4 m.
Height to outer castle: approx. 7.5 m.
The Bremen wreck had only one castle above the poop. The forecastle, smaller and triangular, was used for keeping watch, sounding the sea and checking the course.
Livonian sources (14th century) mention 'cogges' carrying 100 lasts, i.e. about 200 t, and more.
In 1294 the ship carrying cargo from the inhabitants of Saremaa Island (Osel) embarked a load of about 118 lasts of grain (237 t.).

ORGANIZING MARITIME TRAFFIC

The Howker

The 'cogge' was the conventional vessel of the Hanseatic towns between the mouth of the Elbe and the Gulf of Finland.

Sea traffic between the Lower Rhine and the British Isles was effected with another type of ship, the howker (*holk*). Its silhouette, with a rounded bottom and no keel, was rather like a banana or even a crescent. In the 12th and 13th centuries, the howkers were smaller than the 'cogges' but they gradually got bigger. Increasing contacts between the North Sea ports and the Baltic Sea favoured the birth of a vessel combining features of the 'cogge' and the howker and such a ship can be seen on the grand seal of Danzig in 1400 and

160. Ships entering the port of Hamburg, level with the Trostbrücke. Part of a miniature illustrating the chapter *Van Schiprechte* in the *Book of Rights of the Town* (1497), fol. 106.
Hamburg, Staatsarchiv.

The channel of the port of Lubeck was about 3 m deep in the 15th century. In 1425 it was decided that the Koggentief at Danzig should be dredged to a depth of 5 cubits, i.e. 3.4 m.
Because of its tonnage, a 'cogge' was often obliged to drop anchor far from the shore. Its equipment therefore included two or more iron anchors as well as drogues and grapnels. On some reproductions of ships the anchor can be seen on the stem. A hemp rope was attached to the ring of an anchor. A winch situated on the poop facilitated getting under way; it was also used to hoist the yard.
Each big merchant ship had a dinghy or two either on deck or on tow. They were used for dropping anchor when mooring and also saving the crew should the need arise. [K. Slaski]

on the seal of Amsterdam in 1418. This modernised howker had kept its portly silhouette and a very high forecastle. On the other hand, it had borrowed from the 'cogge' the keel, the protruding stem and a wide, flattened quarter-deck.

In the 15th century there were howkers that could carry about 285 lasts, i.e. 560 t. of salt.

This type of boat did not last very long; it was soon overtaken by others of a more modern design.

161. A howker in the port of Antwerp. Part of an anonymous painting, 1513-1540.
Antwerp, Nationaal Scheepvaartmuseum.

ORGANIZING MARITIME TRAFFIC

The Carrack

In the second half of the 15th century, free-board planked ships replaced those that were clinker-built. This enabled them to take greater tonnage. Multi-mast ships also made their appearance.

In 1462 the town of Danzig acquired the famous *Pierre de la Rochelle* which it re-christened *Peter von Danzig*. This served as a model for Hanseatic shipbuilders.

Its deck was about 43 m long and 12 m wide; its capacity was about 1225 t. It carried square sails at the foremast and main mast and a lateen sail at the mizzen mast.

Contemporary sources consider the *Peter von Danzig* as a caravel (*Kraweel*), but it was more like another type of South European ship, the carrack, which in the 15th and 16th centuries became the standard model of the Hanseatic fleet for ocean voyages.

The carrack had a quarter-deck of two or three levels, and an even higher forecastle which jutted out over the stem.

Its masts and spars consisted of two square-rigged masts with a foremast, main sail and two topsails, a mizzen mast with a lateen sail, and a bowsprit carrying a small square sail. Carrack tonnage often exceeded 1,000 t.

162. A carrack.
A burin engraving by the master W.A. who, around 1475, represented a series of ships with remarkable accuracy.
Paris, National Library.

The ship had a double deck.

163. Structure and equipment of a carrack. Drawing by J. Van Beylen, after the engraving by master W.A.
Maritieme Geschiedenis der Nederlanden, G. Asaert, vol. 1, Bussum, 1976, p. 130.

1. Bowsprit	20. Shrouds
2. Foremast	21. Spar blocks
3. Main mast	22. Chain-wale
4. Mizzen mast	23. Top
5. Fore-yard	24. Ladder
6. Yard	25. Top pulley-block
7. Mizzen yard	26. Cannon
8. Foresail jib	27. Grapnel
9. Sail	28. Hawse-hole
10. Studding-sail	29. Cargo door
11. Mizzen-topmast staysail	30. Bend
	31. Clamps
12. Forestay	32. Counter with rudder trunk
13. Broadside	
14. Sheet and fish	33. Forecastle
15. Bowline	34. Raised castle with canopy
16. Brail	35. Poop-deck
17. Topping-lift	36. Raised stern castle
18. Brace	37. Toilet
19. Parrel pulley-block	

164. A four-masted galleon.
Part of the *Paysage avec la chute d'Icare* by Peter Breughel the Elder. Circa 1555.
Brussels, Fine Arts Museum.

The ship is approaching port and preparing to cast anchor. The seamen take in the mainsail and the topsail. The castles, in several tiers, are impressive.

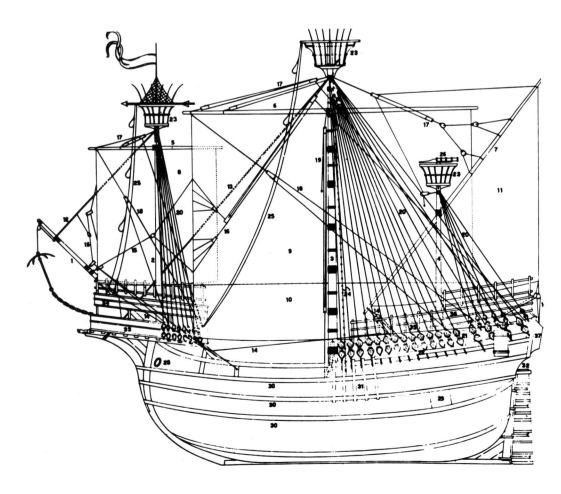

ORGANIZING MARITIME TRAFFIC

The Galleon

In the last century of the existence of the Hanse a type of large ship of Spanish origin appeared on the North Eastern seas: the galleon.
Originally designed as a warship, various variations were made to it to make it suitable for commercial use.
Merchant galleons differed from carracks by their much lower bows ending with a tapering prow decorated with sculptures, above which rose the bowsprit. The stern, on the other hand, was very high, ending flat and decorated in the same way.

165. A three-masted sailing-ship leaving port. Pen-and-ink drawing on paper, water-coloured. By Hans Holbein the Younger (1497-1543) circa 1533, from memories of voyages.
It was a mural decoration project.
Frankfort, Städelsches Kunstinstitut.

THE HANSE SHIPS

Coastal and port boats

Besides the ocean-going ships there were boats for coastal trade and port service.

In the first category came the 'ewer', a flat-bottomed boat which, like the howker, finished by attaining the dimensions of a 'cogge' in the early 15th century. There was a carrier boat called a *kreier* that could take 50 to 100 t., and the 'scuta' (*schute*) with a deadweight of 15 to 30 t which was used for lighterage and coastal trade. The 'enesque' (*Schnigge*), a light sailing ship which was also fitted with oars, acted as a mail and police boat in the 15th and 16th centuries.

For embarking cargo or passengers aboard big ships in the roads, or for disembarking them, as well as for internal port traffic, various kinds of flat-bottomed boats were used, often known only by very general descriptions.

There was mainly the ferry-boat (pram, promptuarium), some wrecks of which, measuring 14-18 m in length and 3.6 m in width, were discovered at Falsterbo in 1911, where the principal herring fishing-grounds were situated in the Middle Ages. There were also the bording, hafkane and eke, which were used on the Weser and the Elbe and are often mentioned in 13th century and later sources. Transport on the Volkhov, as far as Novgorod, was effected in the Middle Ages with native boats (lodis) dug out of popular tree trunks. The oberlaender, which was in use on the Rhine in the 15th and 16th centuries, was of similar conception.

166. The port of Hamburg.
Part of the Elbe-Karte (12 metres), a pen and ink drawing on paper by the painter and cartographer Melchior Lorichs. 1568.
Hamburg Staatsarchiv.

Hamburg, on the right bank of the Elbe, at its junction with the Alster.

167

ORGANIZING MARITIME TRAFFIC

167. Map of herring shoals in the North Sea.
A water colour by Adriaan Coenen (1514-1583) for his Visboec, 1578.
The Hague, Koninklijke Bibliotheek, ms. 78 E 54.

Coenen had a good knowledge of marine fauna and the state of shoals. He was also a keen collector of dried fish. He regularly picked up rare or unusual species on the beach.

It was in 1578 that Coenen started on his book, which was to run to more than 800 pages. He took it to fairs, where he showed it to gapers who paid to see it.

RULE-OF-THUMB TECHNIQUES AND KNOWLEDGE

Before the 15th century the Hanse ships developed an average speed of 6 to 8 knots (7.5 to 11 km/hour). With a favourable wind that speed could easily be exceeded. Sail development in the second half of the 15th century made it possible to cruise even with an adverse wind, and reduced the chances of being becalmed.

To keep on course, one relied on taking the sun and hugging the coast. The high church spires of some Hanseatic towns often served as a landmark.

For entering port there were lighthouses. The Slav port of Wolin, at the mouth of the Oder, had them already in the 11th century. The Hanse copied that example by building lighthouses: downstream of Wismar in 1226, at Stralsund, where the light had to shine from the Nativity of the Virgin (September 8th) till Saint Walburge's Day (May 1st), at Danzig (Weichselmunde), and at Neuwerk on the Elbe in 1300.

In the 14th century, luminous buoys were placed to indicate shallows in channels.

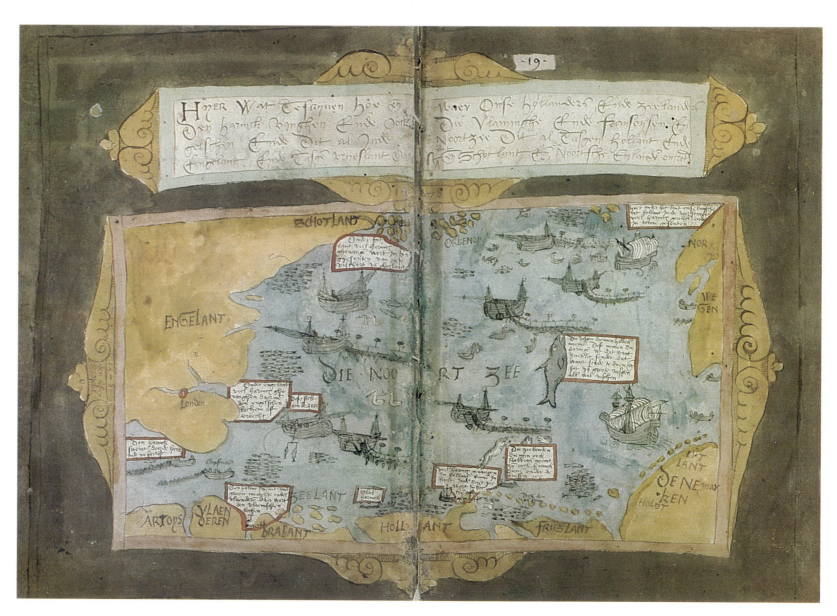

THE HANSE SHIPS

Nautical instruments

On the other hand, until the 14th century, Hanse ships seldom used a compass. In 1460, for the first time, mention is made of a *kraier* from Danzig which had compasses (*kompassen, zeylsteine*).

Because of the configuration of the Baltic and North Sea coasts, the art of sounding had been very highly developed in those regions; the Italian cartographer Fra Mauro spoke very well of the art in 1458.

Sea-charts were unknown. It was only in 1589 that Wagenaer, in his *Spieghel der Zeefhart,* published the first maps of the North Sea, indicating sea depths.

Other nautical instruments in the time of the Hanse were of a very modest nature. From the 14th century a 'log' and a water-clock (Glas) were used to calculate the distance covered. It seems that quadrants and other instruments used by astronomers in the 15th century were not employed for Hanseatic navigation.

The technical development and organization introduced by the Hanse from the 12th to the 14th century greatly influenced navigation and maritime trade in the Baltic. But in the 15th century the Hanse allowed itself to be overtaken in the technical field by Spanish, Portuguese, French, Dutch and English navigators.

168. A sailor sounding the depths.
Part of the *Carta marina* by Olaus Magnus, 1539.

The sounding-lead (Loth, Lyne und Loth, Dieploth) is the oldest known instrument of navigation. It is the only one, before the compass, explicitly mentioned as being aboard Hanseatic ships.
The Italian, Fra Mauro, on his marine map of the world (1458) noted for the Baltic: "On this sea one navigates neither with a marine map nor with a compass, but with a sounding-lead."

169. Using a compass at sea.
Part of a miniature taken from the Livre des Merveilles, 14th century.
Paris, National Library, French Ms. 2810, fol. 188 verso.

At first, the marine compass was only a metal needle which had been rubbed with magnetic iron ore. The needle was suspended in a box – the word Boussole comes from the Italian word meaning a small box – and turned on its pivot, pointing to the north at the end of the movement.
It was only at the end of the Middle Ages that the magnetized needle was suspended over a compass-card, giving the navigator his course according to the terms of the 'thirty-two points of the compass'.

A CONTRACTUAL COMMITMENT

More efficient maritime organization to the North Seas was due to the Hanse.

A right of use, based on Western Europe and local customs, regulated in detail a number of juridical and technical problems. It was progressively supplemented by ordinances emanating from the maritime towns and Diets of the Hanse.

At the beginning of Hanseatic activities, the master boatman was also the owner of the boat. But around 1300 the ship could belong to several owners at the same time. The owners of the cargo engaged the master (schipher, nauclerus) by contract to deliver the goods at the agreed time and place. The master vouched for the preservation of the goods during the voyage, but only within certain limits. If he was not the only owner of the ship, he had to come to an arrangement with the other owners, whilst remaining the sole master. It was he who engaged and paid the crew, composed of ordinary seamen (*schipmans*) and specialists such as the *helmsman* (*stureman*, gubernator), the cook, the carpenter (*timmerman*) and, where necessary, the pilot. 15 to 25 sailors were needed to sail a 'cogge'; more were required to sail a carrack or galleon. The big vessels of the 14th, 15th and 16th centuries also took on board merchants' representatives, passengers and sometimes even a military escort.

The master shared by right in the cargo. The members of his crew had the right to embark a certain quantity of goods as laid down in the contract or in maritime ordinances, for their own account. For instance, Hamburg law fixed that cargo (*fuhrung*) at 5 *schippmunt* (166 kg) for a voyage to Norway or Gotland, and a double sack of wool for a voyage from England to Hamburg.

To avoid bad weather risks, the 1403 Diet prohibited any navigation between Saint Martin's Day (November 11th) and Saint Peter's Day (February 22nd).

170. Loading and unloading in the port of Antwerp.
Part of an engraving by Jost Amann devoted to the *Allégorie du Commerce*. Circa 1585. Brussels, Royal Library, the Print-room.

The Prussian towns, which had bigger boats, protested against that ordinance, and the town of Wismar succeeded in having it accepted that traffic with the southern part of the Scandinavian peninsula would not be prohibited except between Saint Nicholas' Day (December 6th) and Candlemas (February 2nd).

BIBLIOGRAPHY

On certain types of ships

O. CRUMLIN-PEDERSEN, *Cog-Kogge-Kog*, in *Handels-og Sjøfarts Museets Arborg*, 1965.
D. ELLMERS, *Kogge, Kahn und Kunstoffboot*, in *Führer des Deutschen Schiffahrtsmuseum n° 7*, Bremerhaven, 1976.
W.D. HOCHEISEL, *Die Bremer Kogge*, in *Hanse in Europa*. Ausstellung des Kölnischen Stadtmuseum, Köln, 1973.

O. LIENAU, *Danziger Schiffahrt und Schiffbau in der zweiten Hälfte des 15. Jahrhunderts*, in *Zeitschrift des Westpreussischen Geschichtsvereins*, 70, Danzig, 1930.

K. REINHARDT, *Rekonstruktion der Karache 'Jezus von Lübeck'*, in *Zeitschrift des Vereins für Lübeckische Geschichte*, vol. 31, 1941.

On navigation in general and more particularly in the Middle Ages

A. LEWIS, *The sea and medieval civilisations*, collected studies, London, 1978.
H. NEUKIRCHEN, *Seefahrt gestern und heute*, 3rd ed., Berlin, 1972.
A. OLIVEIRA MARQUES, *Navigation entre la Prusse et le Portugal au début du Ve siècle*, in *Vierteljahrschrift für Sozial- und Wirtschaftsgeschichte*, vol. 46, 1959.
W. VOGEL, *Geschichte der deutschen Seeschiffahrt*, vol. I, Berlin, 1915.
W. VOGEL, G. SCHMÖLDERS, *Die Deutschen als Seefahrer*. Hamburg, s.d. (1949).

On ports

History Gdańska, vol. 1: to 1454, reed. by E. Cieslak, Wydawnictwo Morskie, Gdańsk, 1978.
H. SZYMANSKI, *Der Ever der Niederelbe*, Lübeck, 1932.
B. WACHOWIAK, *Port Sredniowiecznego Szczecina*, Gdańsk, 1955.

On shipyards

Historia budownictwa okretowego na Wybrzezu Gdanskim, reed. by E. Cieslak, Gdańsk, 1972.
O. LIENAU, *Danziger Schiffahrt und Schiffbau in der zweiten Hälfte des 15 Jahrhunderts*, in *Zeitschrift des Westpreussischen Geschichtsvereins 70*, Gdańsk, 1930.
M. MALOWIST, *L'approvisionnement des ports de la Baltique en produits forestiers pour les constructions navales, aux XVe et XVIe siècles*, in *Travaux du Troisième Colloque International d'histoire maritime*, Paris, 1960.
K. OLECHNOWITZ, *Der Schiffbau der hansischen Spätezeit*, in *Abhandlungen zur Handels- und Sozialgeschichte*, vol. III, Weimar, 1960.

On maritime law

E. CIESLAK, *Prawa i obowiazki kapitana statku w II-XVI wieku wedlu Rôles d'Oléron i prawa morskiego Zwiasku Miast Hanzeatyckih*, Zapiski Tow. Naukowego w Toruniu, vol. 17, Torun, 1951.
B. JANIK, *Najatarszy tekst prawa morskiego w Gdansku*, 1961.
S. MATYSIK, *Prawo morskie Gdanska*, Warszawa, 1958.

172

Managing the Hanse business houses

In the loose, empirical Hanseatic structure, the business houses played an essential part; they were the vital cores of commercial traffic, encounters and management of Northern Europe international trade.

Business houses sprang up spontaneously around the Hanseatic world: one in the East (Novgorod), another in the West (London), one in the North (Bergen), another in the South-West (Bruges). Those who lived or passed through there were communis mercator hanse theitonice, der gemeine Kaufmann der deutschen Hanse.

An annual general meeting elected the Elders (Aeltermann). Those who were elected took on a burden which became even heavier as the business house flourished, and that office was unremunerated. They had jurisdiction over the merchants, managed the coffers, took the necessary commercial steps for the house as a whole and for individuals, entered into juridical or commercial proceedings with local or national authorities and represented the house on the Hanseatic Diet (Hansetag).

The business house, except in Bruges, was a closed space. All Hanseatic merchants had to reside there, whether they were just passing through or had settled there for a while. They were subject to an austere, strict, closely controlled daily regime from which women were totally excluded as in a conventual entity.

The community was presided over and managed by the Elder and his council. The Elder called the residents together regularly, in particular for the solemn reading of the statutes and bye-laws, the allocation of responsibilities and day-to-day management tasks. Those at the head of the house supervised the quality of goods, the payment of taxes and the honesty of commercial practices.

They also saw that privileges were respected, represented members in disputes at law and levied a certain amount to be used for affairs in common.

The business houses were progressively done away with in the late 15th century.

The Hanse hardly survived. [A. d'H.]

171-173. The arms of the Lubeck merchant companies, intended for the main hall of the Schütting.
Wooden reliefs sculptured by Benedikt Dreyer in 1527.
Lubeck, St-Annen-Museum.

For the Novgorodfahrer: a bearded Russian.
For the Englandfahrer: the double-headed eagle.
For the Bergenfahrer: the cod (stockfish).
The arms of Lubeck bear the double-headed eagle.

JEAN-PIERRE SOSSON
Louvain Catholic University

The Oosterlingenhuis in Bruges

It was fairly late when German merchants appeared in Bruges: at the beginning of the 13th century, at the time when in Flanders, and particularly in Bruges, economic initiative and active trade was passing over to foreigners.

A BUSINESS HOUSE IN 1252

Attracted to the town of Zwin by the fact that it was a centre for Anglo-Flemish trade, foreign merchants became increasingly numerous there in the second quarter of the century. They came from Cologne, Westphalia, Bremen, Hamburg and Lubeck in such numbers that it soon became necessary to regulate their stay.

In 1252 and 1253 Marguerite de Constantinople, Countess of Flanders, granted a series of privileges, the foundation of the commercial strides made by the Hanseatics in Flanders: tax reduction in Bruges; quick proceedings in the case of a dispute; freedom from any collective responsibility for the debts of others; debtor obliged by the local court to pay within three days under penalty of imprisonment and distraint.

During the 1252 negotiations, Lubeck submitted a project to found near Damme a privileged merchant colony equivalent to the London Stalhof or the Novgorod Peterhof.

The project failed and Bruges was then the only one of the Hanse business houses abroad where, having no space reserved for them, the Germans lived with the population. Culturally, this was not without consequence.

174. The house of the Osterlins seen from the north-west.
Part of a painting from the second half of the 16th century, entitled *Septem admirationes civitatis Brugensis*.
Bruges, The Beguinage.

Until 1457 the Hanseatics had no territory or residence of their own in Bruges, whereas they had elsewhere.

A project approved by the Countess of Flanders in 1252 aimed at founding, near Damme, a privileged merchant establishment where the Hanseatics could meet, rather like the Stalhof in London or the Peterhof in Novgorod, but the idea fell through.

The Hanseatics took part daily in the Morgensprachen, encounters which were subsequently held twice a day: at 11 a.m. and between 4 and 5 p.m. (between 5 and 6 p.m. in the summer). All the Germans present in Bruges met there and could discuss their business and problems with the Elders.

In 1457 the city of Bruges allocated to the Hanseatics ground which had become free following the demolition of an old part of the town.

175. Ships and lighters on the Reie, in the outer harbour of Bruges.
A pen and ink drawing, coloured, circa 1460.
Bruges, Stadsarchief.

Germans from Rhineland and Westphalia went to the Flemish towns by road, so they preferred Ghent to Bruges.

Those from the Baltic swept into the Zwin and changed Bruges in the 13th century into an international market, a kind of permanent trade fair replacing previous temporary fairs.

Ships from Bremen and Hamburg generally avoided the high seas. To reach the Zwin they preferred to take the Wattenmeer and Zuiderzee and then Dutch inland waterways.

MANAGING THE BUSINESS HOUSES

176. Key to the safe of the Bruges Osterlins.
The identifying text was drafted on May 28, 1347.
Bruges, Stadsarchief.

177-179. Matrix of the great seal and counter-seal of the city of Bruges.
Bruges, Stadsarchief.
The great seal, sigillum ad contractus, measures 98 mm in diameter. It was made by Jan Inghelbrecht, known as Jan Zeghelmakere, and bears the coat of arms of the city.
SIGILLUM SCABINOR(UM) ET BURGENSIUM VILLE DE BRUGIS AD CONTRACTUS.
The counter-seal, made by the same engraver in 1318, also bears the coat of arms of the city.
+ CONTRA S(IGILLUM) VILLE DE BRUGIS AD CONTRACTUS.
Both matrices and the chain which connects them are of solid silver.

180. Bruges covered market and belfry.
A massive brick construction in the form of an irregular quadrilateral with a central courtyard.
The 83 m tower comes in the middle of the covered market wing alongside the marketplace. It is surmounted by a 27.4 m stone octagon which, until 1741, was topped by a 19 m high wooden construction.
The covered market has three floors. They date either from the late 13th century (before 1280) or from the 14th century.

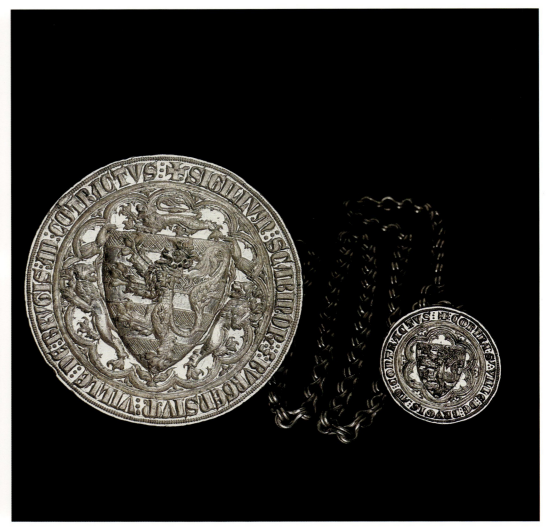

THE STATUTES OF THE BRUGES BUSINESS HOUSE

In the name of the Lord, amen. As it is good and proper to set down in writing the points and prescriptions to be respected, the associated merchants of the Roman Empire of Germany, in the year of our Lord 1347, assembled in the refectory of the Carmelites in Bruges on the day of the apostles Saint Simon and Saint Jude (Oct. 28th), have decided, for the benefit of the associated merchants, to have and keep jointly a book in which shall be entered all the ordinances and regulations to be established and enacted, as well as the customs and usages that are to be observed.

1. Firstly, it is to be known that the above-mentioned community of merchants is divided into three groups as follows: those of Lubeck, the Wendish towns, the Saxons and whatever is connected therewith are grouped in one third; those of Westphalia, Prussia and whatever is connected therewith in another; lastly those of Gotland, Livonia, Sweden and whatever is connected therewith in the third.

2. Furthermore, each year eight days after Whitsun, two Elders are to be elected in each third. He who is elected must accept the office or pay a pound of 'gros' into the coffers of the said merchants, with the risk of being elected a second time and incurring the same fine.

3. Furthermore, if one of the Elders left Bruges, the other five must elect one from the same third to which the sixth belonged, and he must accept under penalty of the said fine.

4. Furthermore, the six Elders shall have the power to assemble the community of Germans on the date they decide and at the place where they are, under penalty of a fine of three 'gros'. (Tariff of fines for defaulters).

5. Should an important matter so require, the Elders may summons to appear whomsoever they wish and inflict a fine as heavy as they wish.

6. Should it happen that an Elder fails to present himself, he is liable to a double fine.

7. If the Elders cannot agree among themselves, the minority must follow the majority.

8. Similarly, if the three thirds do not agree, the third third must accept the decision of the other two.

9. If a matter concerns the whole of the Community, whether within the gates (of Bruges) or outside, it is the wisest and most competent of the six Elders, designated as such by the other five, who must be its spokesman. If the matter concerns one third more than the others, the Elders of the third in question must be the spokesmen.

10. The six Elders, on the very day of their election, must choose six assessors in each third (fine of five sous pursuant to § 2).

11. The six Elders and the eighteen assessors must meet whenever they are convened by the Elders, and they can settle all matters without the joint assembl' of the Germans.

12. When the Elders appoint delegates to local councillors, they must obey under penalty of two sous of 'gros' in town or five sous of 'gros' out of town, if they have to overlap.

13. When the community of the Germans assembles at the Carmelites', at the moment when the Elders go to the refectory they must order their man-servant to go through the church and invite those present to join them. If anyone arrives late after the Elders have begun their speeches, he must pay three 'gros' into the coffers.

14. When the Elders are making their speeches standing at the desk (contoor), if some persons go and sit on the bench or commence to chat with one, two or more others, not listening to what the Elders are saying, they shall pay a 'gros' into the coffers, as many as they are and as often as they do it. The same fine applies to meetings of the thirds.

15. He who opens the doors without the permission of the Elders shall pay five sous of 'gros' into the coffers; he who goes away without permission, three 'gros'.

16. The Elders can require whomsoever is under oath to tell the truth about any matter coming within German law, under penalty of a fine of a pound of 'gros'.

17. If a merchant undertakes an important or secondary deal, whether in Bruges or outside of Bruges, he must carry it through at his own expense. If he cannot or does not want to do so himself, let him ask another to be his spokesman. And the Germans must lend him assistance in his cause according to their power and goodwill.

181. *Hansrecesse I*, vol. 2, pub. K. Koppmann, 1870.

STATUTES IN 1347

It was not until a century after having obtained its first privileges that the Bruges business house became strictly organized. Its statutes were promulgated on October 28, 1347 in the refectory of the Carmelite monastery.
The associated merchants of the Roman Empire of Germany "divided themselves into three groups: those of Lubeck, the Wendish towns, the Saxons and whatever was connected with them; those of Westphalia, Prussia and whatever was connected with them; lastly, those of Gotland, Livonia, Sweden and whatever was connected with them." Each third elected two Aldermen and six councillors, dealt with the town in matters concerning that third, and managed its own finances.

182. The house of the Osterlins.
After Antoine Sanderus, *Flandria Illustrata*, 1614-1644.

Nor was there in Bruges a central place where money matters could be dealt with, although the word 'bourse' comes from the house kept by the Van der Beursens. It is true that Italian banks, by installing numerous subsidiaries and branches there, made Bruges the leading financial place in Northern Europe.
Merchants, to do business and keep themselves informed, went from one place to another. During those comings and goings they thought about business, chatting when they had the opportunity, weighing up the pros and cons with partners who respected and esteemed one another in a professional context which watched over the regularity of transactions, as regards weight, quality and finances.
In 1478 the Osterlins had a bigger residence built for them, int voorgheschreven Cromme Genthof *(the present* Krom Genthof*), of which only a few poor vestiges remain in a Neo-Gothic building erected in 1866.*
The cultural influence of the Hanse business house in Bruges was considerable. It was through it that the Hanseatics perfected their commercial and financial techniques, and that the literary and artistic currents of the West reached Northern Germany. [Ph. Dollinger].

THE IMPORTANCE OF THE BUSINESS HOUSE

The power of the German colony was commensurate to its economic importance; it was in fact equalled only by that of the Italian colonies.

The blockade weapon or, more precisely, the threat to move the business house to another Low Countries town, was formidably effective, for it was liable to plunge Bruges and even Flanders into profound economic stagnation without involving "the complete stoppage of Hanseatic traffic in a sector vital to them" [Ph. Dollinger].

It was effectively used several times in the 13th and 14th centuries. The 'Osterlins' moved to Ardenburg in 1280 and 1307, and twice to Dordrecht. The first blockade, from 1358 to 1360, enabled the Hanseatics to obtain not only the confirmation of their privileges but also the right to trade retail. Then, with less success, from 1388 to 1392, due to Burgundian presence in the Low Countries and the development of Dutch trade in the Baltic. The business house was moved to Deventer in 1450-1451 and to Utrecht from 1453 to 1458.

No figure can be put on the exceptional importance of the Bruges business house in Hanse traffic. An indication is that there were six hundred participants in the 1457 General Meeting.

That importance is explained by three essential factors. The first: the situation of Bruges in the centre of a nebula of textile workshops where the Hanseatics could buy cloth, the main item in their imports. As an example: in Lubeck, out of a total of 339,000 marks for imports, cloth, mostly from Bruges, represented 120,000.

The second: the high demographic density and heavy industrialization of Flanders, making it an exceptional outlet for the products transported by the Hanse: furs, wax, metals, amber, timber and cereals.

The third: the presence of numerous foreign 'nations' in the town of Zwin. Venice, Lucca, Genoa, Florence, Castille or Spain, Biscay, Catalonia and Scotland constituted an almost unlimited potential market for the Hanseatics, adding the North-South dimension to East-West and West-East commercial traffic. In short, the Bruges business house was ideally situated on the major axis of Hanseatic traffic: from Novgorod to London, taking in Reval, Lubeck and Hamburg.

In the urban scene the business house has not left archeological evidence commensurate with its importance.

Contrary to the business houses of Novgorod (the Peterhof), London (the Stalhof) and Bergen (the Tyskebrygge), it had no reserved space of its own. For a long time the merchants lived in hotels or rented houses; the General Meetings were held in the refectory of the Carmelite monastery.

However, in 1442, they rented a house where the secretary could have his office. In 1457 the Magistrate granted them possession of a public place (Oosterlingenplein).

In 1478 the Osterlins built a larger abode, *int voorgeschreven Cromme Genthof* (the present Krom Genthof), of which only a few poor vestiges remain, embodied in a Neo-Gothic building erected in 1866.

FROM 1356 TO 1553

Independent up to the Hansetag of 1356, the business house was then subordinated to the authority of the assembled towns. Its decline, at the end of the 15th century, reduced the number of Aldermen from six to three and the councillors from eighteen to nine in 1486.

The growing competition of Antwerp, the disastrous impact of political events during the infancy of Philip the Handsome and the regency of Maximilian of Austria (from the death of Marie de Bourgogne on March 27, 1482 to the capitulation of Sluys on October 12, 1492), the centralization in Antwerp of trade between England, Cologne, Frankfort-on-Main, Nuremberg and Augsburg precipitated the decline of the town of Zwin and sealed the fate of the Bruges business house.

In 1506 they no longer managed to fill the three Alderman seats and the nine Councillor seats provided for by the reform of 1486. In 1511 there were only a dozen members of the Hanseatic colony left.

In 1553 the Hanse officially transferred to Antwerp.

BIBLIOGRAPHY

RUDOLF HAEPKE, *Brügges Entwicklung zum mittelalterlichen Weltmarkt* (Abhandlungen zur Verkehrs- und Seegeschichte, 1), Berlin, 1908, reed. anast. 1975.
J.A. VAN HOUTTE, *Bruges, Essai d'histoire urbaine*, Bruxelles, 1967 (bonne bibliographie).
L. LENNEN, *Zur Geschichte der hansischen Häuser zu Brügge und Antwerpen*, in *Hansische Geschichtsblätter*, t, 3, 1874, p. 39-74.

THE 'RENEWED' DIET OF LUBECK, IN 1470 THE BRUGES MART

46. No Hanseatic, burgher or resident, no non-Hanseatic, whoever he may be, may bring in any roll of cloth manufactured in Flanders, Brabant or Holland, which has not been bought at or passed through the Mart of Bruges, Antwerp or Berg-op-Zoom at the fair which is held on St. Martin's Day.

51. As regards other goods to be brought to the Mart, the following has been decided upon: all Mart products, i.e. wax, furs, copper, zinc, goat skins and other sorts of skins, wool, fish oil, osmund iron and any kind of iron, woad, linen, vitriol, high boots, linen cloth and all kinds of other Mart products wherever they come from, with the exception of perishable foodstuffs *(ventegud)*, viz. beer, grain, pitch, resin, beams and planks, shall be brought to the the Bruges Mart, the two fairs in Antwerp and on St. Martin's Day in Berg-op-Zoom, as is stipulated in the preceding Article. And if the said Mart products remain unsold at the Antwerp or Berg fairs, they shall be brought to the Bruges Mart.

52. Furthermore, all merchants from Eastern towns, from Lubeck, Rostock, Stralsund, Wismar, the Pomeranian towns, Danzig, Koeningsberg and other Prussian towns, Riga, Reval, Pernau and other Livonian towns and all other Hanseatic towns, anyone, whether a member of the Hanse, or not, who wishes to export (to the Low Countries) these Mart products by the Sund or the Belt, shall swear or certify before the court or with a surety, that he will bring such products to the Bruges Mart or to the Antwerp or Berg fairs, as is laid down.

---

183. *Hanserecesse II*, vol. 6, pub. G. von der Ropp, No. 356, or O. Gönnenwein, *Das Stoepel- und Niederlagsrecht*, 1939; No. 134, p. 216.

JEAN BLANKOFF
Professor at Brussels University

The Peterhof in Novgorod

184. Russian trapper.
Part of the Novgorodfahrer stalls in Saint Nicholas' church, Stralsund. Second half of the 14th century.

Novgorod developed from rural communities. It seems that there were three initially and they probably merged around the middle of the 10th century. It was at that time, or a little later, that a bishopric was established there.

The town was of such economic and political significance that at the beginning of the existence of the Kiev State it was generally given to the eldest son of the Prince of Kiev.

185. Novgorod in the time of the Hanse (15th century).
After P. Johansen, *Novgorod und die Hanse*, 1963, p. 128.

A. *On the Saint Sophia side*
  I. *the Nerevski district.*
  II. *the district behind the citadel.*
  III. *the potters' district.*

B. *On the market side*
  IV. *the Znamenski district.*
  V. *the carpenters' district.*
  1. Goth business house.
  2. Peterhof *and, in the heart of the concession, the* Peterskirche, *a stone construction which was not used only for worship, at first at least, since the Hanseatics stored their goods there, locked up their treasures there and kept their files there. In addition to the residences and halls for merchants and their personnel (about a hundred men in all), the* Peterhof *included a vicarage, a prison, a hospital, a public baths, a community kitchen and a common dining-room.*
  3. Pleskauerhof.
  4. Market.
  5. The Russian merchants' St. John's church.
  6. The ducal court of Jaroslav.
  7. St. Nicholas' church.
  8. The citadel or kremlin.
  9. St. Sophia.
  10. The archbishop's residence.
  11. The citadel moats.
  12. Urban ramparts.

There were two Hanseatic business houses in Novgorod: the Goth one and the German one. They were situated in a populated, animated part: the Goth business house right on the banks of the river Volkhov, just to the south of the prince's residence; the German one not far from there, to the east of that residence, beside Elie street (the lie of that street is approximately that of the present May 1st street).

The German business house, the approximate site of which is known, has not yet been excavated. In addition to the two churches, it housed open sheds, a brewery, a windmill and an infirmary.

Among the hundreds of letters on birch-wood found in Novgorod, one sole German document, No. 488, engraved circa 1400, provides evidence of foreign presence at this place; it contains six lines in Latin, taken from the 94th Psalm.

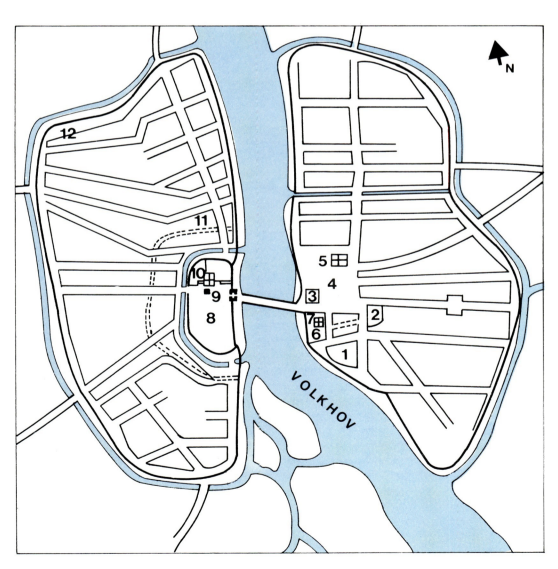

COMMERCIAL TREATY BETWEEN THE PRINCE OF SMOLENSK AND THE GERMAN MERCHANTS

1229. Treaty concluded between Prince Davidovitch of Smolensk, in his name and that of the Princes of Polotsk and Vitebsk, and the German merchants from Riga, Gotland and other towns. Almost all the clauses concerning the Germans in Smolensk comprise reciprocity for Russians in Riga and Gotland.

5. If a Russian buys on credit from a German visitor and that Russian is also the debtor of another Russian, the German shall have priority of payment.

10. No Russian may insist on a judicial duel with a German in Smolensk, nor may a German insist on a judicial duel with a Russian in Riga or Gotland. If German visitors fight between themselves with a sword or spear, that does not concern the Prince or any other Russian. They shall come to terms pursuant to their own laws.

15. If the porterage contractor *(Volok)* learns that a German visitor has arrived for porterage at the same time as Smolensk merchants, he shall without delay send a messenger ordering his men to transport the German visitor and the Smolensk merchant with their goods.

16. Lots shall be drawn to decide which of the two shall be transported first. If a Russian stranger arrives at the same time, he will pass after them.

17. Each German visitor arriving in the town shall offer the Princess a roll of cloth and the porterage contractor shall be given a pair of gauntlets with fingers.

19. Any German in Smolensk may sell his goods without any contestation.

20. If a German wishes to go to another town with his goods, neither the Prince nor the people of Smolensk shall oppose him.

21. If a Russian buys from a German and carries the goods away, he may not bring them back and he must pay for them (and vice versa). A Russian may not bring a German before the general court, but only before that of the Prince. But if a German requests the general court his wish shall be complied with.

27. If a German buys a silver mark and has it weighed, he shall give two squirrel skins to the weigher, but nothing if he sells it.

29. If the weight used for weighing wax is inaccurate, it must be compared and corrected with the weight standards, one of which is to be found in the church of the Mount and the other in the church of the Germans.

31. A German shall pay no toll from Smolensk to Riga or from Riga to Smolensk. Similarly, a Russian shall pay no toll from Gotland to Riga or from Riga to Smolensk.

32. If the Prince of Smolensk goes to war, that shall in no way concern the Germans, unless they ask to accompany him.

33. If, God forbid, a German or Russian ship should be wrecked, its owner may unload his cargo on the bank without obstruction. If he has too few men and is obliged to engage others, the latter shall not receive more than the agreed wage. This applies both to Germans and Russians, on the territories of Smolensk, Polotsk and Vitebsk.

This deed is drafted in 1229 before the Bishop Nicholas of Riga, the priest Jean, Master Volkin (of the Sword-bearers), and numerous merchants from the Roman Empire, whose seal is affixed hereto. The following are witnesses: Regenbode, Dethard, Adam, burghers of Gotland; Member, Friedrich, Dummon of Lubeck; Henry the Goth and Ilier of Soest; Conrad Blödauge and Johann Kinot of Munster; Bernek and Volker of Groningen; Arembrecht and Albrecht of Dortmund; Heinrich Zeisig of Bremen; the burghers of Riga Albrecht Sluk, Bernhart, Walter and Albrecht, a Riga solicitor. If a Russian or German violates this treaty, he violates divine right and the law.

Hansisches Urkundenbuch, vol. I, K. HÖHLBAUM ed., n° 232

186. Novgorod, the new town, Naugarden for the Germans, was the gateway to the Baltic on the Russian continent.

For a long time it was one of the most important of the country's towns.
Situated in the heart of a vast network of navigable waterways, it was linked by water – given portage and trans-shipment at some places – to the Baltic, the great lakes of Ladoga and Onega, Kiev, the Dniepr and Dniestr and, thereby, to the Black Sea, the Crimea and the Byzantine world.
The ships which sailed to Novgorod assembled at the mouths of the Neva, if they had not already been formed into a fleet. An Elder (Aelterman) was then chosen for the rest of the expedition and any cargo was transferred to lighter boats.
The convoy, led by a Russian, proceeded up the river to the mouth of the Volkhov on Lake Ladoga where the Germans also had a concession, with church and cemetery. Here there was a further trans-shipment on to even lighter boats (Vorqchkerlen) capable of shooting the Volkhov rapids.
Some groups made the journey overland (Landfahrer).

The statutes of the German business house were drafted five times between 1225 and 1371.
A new German business house was opened in 1514, and in 1603 the Lubeck merchants sent Boris Godounoff a draft trade agreement.
The Goth business house was excavated in 1968-1970. On the 542 sq.m. that were cleared, they found the foundations of a stone tower, the remains of a palisade and traces of two buildings of 72 and 110 sq.m., very thick beams, assembled by a technique which is slightly different from that of other Novgorod constructions.
It is possible that after the peace of 1617 the Swedish established their trading station in the place of the 'Goth' business house.

NOVGOROD, A TURN-TABLE FOR NORTH EUROPEAN TRADE

Novgorod was the turn-table for North European trade in old Russia for reasons which were both geographical and historical: situated in the North-West of European Russia, on Lake Ilmen, not far from the Baltic and in the heart of a good network of navigable waterways.

Relations going back to the 11th century...
Economic relations between Novgorod and Northern Europe towns very probably went back, in embryonic form, to the 11th century, with great strides being made in the 13th.
It was then that a foreign business house, no doubt that of the Visby merchants, was opened at Novgorod.
A series of political and commercial treaties set out in concrete form and regulated those relations: two in the 13th century, especially that of 1269; seven in the 14th century (1338, 1342, 1371, 1372, 1373, 1376 and 1392); eight in the 15th century, principally those of 1417, 1423, 1436, 1450 and 1466.
Novgorod kept up its links with the Hanse until the German business house closed in 1494.

... and passing through three important moments.
There are in fact three periods to be distinguished, marked by a move in the centres of gravity of trade.
In the 12th and 13th centuries, the merchants of Gotland, an island situated almost equidistantly from the Swedish, German and Russian shores, effected, together with Russian merchants, nearly all the East-North trade. In 1130 the first Novgorod chronicle mentions the presence of Gotland merchants in the town. In 1152 fire in Novgorod ravaged the Gotland 'Varangian' chapel situated on 'Goth' territory. On the island of Gotland, Saint Nicholas' church, and probably a second church, bore witness to the presence and reciprocal role of Novgorod merchants. Russian merchants began going to Lubeck in the 12th century.
At the end of the 13th century the role of German merchants became preponderant and a second business house, the German one, with its St.

187-189. Objects from Novgorod excavations.

The subsoil of the Russian metropolis is a veritable archeological mine. It has been the subject for several decades, especially from 1851, of active excavation campaigns, and no doubt still reserves work for archeologists for 200 to 300 years.

In some places the 'culture bed' is more than 7 m deep, especially in the Nerevski district. The constant humidity of the spongy subsoil is ideal for preserving objects made of organic matter, wood in particular.

The strata, evidence of uninterrupted peopling for several centuries, were formed at an average rate of one centimetre a year. In some places, up to 28 layers covering superposed planks have been found; the planks were used for 'repaving' the streets.

1. *Bone plaquette, most probably French work, early 14th century, found in Novgorod in 1962.*
2. *Copper lilied tongue from the excavations.*
3. *Lead seal from Tournai, found in the 1977 excavations. Diameter: 20 mm.*
   Obverse marked with the fleur-de-lis, surrounded by the inscription: [TOURN]AI.

Novgorod, History Museum.

190. Exchange of gifts, including Ypres cloth.
Miniature illustrating a Muscovite chronicle of the 14th century.
Leningrad, Saltykov-Shchedrin Library, F. IV.LDIX 232, fol. 150.

Ypres cloth was also referred to in a Novgorod charter which Henri Pirenne dates as between 1130 and 1136.
"The fact that it is referred to as a well-known sort of material shows that it must have been widespread for a long time, let us say, without exaggeration, since the end of the 11th century.
Ypres cloth was referred to, not because it was the only one known, but because, being so widespread, it was the best known.
It can be concluded that Ypres was originally what it remained in the 13th and 14th centuries, namely the most complete type that had ever existed of a Middle Ages export industry centre."

Peter's church, was opened. That was the one which carried on the bulk of foreign trade in Novgorod when the Hanseatic League was definitively organized in the 16th century, the 'Goth' house being maintained with a minimum of administrative autonomy but with joint management, particularly financial.

In the 15th century the Baltic towns (Reval, Riga, Dorpat) became the principal intermediary in commercial traffic between Novgorod and Northern Europe. In 1402 Reval rented the Goth business house, a tenancy which was subsequently renewed. In the 15th century, Novgorod also signed treaties with the Livonian Order (1421-1448).

The end of the Peterhof coincided with the surrender of Novgorod by Ivan III in 1478.

THE PRODUCTS EXCHANGED

Novgorod imported woollen cloth from Flanders and Artois. This cloth came from Ypres in the 12th century, especially scarlet cloth, but also from Arras, Saint-Omer, Tournai, Wervick (late 13th century), Dixmude (early 14th), Warneton, Poperinghe (14th) with its imitations of Saint-Omer cloth. Lead seals from Tournai, discovered in Novgorod in 1977 and 1978, furnish evidence of this importation.

The silver which Novgorod had to import was not inconsiderable. The statutes of the German business house as drafted in 1333 also mention the sale of copper, tin and lead.

Secondarily, there are traces of the importation of glassware, particularly glass rings in the 14th century, and some glass plates and dishes, as well as Rhenish ceramic. Western-made chessmen have been found on the territory of the Goth business house.

In the 15th century Novgorod mainly exported wax, furs, skins and leather to the West, perhaps flax and hemp at the end of the 15th century, and natural dyes.

BIBLIOGRAPHY

The principal sources of information about trade in Novgorod, the Hanse customs registers, especially those of Reval at the end of the 14th century and of Lubeck in the 15th century; Russian trade books; minutes of Hanseatic town congresses; merchants' correspondence; the chronicles of old Russia; treaties entered into by Novgorod; material of the highest importance discovered in archeological excavations carried out in Novgorod since 1951.

E.A. RYBINA, *Archeological essays on the history of Novgorod trade* (in Russian), Moscow, 1978.

A. KHOROCHKEVITCH, *The trade of Novgorod the Great in the 14th and 15th centuries* (in Russian), Moscow, 1963.

J. BLANKOFF, *Une campagne de fouilles: Novgorod 1977* (preliminary report). Brussels University Institute of Eastern and Slav Philology and History yearbook, vol. 22, Brussels, 1978, pp. 7-16.

J. BLANKOFF, *A propos des plombs de Tournai trouvés à Novgorod*. Memoirs of the Tournai Royal Society of History and Archeology, vol. 1, Tournai 1980, pp. 13-31.

ALBERT D'HAENENS

The Stalhof or Steelyard in London

There was a smartness about the Stalhof which contrasted with the roughness of the Tyskebryggen in Bergen and the distrustful contraction of the Hanseatics at the Peterhof in Novgorod.

Here in London, on the banks of the Thames, dealings were not in furs or stockfish, but in woollen and linen cloth, wine and other goods which showed a big profit.

London, unlike Novgorod and Bergen, was not situated on the borders of the civilized world but, like Bruges, between the North Sea and the Baltic sea, in the very heart of a network of circulation and commercial traffic which was amongst the densest in the western world.

In the Stalhof, relations with merchants and local traders were just as warm as in Bruges, far more intense than in Bergen or Novgorod, but that did not mean that there was neglect of community life and all that that implied for its satisfactory working.

The statutes required Hanseatics to present themselves and live in the Stalhof with their goods.

Merchants and servants were permanently assigned within the enclosing wall as were some Englishmen who carried out some service or another there. They were forbidden to take out the slightest sample.

It was only when the business house was fully occupied that it was permitted to rent or to take up quarters in the house of an inhabitant.

The merchants were divided into thirds, different from those in Bruges. There were those from Cologne, Westphalia, Saxony and Wend; the Prussians, Livlanders and Gotlanders were under the authority of those from Danzig.

191. London in the 15th century.
Miniature. English manuscript (late 15th century) illuminated no doubt by a Flemish artist.
London, British Museum, Roy. Ms., 16 F II, fol. 73.

In the foreground: the Thames and boats. Then the Tower.
Charles of Orleans, taken prisoner at Agincourt in 1415, was kept imprisoned in the Tower until 1440. He is seen here in three of his occupations: sitting at a table writing his poems; at the window gazing out to the horizon; at the door handing a letter to a courier.
Opening on to the riverside: Traitor's Gate.
In the background: the famous bridge, fringed with street stalls.

192. The city of London, late 15th century.
Part of the miniature of Roy. Ms., 16 F II, fol. 73, British Museum, London.

It is difficult to identify the impressive number of church towers which mark the urban scene. On the right, the Billingsgate houses where the customs were situated: opulent frontages with arches and archways at ground floor level. It was here that the Hanseatics loaded and unloaded and went through the customs. The Stalhof lies along the Thames, on the other side of the bridge. The Hanseatic concession was mentioned for the first time in 1157.

MANAGING THE BUSINESS HOUSES

The thirds had the management of the business house, the coffers and justice in common.

It was an Elder, elected at the New Year for a year, who assumed the management of the community, assisted by a council of twelve. The council met once a week. It checked business deals, rendered justice and managed the finances of the business house.

An early 14th century regulation gives an idea of the severity of daily life for those who lived in the Stalhof. Insulting language and horse-play were heavily punished.

No women; bringing a woman in was a serious offence. Nor could strangers be brought in, except with permission from the *Aeltermann*.

He who took part in supervision and the denunciation of offenders was handsomely rewarded.

The gates were closed at 8 p.m., 9 p.m. in the summer.

A watch was kept during the night.

The premises were kept scrupulously clean and this was regulated down to the smallest detail.

The Stalhof had no church of its own. The Hanseatics attended services at the neighbouring church, All Hallows the Great, where they had their own stalls.

193. The Stalhof about 1555. Part of a plan of London. London, London Museum.

In the foreground, left: the Hausmeisterhaus, *the elevation of which is exaggerated. The* Hausmeister *was responsible for buildings, persons and goods. It was in his imposing residence which no doubt goes back to the very origin of the Stalhof (archeological traces date back to Roman times) that merchants who had not their own warehouse deposited their bales, barrels and chests. Note the crane and animals, whose presence relates to the situation of the river at low tide.*

The big annual feast was on St. Barbara's Day, December 4th. An impressive service was celebrated, with mass for the deceased, and there was a banquet.

As in Bruges, they had *Morgensprachen* in London.

A general meeting was held at the New Year. A fortnight afterwards another one was held at which the statutes and bye-laws were solemnly read out.

Beginning in the 1400's, the business house engaged two or three permanent clerks who dealt with commercial papers, the accounts and business trips to Hanseatic towns abroad.

A particular feature at the Stalhof was that, besides the German *Aeltermann*, there was an English *Aeltermann*. Proposed by the merchants and invested by the King, he had to be a burgher of London, a member of the city council and, in fact, burgomaster. It was usually a German naturalized English. He intervened when there was a clash of interests between the Hanseatics and the English, and he had jurisdiction over Hanseatic trading stations on English soil. He had the right to fees, which were given to him in a pair of gloves at the New Year.

Relations between the Hanseatics and the English were usually excellent. They contrasted with those the Bergen and Novgorod business houses had with the local communities.

194. The Stalhof in 1617.
Part of a view of the city of London by Claes Jansz Visscher the Younger (1586-1652). London, British Museum, Grace Collection.

Aesthetically, this view is the finest one available of the Hanseatic concession, but the Hausmeisterhaus *and its large door are too narrow, the flight of steps too small.*

195. Pewter pitcher and dish (16th century).
Diameter of the dish: 13.75 cm. On the edge: the owner's mark. Diameter of the pitcher: 5.6 cm. Height: 8.3 cm.
London, Victoria and Albert Museum.

These items come from finds in Southwark and Westminster in 1899 and 1903 respectively.
These English pewter productions are very representative of an export article of which the Hanseatic merchants were big purveyors.

196. Silver ewer. Part of the silver table-service of the Stalhof Guildhall.
Bremen, Ratssilberschatz der Hansestadt.

Made in 1562/1563 by a London silversmith, from a drawing by Holbein.
The Stalhof table-service was sold in 1612 and part of it was bought by Hanseatic towns; that explains why this item now forms part of the communal treasure of Bremen.

THE STALHOF IN LONDON

193

197. Portrait of a young Stalhof merchant, by Hans Holbein (1497-1543) in 1541. Vienna, Kunsthistorisches Museum, Inv. No. 905.

Holbein, born in Ausgburg, was the appointed Stalhof portrait painter and artist. He depicted merchants with dignity and luxury comparable to what until then had been reserved for aristocrats and high dignitaries. In doing so he gave the merchant class a prestige and aura which were significant of the profound change in realities: the era of a new humanism coinciding with powers and wealth of a new type, those of new-born capitalism and conquering trade.

198. J.M. Lappenberg, *Urkundliche Geschichte des Hansischen Stahlhofes zu London*, 1851, No. 165.

THE CLOSING OF THE LONDON BUSINESS HOUSE

1598. Ordinance by Elizabeth, 'Queen of England, France and Ireland', addressed to the mayor and sheriffs of London.

Whereas an order has been addressed by the Roman Emperor to all the Electors, prelates, counts and other dignitaries and subjects of the Empire, enumerating various complaints made by the associated towns of the German Hanse, relative to various torts suffered by them in our kingdom; whereas a complaint has been lodged by them against the company of adventurer merchants; whereas no reply had been given to the said Hanseatic towns, such complaints being manifestly unjustified and unable to be supported by any proof; whereas by that order the English merchants, i.e. the adventurer merchants, are forbidden to trade within the Empire and are ordered to leave it under penalty of sanctions, may no longer land, openly or secretly in any port or unloading dock and may in no way recommence by sea or land within the Empire, under penalty of being arrested and having their goods confiscated, not to speak of other extreme sentences pronounced against our said subjects.

And although we have sent letters to the Emperor, the Electors and other princes of the Empire by express, expressing our opinion about this unjust procedure to be put into force by the said Hanse towns, requesting that the said order be revoked or suspended; but not knowing what will come to pass, we feel it a matter of honour, in the meantime, to order all nationals of the Hanseatic towns of the Empire who are present in our kingdom and in particular those who reside in our city of London, whether in the house commonly called the Steelyard or in any other place, to cease any commerce or business and to leave our domains, just as our subjects have received the order to quit the Empire, under penalty of the same sanctions.

And in execution thereof, the mayor of our city of London and the sheriffs shall proceed immediately to the Steelyard, call together the administrators and residents, inform them of our decision and command giving them strict injunctions to leave the kingdom before the 24th of this month – the date on which our merchants must leave Stade – and make known to all the subjects of the Hanseatic towns of the Empire who are within our kingdom that they must leave before the said day.

And you, mayor and sheriffs, together with two of our customs officers, will take possession of the said house on January 24th so that it shall remain sequestered by us until we are informed of more favourable measures on the part of the Emperor, tending to re-establish the traditional trading of our subjects with the Empire.

And this ordinance shall be your mandate for seizing the premises. In testimony whereof we have established these letters patent in our presence on January 13th of the fortieth year of our reign.

BIBLIOGRAPHY

TH. G. WERNER, *Der Stalhof der deutschen Hanse in London in Wirschafts- und kunsthistorische Bildwerken*, in Scripta Mercaturae, 1973, 2.

TH. G. WERNER, *Der Stalhof der deutschen Hanse in London in Wirschafts- und kunstistorische Bildwerken. Eine Fortsetzung*, in Scripta Mercaturae, 1974, I, p. 127-134.

S. H. STEINBERG, *Ansichten der Londoner Stalhof*, in Festschrift F. Rörig, 1953, p. 159-168.

TH. S. HOLMAN, *Holbein's portraits of the Steelyard merchants: an investigation*, in Metropolitan Museum Journal, vol. 13, 1979, p. 139-158.

D. MARKOW, *Hans Holbein's Steelyard Portraits reconsidered*, in Wallraf-Richartz Jahrbuch, Köln, 1978, XI, p. 39-47.

ALBERT D'HAENENS

The Tyskebryggen in Bergen

The 'German quay' (Deutsche Brücke – Tyskebryggen) in Bergen was certainly the least inter-Hanseatic of the four.
Until the 16th century it was essentially in the hands of Lubeck; only a merchant from a town under Lubeck law could be elected Elder, and the appointment of a vicar to the Marienkirche was reserved for Lubeck.
It was in 1343 that the business house seemed to be organized systematically; it was then that the King of Norway confirmed the Hanseatics' previous privileges. Shortly afterwards, the business house was subordinated to the towns, in actual fact to Lubeck.
The German colony in Bergen was made up of merchants and craftsmen. In the 13th century the latter were more numerous than the former (129 in 1451, not counting apprentices).
It was the shoemakers (*Schumacker*), furriers, tailors, gold and silver smiths, barbers and bakers who were designated by the generic name of *Shomaker*. Initially these craftsmen came under a Norwegian magistrate, but at the end of the 14th century they were placed under the jurisdiction of the business house, which made a particular point of forbidding them to do any trading.
German merchants and craftsmen made up about a third of the town's population: 2000 out of 6000 inhabitants circa 1400.
Tyskebryggen and Novgorod had more than one thing in common. They were situated right up in the North, where the Germans appeared as 'Southerners' (*Südmänner*).
As in Novgorod, winter in Bergen isolated the men through an exacting hibernation in a countryside of mountains and fiords which, to men from the plains, was terribly impressive.
Those who went to Bergen stayed there for several years. For them, daily life, especially in winter, was hard, demanding and austere within a community composed solely of men. Long winter nights, games were rare, opportunities for drinking were measured out in miserly fashion, frequent brawls and fights with Norwegians, numerous affairs of morals (it has been said that in the spring whole boatloads of girls could be seen arriving from Bremen or Hamburg).
The initiation rites after which newcomers were integrated in the community were impressive.
The *Bergener Spiele* were held about Whitsuntide, when the fleets came in. At the heart of these 'festivities' were the ordeals of apprentices and greenhorns. They were thrown into the sea several times (*Wasserspiel*). Then, with jeers and gibes, they were taken to the town where they were sentenced by an improvised court and the punishments were carried out without ceremony (*Burgspiel*). After that they were forced into the smoking chimneys of the *Schütting* (*Rauchspiel*) where, on the verge of stifling and suffocation, they had to answer embarrassing, preposterous questions.

199. Shipwrecking of a Bergenfahrer. 1489.
Anonymous painting.
Lubeck, Marienkirche.

The merchant concerned was Hans Ben. During the long weeks of monotonous navigation, the fear of storms or attack by pirates never ceased to haunt travellers, who did not feel safe until they were back in port. So the text on the picture reads: "Let those who embark first go to confession. It took us such a short time to lose our lives."

MANAGING THE BUSINESS HOUSES

200. The double concessions (Doppelhof) are crossed, from one end to the other, by narrow lanes (about 1.5 metres). The streets would be about 4 to 5 m.
This document dates from the end of the last century.
It comes from Bergen History Museum.

201-202. Bergen was ravaged by fire in 1955.
What is now seen is the result of a recent restoration (1981).

203. Ground plan of Bruggen after 1702.
Published by A.B. Andersson, *Bryggen. Das hanseatische Kontor in Bergen*. Bergen, 1982, p. 35.

The Hanseatics obtained the right to build in Bryggen in 1276. Lubeck merchants still had a big majority there and the preponderance of Lubeck was never questioned before the 16th century.
The Hanseatics settled in Bryggen in the form of concessions (Hof, garten or gård): an assembly of rows (up to fifteen) of 1,2 or 3 times 6 metres, height about 7 metres, two floors with outside staircase, galeries and sometimes with a loft (Seespeicher).
They built with tarred rounds and, for the part bordering on the sea, on tree trunks and immersed box-sections.
The buildings were used as residences and warehouses.
In 1403 the Finnegård consisted of fifteen constructions with 75 rooms. The Belgård in 1312 was composed of 90 rooms. The Tyskebryggen could take two to three thousand persons.

204. The Hanseatic business house appears here as it was drawn in 1768 by J.J. Riechenborn, architect and contractor, who provided the urban scene with some of its finest residences.
Published by A.B. Andersson, *Bryggen. Das hanseatische Kontor in Bergen*. Bergen 1982, p. 28.

Between 1581 and 1768 there was the devastating fire of 1702. This explains the much higher houses. But there was no change in the dividing of land into small portions. The same applies to Bryggen from the Middle Ages to the present day. Impressive permanence of an original structure. It is explained both by the weight of property titles and by continuity in the use of identical building materials, in this case: wood.

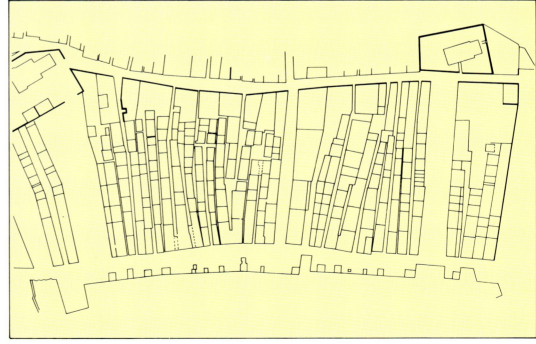

THE TYSKEBRYGGEN IN BERGEN

199

205-206. The Schütting.

Each concession had its community house (Schütting) with two floors and a large room on the ground floor. That was where all those who worked on the concession (Hof) lived, ate and met.
1. *Mantelpiece of the Bredsgården. The Feuerhaus collapsed around 1870.*
2. *The Schötstube of Engelgården, before 1955.*
Bergen. Det Hanseatiske Museum Arkiv.

207. The common room of the Svensgården Schötstube.
Bergen. Det Hanseatiske Museum.

It was kept up at joint expense and closed during the summer. Tables and benches along the walls. Sometimes there were partitions which bounded the sections reserved for each of the concessions, with their own tables, benches, coat of arms and table-service. As from 1702 the room was heated by the neighbouring Feuerhaus where the meals were prepared.

THE TYSKEBRYGGEN IN BERGEN

208. Merchant's business house in the Finnengården.
Bergen, Det Hanseatiske Museum.

The merchant's business house is obviously the central place of the concession (hof or Garten).
The one shown here is as it was in the 17th century. In the foreground, a Baroque table; on the right-hand walls, portraits of Danish and Norwegian sovereigns recalling the links of dependence of the Hanseatics; the big picture depicts an Elder who presides over the destinies of Bryggen.
The merchant's office is on the left, behind the glass panes.

209-210. Merchant's office in the Finnegården.
Bergen, Det Hanseatiske Museum, Seestube No. 1.

The merchant's office – the famous Scrivekamer which figures in so many portraits of merchants, particularly those painted by Hans Holbein the Younger – was the very 'heart' of the concession. It was quite tiny, just enough room for one person, and in the winter it was heated by his own heat, as heating was forbidden in rooms made of wood. Through little windows, the master of the house had a view of the environs. He could keep an eye on everything whilst busy with his inventories and accounts.

201

The authorities tried in vain to forbid that kind of 'merry-making'. They consoled themselves by saying that once the initiation was passed, the young surplus peasants from Mecklenburg, Pomerania, Westphalia or Saxony, initially quite without means of survival, could benefit in the business house by all sorts of apprenticeships: reading, writing, accountancy, music, which would progressively turn them into clerks, then into representatives and independent traders. That happened sometimes.

211. Merchant's bedroom.
Bergen, Det Hanseatiske Museum.

When he went to bed, the merchant took precautions. He shut himself up with his most valuable possessions in a cupboard-bed which should keep him safe from any misadventure.
His servant was not allowed into the bedroom itself; he had to make his master's bed through a little door in the wall.

It was a Bergen merchant, J.W. Olsens, who, in June 1872, founded a Hanse museum on the Finnegården premises. His project was original and brave; his colleagues considered it with scorn. It is thanks to Olsens that these precious traces of the daily life of an exceptionally significant medieval European enterprise are kept here today.

THE TYSKEBRYGGEN IN BERGEN

212-213. Toilet and kitchen utensils belonging to members of one of the concessions using a community house (*Schütting*).
Bergen, Det Hanseatiske Museum.

214. Young clerks' bedroom in the Finegården.
Bergen, Det Hanseatiske Museum.

Both employer and his employees lodged on the second floor. The 'novices', room was austere in the extreme: beds in the walls, a few imbedded cupboards. The sobriety of a cabin-boy's nook!

215-216. Notre-Dame church: the *Tyskekirkene* or *Marienkirche*.

It was the principal church of the business house; it is made of stone and was the property of the business house from the 15th to the 18th century.
There was at one time St. Martin's church, which was burned down in 1702 and never rebuilt; the Halvardskirche, for the artisans, but it was confiscated in 1558.
Notre-Dame church is partly Roman; it goes back to the years 1130-1170. Lombard and English influences are to be found there. It was enlarged in 1248.
The retable dates from the late 15th century and probably came from a Lubeck workshop.

For a Hanseatic, living in Bergen meant austerity, discipline and observance of strict community stringencies. Certainly, life was not so hard as in Novgorod, since there was identity of faith, sensitivity and some culture, though that did not prevent frequent disputes with the locals, often leading to scuffles, especially in the later period of the Hanse, when its members appeared to the Norwegians as agents of exploitation and oppression.
In the Tyskebryggen, as in the other business houses, only bachelors were allowed in.
The initiation and acceptance rites were demanding, as were the stipulations concerning everyday life.

BIBLIOGRAPHY

E. BOWITZ ANDERSON, K. HELLE, M. TREBBI, H. WIBERG, *Bryggen, das hanseatische Kontor in Bergen,* German translation A. Utne, Lübeck, 1982.
K. HELLE, *Die Deutschen in Bergen während des Mittelalters,* in *Hanse in Europa,* Ausstellung des Kölnischen Stadtmuseum, Köln, 1973, p. 137-155.
K. FRIEDLÄNDER, *Bergen Handelszentrum des Beginnenden Spätmittelalters,* Köln, 1972.
F. BRUNS, *Die Lübecker Bergenfahrer und ihre Chronistik,* Berlin, 1900.

217-218. Bergen, Tyskebryggen.

JAN VAN ROEY
Archivist of the City of Antwerp

The Oosters Huis in Antwerp

Antwerp is sometimes spoken of as a Hanseatic town. Generally that is in a political sense and in the economic perspective of relations with Germany. The fact is, however, that the city as such never formed part of the Hanse. On the other hand, Antwerp can be called Hanseatic if by that one means a place where Hanseatic merchants regularly stayed, where they had good business relations and where they felt at home in the place and with its inhabitants.

WHERE TWO EUROPEAN TRADE AXES CROSS

Antwerp had close relations with the eastern hinterland at a very early date – and still has today. Already in the 12th century mention is made of Antwerp merchants on the Rhine, at Coblentz.
When Richard the Lion Heart came back from the Third Crusade and his captivity in Austria, in 1194, he embarked in Antwerp for his kingdom: an eminent example of the city's role as a hinge between East and West. It is known, too, that there were Antwerp citizens in London at the same time.
This East-West link should not make us forget the North-South axis. Holland and Zealand traded for a long time with the present North Brabant and the Antwerp hinterland. That axis between Northern Europe and the most

219. The *Oosters Huis* in Antwerp. Anonymous picture, 18th century. Bremen, Town Hall.

220. The *Oosters Huis* in Antwerp. Anonymous water-colour, late 16th century Antwerp, Stadsarchief.

The business house was built from 1564 to 1568. It measured 80 m × 62 m (approx. 5,000 sq. m.). The Hanseatics had no permanent residence in Antwerp during the 15th century and in 1468 the town placed at their disposal the Kluis (the Hermitage) on the Koornmarkt (Grain Market). The Bruges office controlled that residence which was full only when there were fairs.
"With Antwerp making rapid strides and Bruges declining, the Hanse began to want to transfer its office from the Low Countries to the city on the Scheldt. The Osterlins, who had amassed in Bruges more privileges than any other nation, were firmly decided to insist on as much – if not more – from Antwerp. Negotiations dragged on for years. Bruges put up fierce resistance to the transfer, and some Antwerp merchants did not favour the project. When, in 1553, the wheeling and dealing begun twenty-five years before seemed to be getting somewhere, a hundred of the town's merchants filed a petition declaring that there was no reason to favour the Hanseatics, for the Antwerp merchants met with nothing but ill-natured interference, extortions and arbitrary measures in Hanse towns. The magistrates disregarded them and signed the agreement against their advice, considering that the presence of the Hanse in Antwerp had its importance in the life of the city.
The Hanse merchants brought their files and seals and, as if they wanted to recall the memory of their past splendour, they named the Kluis 'the office of Bruges residing in Antwerp'." [Léon Voet].

northern part of Southern Europe, which was within Hanse dependence, progressively became more important. This situation was singularly favourable in the perspective of the development, in the Middle Ages, of European trade and that of the first world trade in the 16th century. The city on the Scheldt became first of all a European economy centre and later the centre 'par excellence' of world economy.

GERMAN PRESENCE

The oldest 'eastern' partner of Antwerp was Cologne. There was already a warm relationship between the two towns in the 12th century. Initially it was mainly a matter of trade in Rhine wine. That relationship was important if one thinks of the leading part played by that Rhine town in the structuration of the Hanse in the 16th century.

More to the north, Hamburg was another long-standing partner of Antwerp, more so in fact than Lubeck which was generally considered to be the centre of the Hanse.

It was only in the middle of the 14th century, on the founding or definitive organization of the Hanse, that the inhabitants of Lubeck and other Baltic towns discovered Antwerp.

221. The former Town Hall of Antwerp, 1700.
Engraving intended to illustrate the *Annales Antwerpienses* by the Bollandist Daniel Papebroech.
Antwerp, Prentenkabinet.

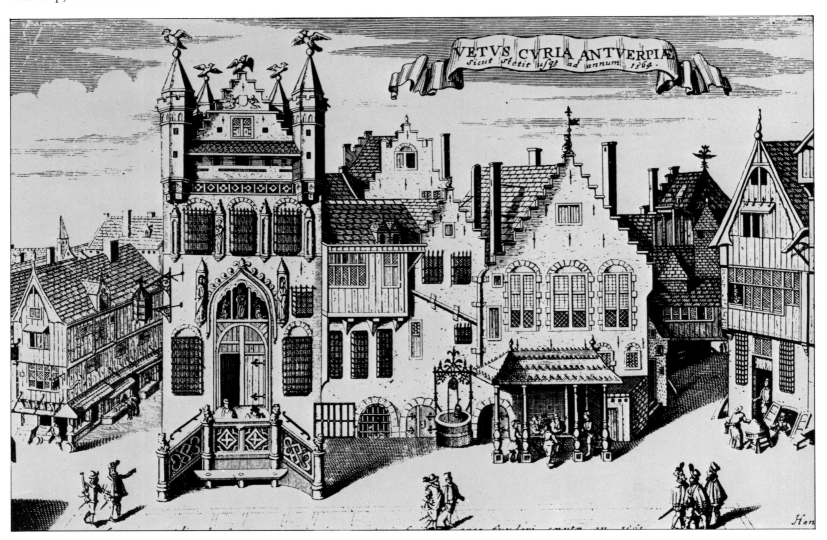

222. Magistrate sitting at Antwerp Town Hall, 1577.
Engraving by Franz Hogenberg (1540-1590).
Antwerp, Prentenkabinet.

223. Antwerp Town Hall. 1567.
Engraving illustrating the *Descrittione di tutti i Paesi Bassi* by L. Guicciardini, published by W. Silvius.
Antwerp, Plantin-Moretus Museum.

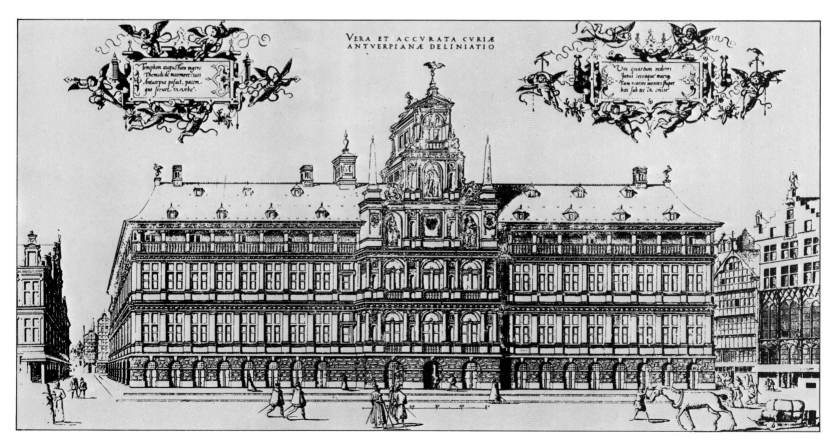

When, in the 15th century, Antwerp gradually supplanted Bruges, the Hanseatic merchants appeared more and more regularly in Antwerp documents.

Even in the absence of a systematic study, the archives clearly show that the Hanseatics, who were still officially attached to the Bruges business house, also did a considerable amount of business with Antwerp and settled their accounts at the annual fairs there.

What is more, the Bruges merchants themselves endeavoured to introduce themselves into Antwerp by buying or renting houses on or close to Antwerp's Main Square, with the manifest aim of checking their rival on the occasion of the economic 'summits', i.e. the fairs.

The City of Antwerp encouraged the movement, which favoured it. In 1448 the Osterlins obtained the *De Cluyse* house on the Old Grain Market, just near the Main Square, the ideal trading centre during the fairs, and particularly suitable for the Hanseatic merchants who could easily and regularly meet their partners from other European countries there.

The concessions Antwerp gave to the Hanseatics and other merchants, especially in the 15th and 16th centuries, throw much light on the keen competition between the city and Bruges.

THE IMPORTANCE OF THE HANSE TO ANTWERP

The Hanse and its merchants formed themselves into a 'nation' in Antwerp. This was also the situation – especially from the second half of the 15th century – of the southern Germans who did not belong to the Hanse, the English, Italians, merchants from different Spanish kingdoms and the Portuguese; the French did not manage to form a 'nation' of merchants.

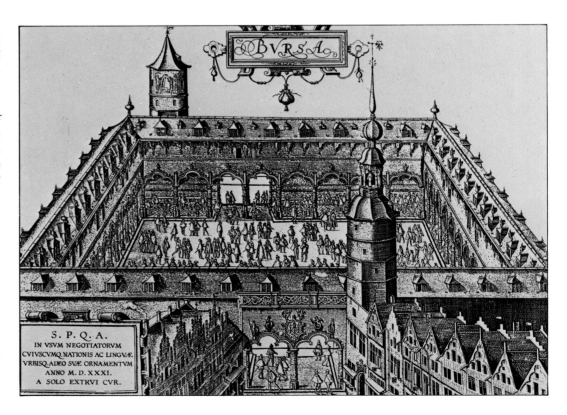

224. Antwerp Stock Exchange, 1581.
Engraving after Pieter Van der Borcht II (1545-1608), illustrating the *Descrittione di tutti i Paesi Bassi*, by L. Guicciardini, published by Plantin.
Antwerp, Plantin-Moretus Museum.

Built in 1531, in the reign of Charles V of Germany (whose coat of arms figures above the entrance) situated in Twaalfmaandenstraat *(street of the Twelve Months), it replaced the former Stock Exchange situated in* Wolstraat *(Wool street).*

225. Crane in the port of Antwerp.
Part of an anonymous picture (between 1513 and 1540): *Zicht op de rede van Antwerpen.*
Antwerp, Scheepvaartmuseum.

THE OOSTERS HUIS IN ANTWERP

211

With the arrival of these merchants, the relative importance of the Hanseatics weakened, although it seems, from 16th century archives, that the weight of the Hanseatics in Antwerp has, until now, been a little under-estimated by historians.

That the City of Antwerp granted land in the new town to build the magnificent palace called the Oosters Huis and heavily subsidized its construction in the 1560's, reveals the importance which Antwerp attached to the merchants from Bremen, Hamburg, Lubeck, Rostock, Stralsund, Stettin, Danzig, Reval and Riga – just to mention the big ports.

The Baltic territories were the granaries of the Low Countries – the 16th century included. Proof: the interest which many historians show in the stagnation of corn transport in 1566-1567; the extent of the shortage, following the iconoclastic troubles. The captain of the first ship that arrived with the first crop of corn was officially received at the Town Hall and a presentation was made to him.

In the tracks of the Hanseatic ships, the Antwerp seamen set off to frequent the Baltic and Scandinavian countries. Similarly, the Hanseatics led Antwerp ships on the route to Brouage on the French Atlantic coast, for salt.

The actions of Sudermann were in themselves very representative of the reality of relations between the Antwerp merchants and the Hanseatics.

Several religious institutions saw the light of day in Antwerp because of him: the convent of the Sœurs Noires, the house of God and the chapel in the Schoenmarkt, which still exist; also the Alexian convent on the Egg Market and the convent of the Third Order, in the Lange Gasthuistraat, both of which have disappeared, as has the Saint-Julien hospice, in the same street, especially intended for women on a pilgrimage.

Sudermann street in Antwerp is a reminder of the good work done by this Hanseatic benefactor.

226. List of the Hanse towns figuring in the statutes of the Antwerp business house, 1579.
Munster, Stadtarchiv.

THE OOSTERS HUIS

The Square of the Hanseatic Towns, the Hanseatic dock, Hamburg street, Bremen street, Lubeck, Rostock and Stralsund roads, recall in toponymy the presence of the Hanse in Antwerp.

The prosperity of Antwerp was tragically reduced to nothing in 1585, two decades after the admirable 'House of the Osterlins' had been built for the Hanse, an organization which was now slowly declining.

227. Flora, with view of Antwerp, 1559.
Painting by Jan Metsijs (1509-1575).
Panel.
Hamburg, Kunsthalle.

THE OOSTERS HUIS IN ANTWERP

228. The Oosters Huis in the snow.
Painting by Lucas van Uden (1595-1672).
Panel.
Antwerp, Koninklijk Museum voor Schone Kunsten.

229. Henri Sudermann (1520-1591), the Hanse syndic in Antwerp as from 1556.
Engraving 1576.
Cologne, Stadtmuseum.

"Now established as a nation, the Hanse wanted to reorganize its new office. As often happens in a period of slump, the most grandiose projects were made and the strength and funds necessary to carry them through were found.
At the core of the project was the syndic from Cologne, Henri Sudermann. He wanted Hanseatics living or staying in Antwerp to have a complex which they could use as an office, hotel, club and warehouse.
A promise was obtained from the town that it would subsidize up to one third of the cost, estimated at 30,000 fl.
Sudermann bore down the fierce opposition by Hamburg and Danzig and obtained vague promises from the League towns concerning their financial aid.
On May 5th 1564, the burgomasters laid the foundation stone of the vast edifice, 80 metres long by 62 wide, containing a hundred and thirty-three rooms, warehouses and a tower.
The town had agreed to advance the necessary funds but suddenly showed reticence when it came to doing so; finally a foremost merchant had to stand surety.
At the same time, Sudermann had been fighting stubbornly to have privileges and preferential tariffs granted. He had obtained very favourable customs arrangements and confirmation of exemption from duties on wine, beer and provisions, something which all the nations dreamed of but few succeeded in obtaining.
So, because of the energy of one man, a small group of foreign merchants whose presence was not vital to the Metropolis, had been able to win a more favourable position than that of certain bigger nations.
The house of the Hanse, the Hansehuis, which housed both business and leisure, became the centre of attraction for tourists who visited Antwerp." [Léon Voet].

In the 17th and 18th centuries this imposing building served several times as a barracks, a meeting place for the Reformed Church, a warehouse...
In 1863, Bremen, Hamburg and Lubeck, heirs in a way to the Hanse, assigned the building to the Belgian State as a contribution to the buying back of the toll on the Scheldt. The City of Antwerp became the owner of the edifice in 1881; from being a ruin it was turned into a corn warehouse, perhaps an involuntary reminder of the extensive Hanseatic traffic of former times.
The building was entirely destroyed by fire on December 10, 1893. In 1912, much more to the north in the port of Antwerp, a fire station was built – today the offices of the port technical department – the outside of which recalled the Oosters Huis to some extent, a sign perhaps of Antwerp's nostalgia regarding its past relations with the Hanse.

BIBLIOGRAPHY

R. HILDEBRANDT, *Die Bedeutung Antwerpens als Börsenplatz 1579*, in Scripta Mercaturae, I, 1974, p. 5-20.
H. VAN DER WEE, *The growth of the Antwerp market and the European economy*, The Hague, 1963, 3 vol.
H. VAN WERVEKE, *Die Beziehungen Flanderns zu Osteuropa in der Hansezeit*, in Die deutsche Hanse als Mittler zwischen Ost und West, Köln und Opladen, 1963.

Dealing with Partners

230. Bernhard von Reesen, a Danzig merchant, 1521.
Portrait painted by Albert Dürer. Oil on oak.
Dresden. Gemäldegalerie.

On the letter which the person is holding: the address partly hidden by his fingers DEM PERNB ZW.
Between March 16 and April 4, 1521, in Antwerp, Dürer wrote in his diary: "Item. I have done an oil painting of Bernhart von Resten.".
As no merchant (a letter with the address of the person was frequently employed in portraits of merchants) bearing this name has been able to be found, the identification with Bernhard von Reesen, of Danzig, (proposed by E. Brand) seems the most plausible hypothesis.

The Baltic, in the eyes of the people of that time, was not a cul-de-sac closed by frozen shores. It was a commercial traffic route opening out on to Russian rivers and to the major markets of Novgorod and Smolensk where rare and fabulous products flowed in from far-off lands, from the White Sea and from the Moslem and Byzantine East.
At the same time as they operated on all the Baltic Sea coasts, German merchants played an active part in founding new towns dedicated to trade, in which they exerted preponderant influence.
Simultaneously they spread along the shores of the North Sea, to Norway, the Low Countries and England, where they strengthened very old trading links between Cologne and London.
In the middle of the 13th century the Hanseatics virtually had the monopoly of traffic in both seas and their trading was organized around a major axis Novgorod-Reval-Lubeck-Hamburg-Bruges-London.
In the 14th century they extended or intensified their ground-based relations with Southern Germany and Italy, and their maritime relations along the Atlantic coasts of France, Spain and Portugal.
Yet it was also at that time that the first signs of resistance to Hanse economic ascendancy appeared.
New rivals, particularly the Dutch, and Germans from the South, successfully attacked the Hanseatic monopoly.
It was largely to ward off that danger that, in the third quarter of the 14th century, the Hanse turned itself into an association of towns, better able to protect the interests of its merchants abroad. But despite a few striking successes, its efforts, both economic and political, failed to check the advance made by its competitors.
By the early 16th century, the decline of the Hanse was manifest.
[Philippe Dollinger].

PHILIPPE DOLLINGER
Professor at Strasburg University II

The Hanse and the Rhine

At the end of the Middle Ages and the beginning of the Modern Era, Germany was animated by two major international trade currents. One, Rhenish, river and land, linked Italy and North West Europe by the Alpine passes. The Hanseatic current ensured commercial traffic by sea and land between the Baltic Sea countries and those of the North Sea, between Novgorod and London, with a prolongation along the Atlantic coasts to Portugal.

231. Disembarking in Cologne.
Panel of the reliquary of St. Ursula, painted by Hans Memling (1425-1494), for St. Jean's Hospital in Bruges, in 1489.
Bruges, St. Janshospitaal.

From Cologne, the Rhine, wider, slower and deeper, enabled the use of more developed ships, sometimes with sails and which, like those seen here on the reliquary of St. Ursula, hardly differed from small sea-going vessels.

232. Portrait of Cologne merchant donor Johann Rinck (died 1462).
Oil on wood by the entourage of the Master of the Life of the Virgin.
Cologne, Kölnisches Stadtmuseum.

It is one of the members of the Rinck patrician family which became rich through trading with England.
Cologne was both a Hanseatic and a Rhenish town.
Apart from Lubeck, no other town had held such an important place in the Hanseatic community from its beginnings to its end.
It participated in the two main Northern Europe trade currents: the Rhenish, from Italy to England; the Hanseatic, along the Novgorod – Lubeck – Bruges axis.

233. Navigation on the Rhine in the 17th century.
Water-colour.
Bâle, Staatsarchiv, Schiffarhrtsakten F3.

Jakob Bettenhauser's boat shipwrecked.
On the left, the boat at the mercy of the waves, with cargo scattered about; it had just struck the Istein rock, centre.
In the background: the Black Forest.
Various types of boats were used for river navigation: simple barques or small, decked sailing vessels, depending on regional conditions.
Where the Rhine was fast-running, flat-bottomed barges, easy to handle, reinforced on the sides against impacts, were used.

THE RHENISH TRADE CURRENT

The older of these two currents was of course the Rhenish one. Without going back to Antiquity, it was prosperous in the 9th century and, after the depression in the 10th, continued to grow as did the towns. The Rhine, navigable as from Bâle, enabled bulk cargo to be carried north in infinitely larger quantities than by land. So it was the carriage of Rhine wine which first founded its fortune, rather than the difficult links with Italy over the mountain passes – the St. Bernard and then the Gothard as from the 13th century.

Wine Wine from Alsace in particular was carried on the river Ill to Strasburg, where it was trans-shipped on to Rhenish boats. It was highly appreciated throughout Northern Europe, and was considered as the most refined of white wines. Cities and lords offered it to their distinguished guests and insisted that it should be delivered 'as God made it grow' and not blended with lesser wines.

Mainz also shipped Rhine wine down the river, as well as some Moselle wine. The quantities progressively increased and by the 14th century overtook exports of Alsace wine.

234. Wine 'measurement' (*Weinverrechnung*).
Water-colour on parchment, by Hans Weiditz. Circa 1530.
Munich, Staatliche Graphische Sammlungen.

Rhine wines, cheaper than those of France or the Mediterranean, were freely drunk in the Hanseatic towns, especially in Ratskeller.

DEALING WITH PARTNERS

235-236. Hermann (III) Rinck (1509-1541) and his wife Sibylle Kannengiesser. Painted by Bartholomew Bruyn the Elder in Cologne around 1525-1530.
Cologne. Kölnisches Stadtmuseum.

The Rincks, who came from Korbach, obtained burgher status in Cologne in 1432. They became rich by trading with Danzig and England. From 1439 they sat on the Council managing the city. Following generations preferred the university and diplomacy.
Sibylle is loaded with ornaments and jewellery, but does not look glowing with joy and health.
On the first finger of his left hand her husband has a narrow gold ring which recalls the usual commercial traffic practices of the 10th centurie (Gewichtsilber).

Cologne

Cologne was the big Rhenish metropolis, thanks to its geographical situation, its nearness to the Low Countries, and the go-ahead spirit of its merchants who radiated in all directions. The town consolidated its primacy when, in the middle of the 13th century, the archbishop granted it a staging right. All foreigners calling at Cologne were obliged to sell their products to natives of Cologne and not to other foreigners: perishable foodstuffs, cattle, wine, iron, steel, cloth, wool, linen. Foreigners bringing in furs paid a heavy tax. So Cologne became the biggest and most diversified market in Northern Germany, leading Frankfort. It added in artisanal production, textiles. And especially metallurgy, active because of the iron in the Siegerland and copper from Harz, imported by the natives of Dinant; from the middle of the 12th century, Cologne-made swords were known in Strasburg.

The Cologne inhabitants

Natives of Cologne were active in Brabant and Flanders, selling their wine and purchasing all kinds of cloth. They attended fairs in Champagne, bringing back spices and Italian luxury products. From the Upper Rhineland they received wine, the foundation of their prosperity; they sent back cloth, salted fish from the southern part of the Scandinavian peninsula and the North Sea, and furs. In Westphalian towns, wine was partly exchanged for linen. Descending the lower Rhine, ships from Cologne sailed the North Sea to Norway where, once again, they sold their wine. A confraternity, the 'Danish fraternity', grouped in Cologne the merchants who visited Denmark and Schleswig from whence they brought back salted herrings, furs and wax; natives of Cologne were even sighted in Russia. Lastly, it was in England that their economic expansion was best seen. In 1157 Henry II granted them the privilege of selling their wine in London at the place where French wine was sold; he took them under his protection, which extended to their goods and particularly to their house on the banks of the Thames, the Guildhall. In that warehouse they sold their metal wares and furs, and brought back wool and probably tin, too.

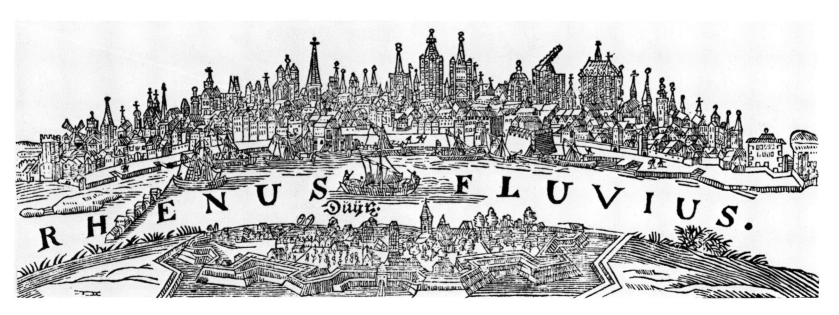

237. Cologne circa 1550.
Wood-engraving.
Cologne, Kölnisches Stadtmuseum. Inv. AI/2/8.

THE HANSEATIC CURRENT

Actually, the trading network of the Cologne merchants, which extended in its northern part from the Baltic to England, foreshadowed to a large extent that of the Hanse as constituted at the end of the 12th and in the 13th century. So Cologne had a Hanseatic vocation whilst conserving its Rhenish vocation. Its merchants shared, in fact, the Hanseatic privileges, especially in the east, before the town itself became a member of the Hanse towns when it was formed (1356).

Complementarities and antagonisms

So the two main trading streams in Germany supplemented each other and benefited each other, but they did not merge completely, each keeping its special interests. It was even found that harmonization between them sometimes gave rise to difficulties.

For instance, when the natives of Lubeck, early in the 13th century, came to trade in London, they ran up against the ill will of the Cologne natives, who considered them as intruders and refused them access to the Guildhall. Frederick II had to intervene, summoning them to put an end to their differences and recognize that the Lubeck natives had equal rights with those of Cologne.

So far as the English sovereigns were concerned, they extended a favourable welcome to the East German merchants, who brought Russian products, furs and wax to England. Henry III, in 1266, conceded to the Hamburgers and the following year to the Lubeck merchants the privilege of forming their own Hanse on the lines of that of the Cologne natives. The existence of these three more or less rival groups was prejudicial, however, to all the Germans, so that finally in 1282 the three Hanses managed, if not to merge, at least to associate in forming one sole business house in London.

Both the interests of the Rhinelanders and the Hanseatics sometimes remained distinct, as was seen two centuries later when the Anglo-Hanseatic war broke out. Cologne was granted special privileges. That led to its exclusion from the Hanse (1471), to which it was not readmitted until three years later, after peace had been declared.

The Frankfort fairs

The Hanse showed great interest in Rhenish products, especially the wine, which was sought after by all the North Eastern towns, Scandinavia and even Russia. Its commercial traffic particularly expanded in the 14th century as a result of a new factor which substantially altered the structure of Rhenish economy: the big strides made by the Frankfort-on-Main fairs.

Frankfort was the venue of an international market in the 12th century, but it was principally the privilege granted by Louis of Bavaria (1330), subsequently enlarged by others, which ensured its prosperity. So it can be said that twice a year, at Lent and at the end of summer, goods from all over Europe flowed into Frankfort which was, in part, the heir of the Champagne fairs which had declined since the end of the 13th century.

Its heyday was reached at the end of the 14th century, but the Frankfort fairs remained important in the 15th and 16th century, despite numerous crises and the efforts of Mainz and Nuremberg to attract the fairs to their towns. These fairs were of course frequented by merchants from all over Germany, from the Centre and the South, but also by foreigners: the French from Paris and Avignon, Italians from Milan, Genoa and Venice, men from the East: Buda and Cracow, and by the Hanseatics.

The principal wares were wine, carried in Strasburg and Mainz boats, cloth from the Rhineland, Brabant, Holland and England, new textile fibres, Milan fustian, linen from the Ulm and Saint-Gall regions, salted fish from the North Sea and the southern part of the Scandinavian peninsula, spices, luxury products from Italy. At the end of the 15th century Frankfort was the leading European printed book market.

There were many Hanseatics in Frankfort. The closest relations were those of Cologne, some of whose factors had settled permanently and owned houses and shops. They mainly sold cloth and salted herrings; they still bought wine there but that did not prevent them from also having representatives in Alsace and around Mainz to buy direct from producers and ship the barrels to their town.

Lubeck Lubeck also developed its relations with the Rhineland area. Its merchants generally took the overland route via Thuringia to reach Frankfort. In 1366 one firm disposed of seven thousand furs there and brought back fourteen bales of fustian worth more than 1600 florins. At the beginning of the 15th century the Veckinchusen firm sent salted fish, Prussian amber and furs to Frankfort. At the end of the century, the purchases book of the Lubeck firm Mulich listed all the products bought at the Lent fair in 1495, to a total value of more than 7600 florins. They were largely luxury objects: pearls, gold and silver ware, velvet from Milan and Genoa, but also arms, cuirasses and spices. Other documents show the continued interest of the Lubeck people in Rhine wine. Around 1575 the managers of municipal wine cellars in Lubeck, Hamburg and Greifswald were to be found in Strasburg where they bought wine for their towns.

BEGINNING IN THE 15TH CENTURY: THE DECLINE

However intense and lasting may have been the economic activities of the Hanseatics in Southern Germany, there is no doubt that at least a relative decline in their participation in Rhenish trade began in the 15th century.

The main cause, in this sector as in others, is to be found in the great strides made by their competitors, in this case the Germans from the South and from Nuremberg. They were more individualist, more go-ahead, less constricted by niggling regulations, and they progressively outclassed the Hanseatics by their technical and financial superiority.

Cologne comes out of it well Of the Hanseatic towns, Cologne best defended its position. It kept its almost absolute mastery of the Rhine wine market. It also continued to despatch salted herrings to the South, buying them far more from the Dutch than from Lubeck.

It was partly the same for cloth, but the Nurembergers captured a large part of the carriage of English wool and cloth to Italy. Even more clearly, Cologne iron and steel products ran up against Nuremberg competition; as from the middle of the 15th century it can be said that the whole of Southern Germany bought its arms, cuirasses, tools and hardware almost solely from Nuremberg. Lastly, the Frankfort fairs and their vast zone of influence were principally supplied with spices, Italian and exotic products (saffron) by the Nurembergers and other Upper Germany companies such as those of Ravensburg, Diesbach-Watt and the Fuggers.

The Baltic towns succumb The decline in Hanseatic participation in Rhineland trade is far more pronounced as regards the Baltic towns and especially Lubeck. Perhaps their weakening was principally due to the development of a new East-West route: Breslau-Leipzig-Frankfort, outside the Hanseatic area. Products from the East, Russian furs and wax and Slovak metals increasingly came into Southern Germany by that new route, to the benefit of the Nurembergers and the detriment of the Hanseatics.

At the same time the conquest of Novgorod by Ivan III and the closing of the German business house in that town in 1494 both seriously harmed Lubeck's trade in the East.

In the 16th century the progress made by the Leipzig fair, which had become the market for Eastern products, clearly showed the shift in the main trading currents.

Furthermore, another article, which had so far contributed a lot to the trade of Lubeck and the Baltic towns, namely salted herrings from the Southern part of the Scandinavian peninsula, became scarce due to the decline of the fair there and the migration of fish to the North Sea. Although some towns such as Hamburg and Bremen profited by the situation, the main part of the fish trade, much sought after by all the Rhenish towns, went to the Dutch.

Lastly, Nuremberg firms succeeded in establishing themselves in Danzig and Lubeck and cornered part of the trade with Southern Germany.

It is therefore clear that the slow decline of the Hanseatic trading system was particularly early and accentuated in the Rhineland area.

238. The landing-stage at Cologne. Part of the reliquary of St. Ursula, painted by Hans Memling for St. Jean's Hospital in Bruges. 1489.
Bruges, Sint-Janshospitaal.

BIBLIOGRAPHY

PH. DOLLINGER, *Relations directes entre Strasbourg et les villes hanséatiques; XIVe-XVIe siècles*, in *Aus Stadt- und Wirtschaftsgeschichte Südwestdeutschlands. Festschrift für Erich Maschke*, Stuttgart, 1975, p. 118-136.

F. IRSIGLER, *Die wirtschaftliche Stellung der Stadt Köln im 14. und 15. Jahrhundert. Strukturanalyse einer spätmittelalterlichen Exportgewerbe- und Fernhandelsstadt*. Wiesbaden, 1979.

DEALING WITH PARTNERS

228

SIMONE ABRAHAM-THISSE

The Hanse and France

It was until the 13th century that Hanseatic sources made mention of French products, yet many favourable factors ought to have attracted the Hanseatics to the territories which make up France today, and in particular products which the Hanse and its hinterland lacked: salt, for example. Before then, however, Luneburg salt, for which Lubeck held the monopoly, had sufficed for the needs of Baltic and Eastern Europe. There were French wines, too, but they were expensive and Rhine wines sufficed for local consumption.

As regards Hanseatic products, most of them had sure markets in Northern and Eastern Europe, so there was no real outlet problem.

It is true that the Bruges and London marts enabled the Osterlins to procure Flemish and English cloth, spices and other Oriental products sought by their clientele. Both those big markets offered the Hanseatics the possibility of meeting the French, who were attracted by Russian wax and furs. It is known that there was a House of Rouen merchants and a House of France in Bruges. Robert Fancillion was the representative of France at the Bruges business house when it was transferred to Deventer.

239. A shopping street.
Miniature placed on the frontispiece of the translation of *Aristotle's Ethics*. Painted by a Flemish or Northern French artist between 1460 and 1470.
Geneva. Public and university library. ms. fr. 160. fol. 82.

Artisan's shops. From left to right: shoeing-smith, hatter, roast meat seller (a curtain is used to keep flies off his dishes), grocer (in centre). A mediaeval shop looked like a room opening on to the street and closed by shutters (generally movable); the lower shutter could serve as a flat surface for the shop window.

On this street, typical of Northern France or Flanders, with its narrow, gable-ended houses, two allegorical personages stand out: Strength holding a diamond, and Justice holding a sword in one hand and an emerald in the other. These two personages, with Prudence and Temperance, are the four virtues about which the book teaches us.

240. Weaving in Ypres in the 14th century. Copy of a drawing taken from the *Livre des Métiers* of the town of Ypres, destroyed in 1914.
After A.-L. Gutman, in *Revue Ciba*, No. 14, 1938 (cover).

Here we read of the stages in cloth making: spinning with distaff and spindle; winding off with the spinning-wheel; warping or preparation of the warp yarn; weaving on a horizontal loom, so wide here that the weaver needs an assistant to catch the shuttle and return it.

241. The Champagne fairs seal (1267). Archives du Nord, Chambre des comptes.

Cotised band escutcheon, accosted by two intaglios; the one on the dexter side represents Apollo shooting an arrow.
SIGILL': NUNDIN... H: DEI: GRA: REGIS: NAVARRE CAMPANIE
(*and in the Field*) ET BRIE: COMITIS PALATINI.
(*"Seal of the fairs of Thibaud, King of Navarre by the grace of God, Count Palatine of Champagne and Brie"*).

THE HANSE AND FRENCH ECONOMY

In the 13th century the Hanseatics were welcomed at the Champagne fairs, especially those from Cologne, to be joined at the end of the century by the Westphalians and by Lubeck merchants coming via Bruges. These fairs encouraged contacts between the men of the League with Germans from the south and Italians, whom they had already met in Bruges. Certainly, merchants from the north were not very numerous, and the case of a Lubeck merchant installed in Troyes was a rare one. In the 16th century they were again in Champagne and Bonaventure Bodecker, a Stettin bourgeois installed in Antwerp, had sums due in Reims.

The policy of the English and French sovereigns worked on these *rapprochements* between merchants.

In 1377 Richard II of England attracted Hanseatics and men from France, Provence, Toulouse to the London Stalhof.

In 1294 Philip the Fair of France protected Hanse merchants attending the Champagne fairs; he exempted them from passing through Bapaume if they were carrying German products. In 1392 Charles VI accorded privileges to men from Kampen and Prussia. Louis XI showed the same attachment for this policy in 1464 by affording various forms of protection to Hanseatics frequenting La Rochelle, Harfleur, Honfleur, Dieppe and Cherbourg. Letters patent from Charles VIII placed Hanseatics and subjects of the kingdom on an equal footing by offering the former appreciable guarantees in the event of war. François I and Henri IV showed much interest in them.

The aim of the French kings was of course both economic and political. Philippe IV would have liked to have found in the Hanse an ally against the English; Louis XI, against Burgundy, whose economy he hoped to turn towards the kingdom of France; and even François I against Charles V of Germany. Not concerned with the causes of those conflicts, the Hanse desired to be able to continue its trade in full neutrality. During the Hundred Years' War, merchants from Prussia, Livonia and the Wendish towns tried to act as commercial intermediaries between the belligerents. The Hanse would seem to have taken advantage of the wars to develop its activity. Unfortunately, neutrality was not possible: any traffic with England signified betrayal for France, and vice versa.

So agreements were periodically called in question. The Hanseatics could not accept the clause closing, even partly, their trade with England: the interests of the London and Bruges business houses would have been too compromised. Such positions led to open war between the Hanse and France from 1470 to 1473.

Truth to tell, all the conflicts which tore Western Europe apart threatened Hanseatic trade and strengthened the endemic scourge of piracy. The Dutch and the English captured Hanseatic ships. In France, before the natives of Bayonne and the Bretons, the Normans, especially from Honfleur and Dieppe, showed themselves to be the most aggressive. Confusion arose, too, from the fact that the Hanseatics often chartered English ships. Corsairs sold the stolen goods in Normandy. During the last twenty years of the 15th century there were daily complaints about French pirates.

Solutions proved ineffective. Charles V proposed compensation in 1378, but

THE HANSE AND FRANCE

in vain. It was in vain, too, that the Hanseatics offered King Louis XI sables, ermine and weasel furs, the pirates continued to scour the seas. Charles set his Normandy magistrates in action, and ordered that prize trials were unceasingly to be judged at the Paris special court known as the 'Table de Marbre'. Goodwill and diplomacy failed to overcome the difficulties. Little by little the Hanseatics preferred to leave part of the traffic to the Dutch and the Bretons.

Despite these often difficult conditions, Hanseatic trade with France developed quite well from 1350. Luneburg salt, of good quality but expensive, had become insufficient to meet the Baltic demand.

242. Artisan tailors.
Drawing illustrating a manuscript of the *Postillae Nicolai de Lira supra Pentateucho, Josue et Judicibus*.
Arras, Municipal Library, Ms. 252 (formerly 2).

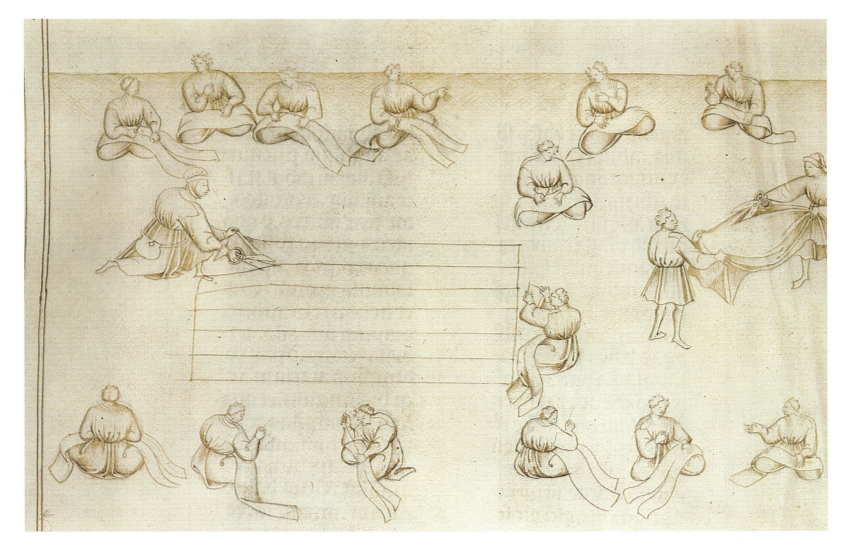

231

DEALING WITH PARTNERS

COMMERCIAL TRAFFIC

Hanseatic trade was, above all, one of intermediaries and redistribution. Most of the products bought in France were disposed of in England (wine), Flanders and, especially, in Central and Eastern Europe, Poland and Russia, whence in return came timber, wax and furs.

Cloth From towns in Northern France the Hanseatics exported cloth known as Flemish.
The Teutonic Order traded in cloth from Arras, Lens, Maubeuge, Comines and Valenciennes. These fabrics were sold in Hamburg, Lubeck, Danzig, Reval, Riga and even Pernau; in all these towns Saint-Omer cloth led, followed by that from Cambrai. These cloths played a not inconsiderable part in the cloth trade of one of the biggest Hanseatic merchants of the 15th century.

Salt The Hanseatics hardly confined themselves to the North Sea coasts, they sought salt everywhere.
Normandy was the first to come forward. It is true that relations between the two communities were not always all they might have been. Therefore, a lot of ships coming from Brittany or Vendée preferred to hug the English coasts to escape piracy; no doubt that contributed to keeping the Hanseatics away from this province. Also, Flemish, Zealand, Dutch and then Breton ships served as intermediaries for them.
Nevertheless, in 1425, Dieppe accounts mention two German ships and a Danzig howker requisitioned in Rouen. Some Germans, Thildemen Bonhors and Gerhart Vannarden, lived in Dieppe and Rouen in the early 15th century.

243. Articles of dress workroom.
Drawing taken from a *Tacuinum sanitatis*. Liège University Library. ms. 1041, fol. 73 verso.

244. Sea fishing.
Part of an engraving by Gérard Mercator, in his edition of Claude Ptolémée's *Geographia*, Cologne 1584.
Greifswald, Universitätsbibliothek.

They were looking for salt, Spanish iron, figs, alum, liquorice and tallow candles. Normandy was a province for the redistribution of southern and even oriental products, thanks to the Spanish and the Bretons.

The Teutonic Order bought Normandy cloth (Normediessche laken) and Montivilliers cloth of poor quality to protect furs in casks. These Norman cloths were to be found on Danzig and Torun markets. The Libri antiquissimi of Cracow, in the early 15th century, mention Monstir de lira in Poland, which can be likened to Montivilliers cloth. Hildebrandt Veckinchusen included this quality among the wide range of cloths in which he dealt.

245. Rouen in the 15th century.
Miniature illustrating a manuscript of Aristotle's Ethics.
Rouen, Municipal Library.

DEALING WITH PARTNERS

246. Fishermen at sea.
Uncoloured pen-and-ink sketch.
Taken from the *Mirakelboekje*. End 15th-early 16th century.
Bruges, Stadsbibliotheek.

247. Salting fish.
Drawing taken from a *Tacuinum sanitatis*.
Liège University Library, ms. 1041, fol. 60.

Fish was the foodstuff 'par excellence' for Fridays, Lent and people of modest means. It was mainly from Bergen that the Hanseatics brought it back. To prepare it for the journey and preserve it, salt was needed. Lubeck was the leading salt supplier.
Scandinavian herrings were salted around Skanör and Falsterbo, on sites occupied each fishing season by the Hanseatic Schonenfahrer and where a bailiff from each town concerned exercised ordinary jurisdiction.
The finished product was shipped to the East, West and South in thousands of barrels.

Corn and more especially herrings arrived from the Baltic. It was not until 1503 that the Sound tolls attested the passage of Rouen natives. Normans settled in Danzig at the end of the 16th century, attracted by the cereal market: there were sixteen of them in 1587, a hundred in 1595. Henri IV appointed Jean de la Blanque to be the French consul in Danzig.

Hanseatic trade turned more towards Brittany; the Bourgneuf lords multiplied privileges, firstly in favour of the people from Kampen (1430) and then for all the Hanseatics in 1433.

Bourgneuf salt appeared for the first time in a German document dated 1276. In the 13th century, Bourgneuf was still a little port, mainly frequented by Flemings and Kampen merchants. In 1369, Hamburg's customs registers still showed only small quantities.

Traffic really began to be organized in the late 14th century. Whilst the Hamburgers were the first to be interested, the Livonians and then the Lubeck merchants turned towards this new source of procurement, for the salt was cheap even if it was not always of good quality.

In order to cope with pirates, the ships formed a convoy protected by warships fitted out at the expense of the participants. The fleet from the Bay arrived in Zwin in the autumn, stayed in Bourgneuf from December to March and returned to the Baltic in May.

In the 15th century, more than a hundred ships went through the Sound every year. Prussian ships, armed by the Teutonic Order, were often the most numerous, but in 1442 the town of Reval alone sent 59 ships. This number, still insufficient for requirements, explains the presence of Dutch ships, which worked first of all for German merchants before doing so for their own account.

Large quantities of salt were carried in this way. In 1383 Reval imported 1350 lasts; between 1426 and 1448 an average of 2500 lasts a year. H. Veckinchusen bought this salt from the Bay. In 1420 he tried a speculation on salt in Prussia and Livonia. He failed, because the arrival of Dutch salt caused prices to collapse. He imported some direct from Riga. Merchants from that town often went to Reval for salt before buying it in Dorpat, Narva. Polotsk was the biggest salt mart for Lithuania.

In Bourgneuf the Hanseatics also obtained products from the south, but especially those from the Nantes hinterland (canvas, Loire wines) which became a big market. In 1448 the Hanseatics sold a lot of furs there without passing through the Bruges mart. Some settled and married there in 1426.

As the approaches to Bourgneuf were becoming difficult, because of a lack of upkeep, the Hanseatics frequented Brouage more assiduously around 1450.

Wine More especially, the hinterland offered more goods, particularly the wines of La Rochelle, Saintes and Saint-Jean d'Angély (the last-named was available on Polish markets in 1336).

La Rochelle wine is mentioned for the first time in the Lubeck maritime statute-book in 1270. It was available in Luneburg in 1278, and the Lubeck maritime state-book again mentions it in 1292.

La Rochelle became one of the principal centres of activity for the Hanseatics, guided by the Kampen merchants. The people of La Rochelle were generally favourably disposed towards them and sometimes transported the wine for them (e.g. Jean Barrat in 1402 for two Hanseatics); they attempted to mediate between the Hanse and Spain in 1436. In the 16th century, Hamburgers settled in La Rochelle. After 1440, relations seemed to weaken.

In town, Hanseatic merchants still procured wine from Poitou, but also from 'Malvoisie' and 'Romanie'. Veckinchusen bought some in 1408. That merchant's clerks frequented La Rochelle, though it is not known with what regularity.

The activity of the Hanseatics in this sector constituted keen competition for the Bretons and Spanish who were in open warfare with the Hanseatics in 1419. Castilian piracy handicapped Hanseatic navigation.

Generally speaking, wine served as a complementary product for the salt fleets which did not always return fully laden. French wine remained dear and could be found only on the tables of the rich.

Bordeaux wine was mentioned in 1375. Whilst the Hundred Years' War was on, London Hanse ships ensured the Gascony wines trade. Returned to the kingdom of France, the province willingly opened up to direct trading with Hanse-linked towns: Cologne, Lubeck, Stettin, Danzig and Marienburg.

At the end of the 14th century the Hanseatics had set up in Bordeaux one of the rare trading stations in France, but it did not last long. Heinrich Warendorp, the Lubeck partner of Veckinchusen, went to Bordeaux and from there to Brest, 14 days at sea; he left for Bayonne and was back in Bordeaux in two days.

Bordeaux wine was often sold by the Hanseatics in Flanders and England. This time it was the English who considered themselves wronged by Hanseatic trade. By an Act of the London Parliament in 1490 they tried to oblige the Hanseatics to use English ships to import Gascony wines to England.

The Osterlins then forsook wine a little, in favour of silk and cloth from Languedoc, pastel-dyed in Toulouse.

Other products Apart from salt and wine, the Hanseatics procured from France: fish (salmon and lampreys from Nantes), oil, soap, silks, honey, raisins, fruit, vinegar, figs and, as we have seen, cloth and canvas. All that would seem to have played only a secondary role.

In exchange, the Hanseatics brought herrings, pitch, tar, Prussian ash, building timber, Hamburg beer, madder from Wroclaw, metallurgical products from Solingen, copper or brass wares and, principally, wax and furs.

The search for cheaper products led the Hanseatics to the Portuguese coasts.

In Lisbon they took on board salt from Setubal, the price of which in Danzig became competitive around 1495. No doubt it competed with French salt and contributed to a slowing-down of commercial traffic between France and the Hanse. Already in 1410 H. Veckinchusen shipped salt from Lisbon to Riga.

The Hanseatics also found products from the Orient in Lisbon, such as spices which until then they had bought in French towns, and, of course, Bruges.

TECHNIQUES AND METHODS OF COMMERCIAL TRAFFIC

From a recent thesis by R. Delort we learn that Prussian fur-skins intended for the Genoese transited through Bourgneuf; the Germans also brought some to Rouen and Bordeaux.

Dine Raponds of Paris ordered his valuable furs direct from Prussia, without going through Bruges. He also supplied the Duke of Burgundy with Russian sables.

H. Veckinchusen sold furs to a man in Abbeville. One of Veckinchusen's good customers was Th. de Bompuis, a future Paris councillor and Prevost of the merchants.

In 1396, Bourdon and Poullier, both from Mons, paid Hildebrandt nearly 3,000 pounds of *gros* for furs which they intended for the King and Queen of France.

Other merchants, individuals or partners, in Arras, Saint-Omer and Valenciennes, were also his customers.

The Hanseatics and their brokers frequented the Lendit and St. Denis fairs, so

Paris was not set aside from their activities after the decline of the Champagne fairs. The Statement of Lendit speaks of six Germans installed in Paris. The Cologne merchants brought in the products of their industry: leather, jewellery, metals and arms (from Solingen).

What could the French capital offer in return? Silks? Fabrics?

It is known that textile artisanry existed around Paris, whence perhaps came the Tyschlaken of the Teutonic Order (whose representative often came to Paris), and Seynisch cloth consigned by the treasurer of the Order to Marienburg.

However, Paris and its fairs figured primarily as a place of payment. Payment for furs was generally made on returning from the fairs.

In that field, the Hanseatics still employed techniques which may seem archaic. They made little use of the bill of exchange and often imposed lengthy credit times on their creditors.

It is interesting to note that French currency, the Frankesche Crone, which can be identified as a gold crown, is often found in the affairs of H. Veckinchusen. He received some in payment for salt and fur-skins and he sometimes used them to pay for Saint-Omer cloth. In 1420 he paid 25 francs

248. Portuguese caravel.
Drawing by Cornelis Cloot in *Livre des Privilèges* of the town of Dordrecht, from 1564-1572.
Dordrecht, Gemeentearchief.

249. Arras. Main square: 175 m × 100 m.
The present condition of the centre of this medieval town which was particularly active in the cloth production field echoes the reconstruction of the municipal site following its destruction in 1914-1918. What was destroyed then dated back to the 16th and 17th centuries.
However, its spatial configuration, parcel structure and symbolic dimension still provide admirable evidence of what this impressive urban accomplishment was like in its original state in the 12th and 13th centuries.
Here, more perhaps than anywhere else in Northern Europe, the central space of the town attains masterly proportions, revealing the rationality and power of these medieval industrial cities which made great strides under Flemish influence.

for five rolls of black cloth from Lierre. The clerk Jean Olva signed an acknowledgment of debt of 18 scuta auri monete Francie.
It was in 1415 that a payment of 16,000 florins by Lubeck to the Emperor Sigismond was arranged to be made in Paris or Bruges, showing that Paris was an important financial place.

There were active relations between Hanseatic merchants and the French, although Hanseatic legislation forbade them to associate.
This constraint seemed to be less and less respected. Rouen merchants associated with merchants from Lubeck and Danzig. In 1401, Veckinchusen spoke of a François van den Bunen, myt ene manne van Parijs. What was the link between the two men?
Although one cannot be certain of the existence of contracts, a number of French and Hanseatics dealt directly with each other: Arras merchants with those of Hamburg and Brunswick; Pierre des Essarts, of Abbeville, with an man from Reval.
We have seen that Hanseatics settled in France, but few French went to the Baltic, at least before the 16th century.

At that time, Lille merchants were in Duisburg, Soest, Hildeheim, Brunswick and Bremen. Jean Baillet was in Lubeck; Hubert Deliot in Danzig; le Moisne was in Reval, as were merchants from Valenciennes and Cambrai in 1556; the sister of one of the latter married a Lubeck burgher in 1585. Thierry Badoire, of Paris, brought back a stock of furs from Narva.
Were these economic links accompanied by a cultural exchange?
In France, little remains of Hanseatic presence, but French influence was substantial in their towns. The Oleron registers may have inspired the navigation laws of Visby, Hamburg and Lubeck.
In the 16th century, Danzig, Lubeck and Hamburg sent apprentice merchants to study French in Paris.
It was mainly in the architectural sphere, however, that French influence was found. The archbishop of Magdeburg had studied at Paris University; the chancel and transept of his cathedral were modelled on those of Laon. Lubeck Marienkirche had the same dimensions as Notre-Dame of Paris and was connected with Soissons cathedral.
Relations between the Hanse and France were not inconsiderable. The political difficulties of the times, conflicts born of competition, piracy, the Bruges mart and, later, the almost permanent Antwerp fairs, no doubt partly explain why commercial traffic was not developed more fully.

BIBLIOGRAPHY

D. HELD, *Die Hanse und Frankreich von der mitte des 15 Jht bis zum Regierungsantritt Karl VIII*, in *Hansische Geschichtsblätter*, 18, 1982.
CH. VERLINDEN, *Le trafic et la consommation des vins français. Une question de méthode pour l'utilisation des sources quantitatives du commerce maritime à la fin du moyen âge et au début de l'époque moderne*, in *Les sources de l'histoire maritime*, Actes du 4e Colloque d'histoire maritime, Paris, 1962, p. 345-355.
E. NORDMANN, *Die Veckinchusenschen Handelsbücher*, in *Hansischer Geschichtsblätter*, 66, 1942.
P. JEANNIN, *L'économie française du XVIe siècle et l'économie russe*, in *Annales E.S.C.*, 9, 1954.

ARCHIBALD LEWIS
Professor at Massachusetts University

The Hanse and England

In 1281 three groups of German merchants who had been trading with England for more than a century and who came from Cologne, Westphalia and the Western Baltic, united to form a single federation or *Hanse* centred in London.

These merchants succeeded in obtaining their own trading quarter known as the Steelyard or Stalhof for which they paid forty shillings rent a year. They enjoyed extensive trading privileges which they had secured over a period of years from a number of English monarchs and which allowed them to trade freely not only in London, but in a number of other towns in Eastern England of which Newcastle, Yarmouth, Lynn, Ipswich, Hull and especially Boston were the most important.

During the ensuing reigns of Edward I, II and III, the Hanseatic merchants expanded their activities by importing increasing amounts of timber, grain, furs and wax from the Baltic and wine from the Rhineland in return for wool and metals of various sorts. During these years Boston, rather than London, was the principal port involved in exporting wool which reached a level of 3,500 bales in 1303. Some of these merchants also served as bankers who made large loans to the English monarchs of the time, especially to Edward III when he was beginning his assaults upon France, which began the Hundred Years War.

250. *Holbeinteppich*.
Anatolia. 16th century.
Berlin, Museum für Islamische Kunst.

This carpet forms part of a series, the 'Holbein Carpets', one of which figures in the portrait of Gisze, a Hanse Stalhof merchant, painted by Holbein.

251-252. Funeral tears.
1. Tideman Berck (deceased 1521), Burgomaster of Lubeck, and his wife, Elisabeth.
Lubeck, St-Annen-Museum.
2. Boston, England.
Johann Luneborch (deceased 1467), Burgomaster of Lubeck, and his son, of the same name.
Lubeck, Katharinenkirche.

DEALING WITH PARTNERS

THE CENTURY, CONSTANT EXPANSION

During most of the fourteenth century trade with England conducted by the Hanse increased steadily, especially traffic in woollen cloth which replaced wool as an export of great value. Such exports rose five-fold from an average of 1,690 lengths per year between 1366 and 1368 to one of 7,827 from 1392 to 1395.

Hanse merchants also began to sail their ships to the Bay of Biscay where they loaded them with large cargoes of salt and wine, some of which they landed in London and English Channel ports on their way to the Baltic. The London Steelyard exerted considerable control over other Hanseatic factories in England and a feature of this control was the selection of a new Alderman who, though German by birth, had English nationality and exercised special authority over the entire German community in Britain.

Despite this growth in trade and commercial influence, the last years of the fourteenth century saw periods of tension develop between the Hanse and England. They were essentially the result of the refusal of the Hanseatic towns in the Eastern Baltic to allow English merchants to live and trade there as freely as they could in England. Though these tensions never resulted in outright war they threatened to do so between 1385 and 1388 during the reign of Richard II.

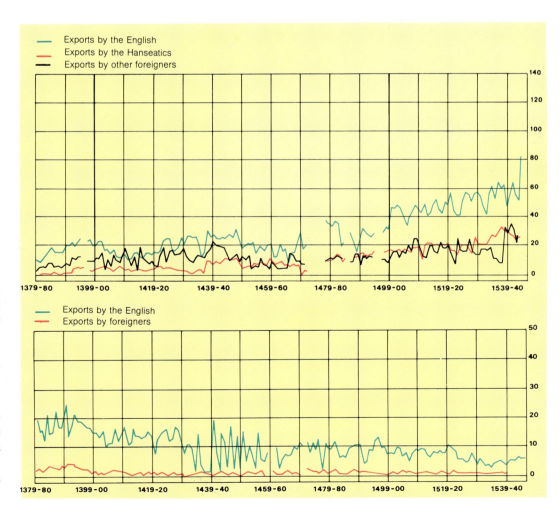

253. Exports of English cloth (1379-1540). Thousands of rolls of material. The annual accounts ran from Michaelmas Day to Michaelmas Day.
After E.M. Carus-Wilson and O. Coleman. *England's Export Trade, 1275-1547*, Oxford, 1963, pp. 138-139.

254. Exports of English wool (1379-1540). Thousands of sacks. The annual accounts ran from Michaelmas Day to Michaelmas Day, except for the period 1279-1290, when they were opened around Easter.
After E.M. Carus-Wilson and O. Coleman, op. cit. pp. 122-123.

THE 15th CENTURY

After Henry IV became king in 1399 he ushered in a period of peace that lasted some seven decades during which the commercial trends of the fourteenth century continued to prevail, though exports of cloth by Hanse merchants did not reach the levels of 1392-1395 until almost the middle of the fifteenth century. The value of Hanseatic trade had reached about £47,000 of which £26,000 represented English imports and £21,000 represented exports. This was about one seventh of England's total foreign trade – no mean figure. Then as the Hundred Years War drew to a close and the Wars of the Roses entered a period of lull with the accession of Edward IV, tensions rose again. These were the result of continuing resentment on the part of the English merchants at their exclusion from trade in the Eastern Baltic, and degenerated into open warfare between 1469 and 1474. Despite the defection of Cologne the Hanse successfully weathered this war which ended in a treaty signed in Utrecht in 1474.

In England the Hanse was stronger than ever. Its property in the Steelyard, confiscated during hostilities, was returned to them and their privileges in Britain were reviewed without English merchants gaining much in the way of reciprocal trading advantages in Baltic waters. By the 1480's Hanseatic merchants had managed to double the value of the English cloth they exported. The total value of their commerce rose to £61,000 a year, about one half in the form of exports and one half in the form of imports. This figure still represented about one seventh of England's foreign trade. During this same period the Hanse's monopoly of wax imports enabled it to double the quantities imported: almost 140 tonnes a year.

255. After G. Schanz, *Englische Handelspolitik gegen Ende des Mittelalters*, vol. 2, 1881, p. 155.

256. After E. Power and M. Postan, *Studies in English trade in the fifteenth century*. 2nd ed. 1951. p. 407. G. Schanz, *Englische Handelspolitik gegen Ende des Mittelalters*, vol. 2, 1881, p. 103.

IMPORTS OF WAX BY THE HANSEATICS

Annual average

1476–1479	1107
1480–1483	2750
1510–1514	4064.6
1515–1519	3658.2
1520–1524	2798.4
1525–1529	6361.2
1530–1534	2561
1535–1539	1630.6
1540–1544	926.6

EXPORTS OF ENGLISH CLOTH BY THE HANSEATICS

In rolls of cloth

1366–1368	1,690	1451–1455	7,682
1377–1380	2,028	1456–1460	10,176
1392–1395	7,827	1461–1465	8,734
1399–1401	6,737	1465–1470	5,733
1401–1405	5,940	1471–1475	3,360
1406–1410	6,160	1476–1480	9,820
1411–1415	4,990	1481–1482	15,070
1416–1420	5,686	1510–1514	21,607
1421–1425	7,238	1515–1520	20,400
1426–1430	4,495	1521–1525	18,503
1431–1435	4,016	1526–1530	20,372
1436–1440	9,044	1531–1535	24,266
1441–1445	11,480	1536–1540	30,740
1446–1450	9,292	1541–1545	27,329
		Jan.–Sept. 1554	27,903

THE 16th CENTURY

Under the first two sovereigns of the Tudor dynasty, Henry VII and Henry VIII, prosperity continued to be enjoyed by Hanse merchants in England, which was in contrast to the decline of markets in other countries such as Holland, Scandinavia or Russia. Their exports of English cloth rose from an average of 20,000 lengths between 1500 and 1525 to double that in 1548 and in 1529 they imported about 432 tonnes of wax. They also continued to transport large cargoes of wine and salt from the South-West of France to British ports, as well as indispensable timber and tar from Livonia and Norway for shipbuilding. During these prosperous years the Steelyard in London became the centre of all Hanse trading activities, whilst Boston and other English Eastern ports lost much of their importance. These years were the high-water mark of Hanse commerce with an England which considered Hanseatic trade as essential to its prosperity — again in contrast to a decline in such trade with the Low Countries and especially with Antwerp, despite that town's growth.

257. The triumph of Poverty.
Copy (circa 1670) by Jan de Bisschop of an oil painting, subsequently lost, by Hans Holbein the Younger.
London, British Museum.

The oil painting, which measured 222 × 301 cm, adorned, with The triumph of Wealth, *the walls of the Guildhall Banqueting Room in the Stalhof in London.*
Both paintings were inspired by a dialogue written by Hans Sachs in 1531.

1598: THE END OF THE STALHOF

Then the Hanse suddenly began to lose importance in England. This seems to have begun when the English crown decided to support English Merchant Adventurers' efforts to expand their trade to the Continent and especially to the Baltic. As part of this effort Edward VI's ministers in 1553 ended all Hanse trading privileges in his realm. And although they were renewed by Elizabeth when she came to the throne, the latter also gave firm backing to the Eastland Company's effort to trade in the Baltic and make Elbing the English trade terminus. When Lubeck used its influence in the Diet to retaliate and persuaded the Emperor Rudolph II to ban admission of English Merchant Adventurers to Germany in 1597 the end of the Hanse came swiftly. In 1598 Elizabeth ordered the Steelyard to be closed and refused to allow Hanse merchants to trade with England or remain in her realm. Though the Steelyard was returned to its owners a few years later (1606) its days of glory were at an end. And even the Steelyard itself, that symbol of the Hanse in Britain for more than three centuries, disappeared when the Great Fire of London in 1666 reduced it to ashes and ended its physical existence.

What were the causes of the Hanse's failure to maintain itself in England beyond the end of the 16th century? One cause, seldom emphasized, lies in the Hanse's reluctance to make use of more modern vessels such as the carrack and stuck to the old type of argosy which, though better than the shallow hulks of the Baltic and North Sea, was at a technical disadvantage in the open ocean. Hanseatic merchants also failed to match Dutch skill in the construction of small, cheap, flat-bottomed vessels and, in the North Sea, they used herring-fishing boats which were hindered by Holland's large foreign trade vessels.

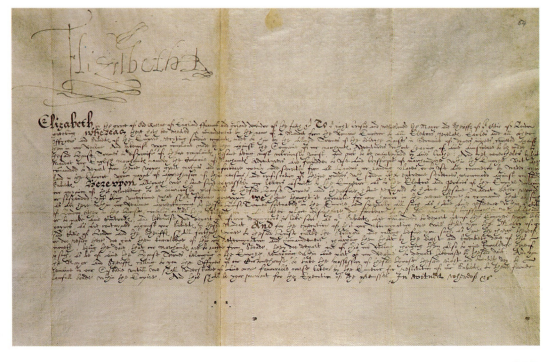

258. Elizabeth, the Queen of England, ordered the expulsion of the Hanseatics and the requisition of the Stalhof. 1598. London, British Museum.

The Queen's decision was a response to the imperial mandate forbidding the activities of the Company of Merchant Adventurers on the territories of the Empire, following harsh treatment inflicted on the Hanseatics in England.
England was now able to manage without the Germans for iron and steel imports and cloth and tin exports.

DEALING WITH PARTNERS

Equally important is the failure of the Hanseatic merchant community to keep up with more modern financial and business methods which originated in Italy and which by 1450 had spread to the Low Countries, France, England and the Southern Germany of the Fuggers and Welsers. The Hanseatics did not interest themselves sufficiently in the field of banking or limited companies which had become very important in the Antwerp of the late 15th century. Instead they waged a war against all credit transactions and forbade partnerships with foreign merchants. They deliberately chose to trade with England in ways which avoided the newer mechanism of credit, banking and joint stock companies which Dutch, French and English capitalist circles were finding so attractive.

SOCIAL-CULTURAL BEARING OF HANSEATIC PRESENCE IN ENGLAND

Extensive commercial traffic developed. For three centuries it strengthened links between England and the merchants who provided such important products as cereals, timber, tar, wax, and other things needed for shipbuilding. These goods came from Baltic, North German and Scandinavian countries.

The Hanseatics also brought in wine and salt from South-West France. At times, and especially during the early 15th century, they financed English monarchs as well. They helped to foster a market for English wool and cloth in much of Northern Europe. But they failed to introduce new trading and financial techniques in England and instead did everything they could to discourage such techniques.

As far as the influence of Hanse merchants on English culture is concerned, one must conclude that it was negligible. The Hanse had no influence on

259. The triumph of Wealth.
Copy (circa 1670) by Jan de Bisschop of an oil painting, subsequently lost, by Hans Holbein the Younger.
London, British Museum.

The oil painting, which measured 244 × 616 cm, adorned, with the Triumph of Poverty, *the walls of the Guildhall Banqueting Room in the Stalhof in London.*
Both paintings were inspired by a dialogue written by Hans Sachs in 1531.

260. Weights struck with the imperial eagle.
London, British Museum.

This type of weight has been found in several places in England, imported by Hanseatic merchants.
The size of a fist, they were probably cast in Cologne which, the heir to Roman weighing techniques, had an international reputation in this field.

English literature or architecture, at least prior to 1500. Only at the end of its existence did it play a somewhat accidental role by encouraging and patronizing Hans Holbein the Younger, who painted important pictures for the Guild's meeting-room in the Steelyard. They have unfortunately disappeared. But having painted the portraits of important Hanseatic merchants, Holbein acquired fame which enabled him to become the court painter of Henry VIII and influence the art of English portraiture for all time. Just before its demise in England, the Hanse also influenced culture of a Tudor England whose foreign trade it had done much to shape and dominate for so many years. Until then, however, the Hanse's economic and socio-cultural role was much less important than one would have thought to be the case.

BIBLIOGRAPHY

E. M. CARUS-WILSON, *Die Hanse und England*, in *Hanse in Europa. Brücke zwischen den Märkten 12-17 Jahrhundert* - Ausstellung des Kölnischen Stadtmuseums, 9 juni-9 september 1973, Köln, 1973, p. 85-105.

D. PURCELL, *Der hansische 'Steelyard' in King's Lynn, Norfolk, England*, in *Hanse in Europa; Brücke zwischen den Märkten 12-17 Jahrhundert* - Ausstellung des Kölnischen Stadtmuseums, 9 juni-9 september 1973, Köln, 1973, p. 107-111.

K. FRIEDLAND, *Hamburger Englandfahrer*, in *Zeitschrift des Verein für hamburgische Geschichte*, 1946, 6.

M. M. POSTAN, *Partnership in English Medieval Commerce*, in *Studi in honore di Armando Sapori*, Milano, 1957, p. 521-529.

GABRIELLE ROSSETTI
Professor at Pisa University

The Hanse and Italy

In the matter of research, the question of the presence of the Hanseatics in Italy, and the links which existed between the Baltic and the Mediterranean, is quite new and very interesting.

Archives kept in Italy and throughout Europe are much richer than what is usually said about relations between Venice, Genoa, the Po, the Curia, the Mezzogiorno and the transalpine world.

The Hanseatic question should be a means of going beyond and renewing debates concerning the vitality and then the loss thereof of Italian merchant cities. Political causes: the increasing heaviness of the aristocracy; economic causes: too great a disparity between urban and rural economics – each of these explanations has its merits, but also its weaknesses.

When studying the political and social history of a specific town, insufficient account is taken of the incessant contribution in men, capital, work and initiatives from the near countryside, from other towns, from overseas and from beyond the Alps.

There is failure to recognize the financial and commercial activities of merchants outside of their town of origin; the importance they had elsewhere where they settled for a while or permanently; the social and economic links

261. Map of the world in two hemispheres by Fra Maura. 1459.
Vellum mounted on wooden board.
Venice, Biblioteca Nazionale Marciana.

"In order to obtain a conspectus of its competitors' knowledge of the world, the Portuguese government engaged the services of a foreigner, one of the most eminent cartographers of the time, the Venetian monk Fra Mauro.

His original map was sent to Portugal in 1459. No trace of it remains, but another map of the world, attributed to Fra Mauro and the same year, is preserved in Venice.

Fra Mauro's map of the world in two hemispheres is circular, with a diameter of nearly two metres. It is the last of the big maps of the world of the Middle Ages: medieval by its border, modern by most of the data represented; a curious mixture of classical, biblical and medieval items and of commercial and nautical realities.

Europe can be recognized, with Southern Scandinavia, Africa, the coast and the islands of Southern and Eastern Asia. But despite the tradition that Fra Mauro possessed detailed maps of Portuguese discoveries, the drawing of Africa bows to the circular border of the map and furnishes no indications about the distances covered and the discoveries made by the Portuguese in West Africa. By a further consequence of the 'policy of silence' adopted by Portugal, Fra Mauro's map of the world in two hemispheres represents Africa, not as a reality, but as an abstraction." [Georges Kisch].

262. Italian foreign exchange office. 15th century. Engraving on wood.
Florence, Biblioteca Nazionale Centrale.

DEALING WITH PARTNERS

263-264. The family of Thomas Portinari, representing the Medicis in Bruges. Circa 1474-1475.
Side volets of the retable of the Adoration of the Shepherds, by Hugo Van der Goes (circa 1440-1482).
Florence, Uffizi.

The retable had been ordered to decorate the Santa Maria Nuova hospital church in Florence.
The donor and his sons are protected by St. Thomas and St. Anthony: his wife and daughter by St. Marguerite and St. Madeleine.

they maintained with their country; the role they continued to play despite their absence or because of it.

As regards economic history, they sometimes conceptualize excessively.

The wool, corn or salt routes, the networks of commercial traffic systems, banking techniques and the social course of a family do not provide an accurate account of life as lived by individuals and groups.

Links were forged in the Middle Ages throughout Europe and have continued since.

I do not think one should seek the basic element of those links in international trade routes, the trade God that builds salt, corn or wool roads on which, from abstraction to abstraction, it always ends up by seeming that only products have travelled and not men.

The merchant is uprooted by vocation. Travelling the world, he entrusts to the little town of his birth the custody of his affections, the fruit of his trade, the memories of his adventurous life.

That is why I especially think of towns as being the essential element of European relations – the urban community.

Medieval towns must have been similar to compass-cards, compasses with the point situated in the heart of towns and the leg extending to the place the men from those towns go to, supported by the political structures and will of their free town. Polarity that blended with others, a place where men from different parts met and talked of their relations with their first town. Really a European network.

A census needs to be taken of foreigners in medieval Italian towns, with an in-depth study of the presence of Hanseatic merchants; encircle the different forms of material, social, cultural and political rootedness. What is really meant by the notion of representative? Contributions and loans and, what is far more, business relations, and that also presupposes force and violence. Commercial attitude is then no longer considered in relation to itself but in relation to other groups and all the vitality which, long term, animates the cities of Europe.

Attention to the links which progressively wove Europe in the Middle Ages makes it possible to study the political history of modern times with a much lesser feeling of triumph or respect vis-à-vis established powers. War itself could well be read as being the consciousness of belonging to the same economic and cultural zone.

A history of everything that the Reformation implied would also be extremely enlightening.

The Reformation profoundly upset the existing social balance, but it needs to be better known. It interrupted the spontaneous movement of populations between the Mediterranean zone and the transalpine regions. It changed old yet constantly renewed migrations into definite settling. It cut the umbilical cord which still bound old and new emigrants to their country of origin through family ties, customs, religions or economic and political interests. All that is true, but the elements have survived, changed and lasted; they need studying.

One should reflect, too, on the meaning of the division of Europe into two religious areas hostile to each other.

265. Italian grain trade. First half of the 14th century.
Miniature by an anonymous Florentine in the *Spechio umano*, by Domenico Lenzi, a corn merchant who, from 1320 to 1335, noted therein the prices of cereals on the Or San Michele market.
Parchment, First half of the 14th century.
Florence. Biblioteca Laurenziana.

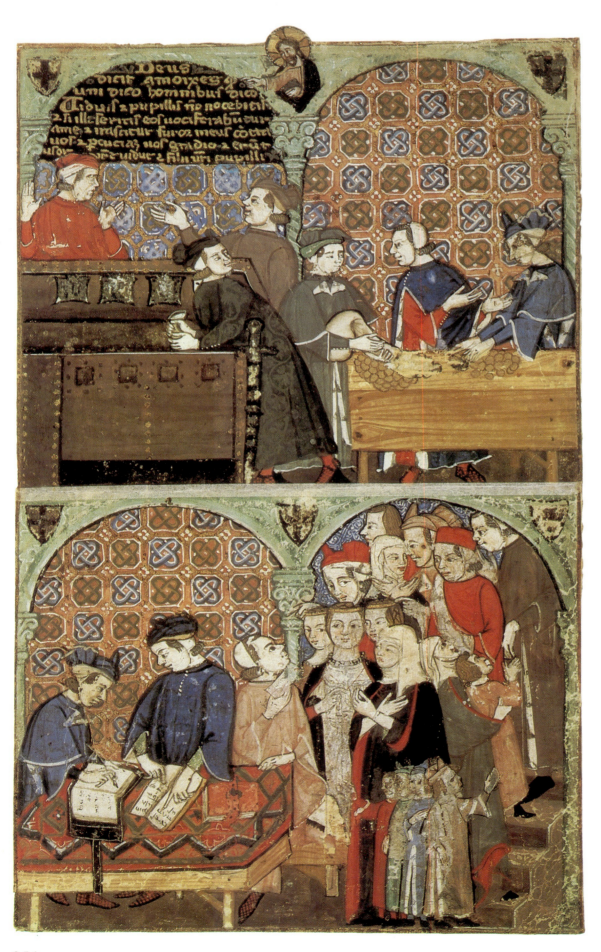

266-267. Italian banker's office. End of 14th century.
Miniature taken from a treatise *De septem vitiis*.
British Museum. Ms. Add. 27695. fol. 8 verso.

Above: the counter and safes.
Below: customers and account books.

268. Genoa, circa 1480.
Oil painting by Cristoforo Grassi who, in 1594, copied a view of 1481.
Genoa, Civico Museo Navale.

The Reformation may well have been a decisive moment in European history, because differing visions of the world developed among Catholics and Protestants, because there was intolerance – and also political recovery.
The presence of Hanseatics in Italy was small.
Italian notaries spoke of *transmuntani* or specified the name of the town of origin of merchants, often a very small locality, but there is very little reference to the Hanse itself. Perhaps that was because the Hanse, as an association, played but a very small structural part in Baltic-Mediterranean relations. Even the *Fundaco dei Tedeschi* in Venice is not representative of the Hanse.
The designation of *transmuntani* also revealed other things. All sorts of men came from beyond the Alps – from Flanders, France, the Low Countries and Germany. Similarly, the kings of France, counts of Flanders and dukes of Burgundy granted privileges to *mercatores italici*, without specifying, wholly or in part, whether the merchants were Genoese, Milanese, Venetian, Tuscan or Roman.
This should be an invitation to go beyond a national framework and study European history – especially economics – in terms of regions. Was the Hanse an important or relatively weak influence in relations between the North Sea and the Baltic and Mediterranean Europe?

DEALING WITH PARTNERS

269. The Fondaco dei Tedeschi.
An engraving by Raphaele Custos. 1616.
Paris. National Library.

"In Venice, the Lubeck and Cologne merchants had their recognized Chamber in the Fondaco dei Tedeschi.
Lubeck trade there is mainly known through the transactions of the Veckinchusens in the first quarter of the 15th century.
Russian furs were and remained by far the principal articles. In 1447 the city of Bruges complained that 'for some years' Lubeck had been sending furs to Genoa and Venice, which detracted from its mart privilege.
In addition to furs, the Lubeck merchants brought to Venice amber jewellery, which was particularly appreciated, Westphalian linen cloth – mentioned in Alexandria – and dried fish.
They brought back spices, silks and southern fruit.
Though Lubeck merchants were still to be found in the Fondaco at the end of the 15th century, it is nonetheless true that at that time they were increasingly ousted by Germans from the South who took over all the traffic between Venice and Lubeck.
The Cologne merchants had arrived earlier and they remained longer.
In 1535 there was some talk of a tax levied by Venice on goods from Cologne, by way of reprisal for prejudices suffered by the Venetians in Germany and Flanders. Such goods included golf-leaf and jewellery, regarding which the town informed the Most Serene Republic, forty years later, that it wished to keep a strict control, and sent it a specimen of its hall-mark.
In the 15th century it sent it large quantities of cloth.
Venice took offence at the wrong done to its merchants and placed a tax on cloth imported overland. A delegation sent by Cologne pointed out that overland traffic was more costly and dangerous than sea traffic, and no other German town supplied Venice with so much English cloth. It is not known whether it obtained satisfaction."
[Philippe Dollinger].

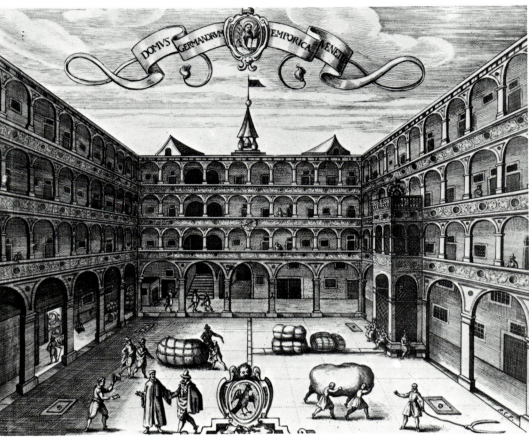

270. The Fondaco dei Tedeschi, on the Grand Canal, Venice.

The present palace dates from the beginning of the 16th century (Giorgio Spavento and Scarpagnino, 1505-1508).

It was built at the expense of the Republic to replace the former building which was destroyed by fire.
Today it is the central Post Office.

271. The sign of the Venice Arsenal Carpenters Association. 1753.
Venice, Venetian History Museum. (Correr Museum).

The gastaldo *is the head of a group of craftsmen.*
Here, in private shipyards around the Arsenal, single-masted square-sail rigged ships were built specially to carry heavy, bulky products.

BIBLIOGRAPHY

P. JEANNIN, *Entreprises hanséates et commerce méditerranéen à la fin du XVe siècle*, in *Mélanges Fernand Braudel*, vol. I, Toulouse, 1973, p. 263-276.

H. SAMSONOWICZ, *Relations commerciales entre la Baltique et la Méditerranée aux XVIe et XVIIe siècles. Gdansk et l'Italie*, in *Mélanges Fernand Braudel*, vol. I, Toulouse, 1973, p. 537-545.

P. BRAUNSTEIN, *Venise et son arrière-pays: les routes du commerce allemand (XIIIe-XVe siècles)*, s.l., 1969.

H. SIMONSFELD, *Der Fondaco dei Tedeschi in Venedig und die deutschvenezianischen Handelsbeziehungen*, Stuttgart, 1887, 2 vol.

H. KELLENBENZ, *Rheinische Verkehrswege der Hanse zwischen Ostsee und Mittelmeer*, in *Die Deutsche Hanse als Mittler zwischen Ost und West*, Köln, 1963, p. 103-118.

HERRYK SAMSONOWICZ
Professor at Cracow University

The Hanse and Poland

Constituted as a State in the first half of the 10th century, Poland occupied an interesting position in the network of trading lanes connecting the Baltic to the Mediterranean, the Black Sea to the German regions. That network came very much to life with the appearance of monetary economy. The Hanse, an association of powerful merchants, was born of the expansion linked with that monetary economy, and integrated the peripheries of developed countries in the network of European commercial traffic. However, that traffic involved only a relatively small group of big merchants, who found in it an appreciable source of income and ground for activities enabling them to reach the highest social positions.

272. Torun. The town, St. John's church, the Vistula.

273. Birth of the Virgin.
Alabaster sculpture. 14th century (?)
From England.
Torun, the Town Hall Museum.

DEALING WITH PARTNERS

THE HANSE AND THE BALTIC IN THE 13TH CENTURY

It was in the 13th century that the newly constituted Hanse extended its activities to the Baltic countries.

What it was in Poland that interested the Hanseatics

At that time the territories were organized in dukedoms. Some of these were not even in the hands of the autochthonal Piast dynasty, for the ancient kingdom of Poland had become coveted by certain Western communities.

The poor Saxony nobility, Dutch, Flemish, Rhenish and Saxon peasants, representatives of the merchant class from the big Hanseatic towns, came to make their careers in Pomerania and in Greater and Lesser Poland.

These regions interested them for more than one reason. Poland formed part of the European monetary circulation zone. It produced an abundance of cereals which were much appreciated by the Hanseatics. It gave access to Russian markets which were keenly sought after by German merchants.

The insertion of Poland in the European monetary zone followed from the German colonization, from the *Drang nach Osten*, after which Western law was imposed on town and country. So currency became widely available there and commercial production began to find its way into the countryside.

274. Delivery of grain.
Scene illustrating the activities of a rural seigniory, 14th century.
Drawing on vellum in a manuscript of the *Postillae Nicolai de Lira supra Pentateucho, Josue et Judicibus.*
Arras, Municipal Library, Ms. 252 (formerly 2), fol. 96.

THE HANSE AND POLAND

Cereals — Poland was therefore ready to take part in major international cereal traffic once corn became worthwhile commercial produce, in the 13th century. Cereals were then exported to Norway and Iceland to make up for the seasonal shortages of Western city centres. So Pomerania and Greater and Lesser Poland progressively changed into a kind of Western hinterland which, although secondary, counted for a lot in the trade balance of Lubeck.

Russian products — It was also the Germans who, in the 12th century, exported Russian goods to the West, mainly furs and some other specific products. The traffic mainly operated through the ports of Livonia, but the overland routes which traditionally linked the mouths of the Oder and Vistula to the Russia of Halicz continued to be used.

It was in fact along that traditional route that Prussian, Mazovian and Polish towns such as Warsaw, Sandomir and Lublin were established.

Immigration — Together with these Hanseatic activities went the expansion of the gentry associated with the Teutonic Order. For the Teutons, the Hanse ensured the safety of their communication network with the West. In return, it benefited by the military expeditions of the Order; newly conquered territories were given to the representatives of the burghers of Westphalia, the North Sea littoral and the Baltic coast for colonization. In this way, pursuant to the law of Lubeck and with Western settlers, the towns of Danzig, Tczew, Braunsberg and Frankenburg were founded.

The mouth of the Vistula — The natives of Lubeck were particularly concentrated the mouth of the Vistula. It is known that about 1230 they brought salt, Flemish cloth and herrings to Danzig and then, sailing up the Vistula, they sold these goods in the hinterland.

In 1298, Ladislaus the Short guaranteed them free trading on his territory. In addition, he granted them, exceptionally, the right to build a business house within the urban surrounding wall of Danzig. So there was one more Hanseatic business house: after those of Norway, Flanders, England, Ruthenia and Saxony, came that of Danzig in Polish Pomerania, about which little is known.

In the 13th century the Lubeck community in Danzig occupied an important position in the Hanse: it formed part of the Hanseatic members who decided activities from Peterhof to Novgorod. But it was eliminated in 1308 by Teuton knights; Lubeck-controlled Danzig was too dangerous a rival to Elbing and the other monastic State ports.

DEALING WITH PARTNERS

THE HANSE AND POLAND IN THE 14th CENTURY

An economic slump in the first half of the 14th century substantially changed relations between the Hanse and Poland.

The monopolization of commercial traffic between East and West

With the corn trade flagging, other ways of making a fortune had to be found.
The Hanse then attempted to obtain sole rights in East-West commercial traffic. It progressively monopolized traffic in cloth, herrings, salt, spices, furs, honey, wax, hemp, Hungarian copper and Swedish iron.
Now at last the Teutonic Order, which had become master of Pomerania and therefore the biggest political power on the Baltic, found itself in the very heart of the interests and politics of the Hanseatic towns.

New relations with Poland

As regards Poland, its sovereigns had loosened their relations with the Hanse. They had not been able to integrate either Pomerania or Silesia in their new State. This deprived them of access to the Baltic littoral and hampered direct, intensive relations with the Hanseatic towns.
Starting in the 30's, efforts were made to have closer contact with Lubeck, particularly by Casimir the Great (1310–1370) who succeeded in bringing together the two economic zones which until then had been almost strangers to each other.

275. Threshing and warehousing the grain.
Scene illustrating life at a rural seigniory, 14th century.
Drawing on vellum in a manuscript of the *Postillae Nicolai de Lira supra Pentateucho, Josue et Judicibus*.
Arras, Muncipal Library, Ms. 252 (formerly 2), fol. 96.

One zone took in the Carpathian and Sudetan regions and was linked with the Balkans where they mined non-ferrous metals – copper, silver, lead – and operated in yarn, corn and cattle from the Hungarian and Moldavian steppes. The other zone, the Baltic, exported furs, linen, yarn and hops in the first half of the 14th century. Casimir managed to join these two zones and it was they that were to fashion Polish culture and the economy.

In the second half of the 14th century, after the Peace of Stralsund (1370), two towns in the south became members of the Hanse for a short time: the capital of the kingdom, Cracow, and Wroclaw, the principal town of Silesia which was Czech at that time.

A Hanseatic saying, probably of that time, perfectly characterized the role of the Polish towns in the then international trading system: Cracow was the copper house, Stetting the fish house and Danzig the corn house.

FROM THE END OF THE 14th TO THE END OF THE 15th CENTURY

The union of Poland with Lithuania, the Hussite revolution in Bohemia and the Turkish invasion of the Balkans were all elements which displaced economic and political centres in Europe north of the Carpathians.

A new economic situation encouraged the formation of new social groups seeking national and international confirmation of their promotion. Also, production was developing in the West, which ensured a wider choice of goods likely to interest the East but increased the need for raw materials, especially those indispensable for shipbuilding and the drapery industry: timber, ash, tar, pitch, hemp, linen, wax and honey. These were the main items which the Hanseatics exported from Poland, Pomerania, Teutonic Prussia and Mazovia, together with furs, and corn which Polish territories supplied in increasing quantities from about 1450.

The Danzig merchants gradually withdrew from direct commercial activity and contented themselves with buying cereals through business houses which granted the nobility payments on account guaranteed by future harvests.

Despite laws which were unfavourable for towns, they could now allow themselves very broad local self-government. Danzig showed increasing autonomy in conducting its foreign policy. Royal power was relatively weak in royal Prussia, the king needed his financiers, the other towns and Prussian States systematically isolated the big port on the Vistula.

IN THE 16th CENTURY

When an attempt was made to reform the Hanse in the 16th century, the King of Poland was even thought of to be the principal protector of the League. But there were various obstacles: growing differences between the Prussian and Wendish towns, the weakness of Polish policy on the Baltic, and the fear of complicating problems posed by navigation on the Narew and by contacts with Russia.

The decline of the Hanse went hand in hand with the development of Danzig, which benefited considerably by the situation favoured by the new Baltic economy.

The conflicts which opposed Danzig to Kings Augustus Sigismond and Stephen Batory did not come within the struggle by the Hanseatic confederation against the Polish sovereigns, even though Lubeck came down on its side. It was far more a quarrel between the town and the other Polish members of the Hanse. It is true that even Elbing and Torun had less and less contact with the German confederation. In any case the Polish State was so weak that there could be no question of an active policy by Poland either on the Baltic or with the Hanse, especially from the end of the 16th century, with conflict between Poles and Swedes.

For close on 400 years the Hanse merchants fashioned, up to a point, the commercial and self-governing activities of towns situated on the territories to the north of Poland.

They were the promoters and agents of an international culture, by integrating the great plains, the lake regions and the Baltic littoral territories in an economic sphere which used the same business language and common currency and where the architecture was identical.

The Hanse facilitated relations between East and West, from Novgorod to Lisbon. In the 14th and 15th centuries it introduced bourgeois social structures into Prussia and Pomerania.

The Hanse engaged the little towns which predominated in Poland, but hardly played any national political role, in a big network of credit and commercial traffic which structured the West, resulting in the inhabitants of those towns often adopting the way of life of the patriciate of Danzig or Torun as the model for their behaviour.

Poland was able to adapt its economy to the needs of modern Europe. It owes that in particular to the Hanse and the forms of action it set up.

EVOLUTION OF RELATIONS BETWEEN THE HANSE AND POLAND

Stage	Period	Polish balance of Hanseatic trade	Principal goods		Principal trading areas	Principal contracting parties
			exports	imports		
I	mid-13th c. to early 14th cent.	Favourable	Corn	Cloth	Pomerania	Wendish Hanse merchants
II	up to the close of 14th cent.	Adverse	Furs	Cloth Salt Herrings	Teutonic Prussia Mazovia	Prussian Hanse merchants
III	up to third quarter of 15th cent.	Adverse	Timber	Cloth Salt Herrings	Prussian Couiavia Mazovia	Prussian Hanse merchants
IV	up to close of 16th cent.	Favourable	Corn	Cloth Salt Herrings Spices Precious wares	All the Vistula basin	Prussian Hanse merchants. Polish nobility

THE HANSE AND POLAND

276. Weighing goods.
Relief sculptured in granite, attributed to Adam Kraft (1460-1508) and placed on the fronton of the Nuremberg Public Weighing building.
Nuremberg, Germanisches Nationalmuseum.

The arms of the town are connected by a banderole bearing the date: Anno 1497.
The Master of the Weights is checking the weighing. His assistant is waiting to be told to add or take off a weight.
On the right, the merchant goes into his purse in order to pay up.
On the banderole in the middle: "dir als (so wie) einem andern". ("For you as for another". "The same for everybody").

BIBLIOGRAPHY

Hanse und der Deutsche Orden. Ausstellung Staatliches Archivlager Göttingen, Göttingen, 1966.

R. KÖTZSCHKE, *Deutsche und Slawen im mitteldeutschen Osten*. Reed. W. Schlesinger, Darmstadt, 1961.

J. HERMANN, *L'approvisionnement des ports de la Baltique en produits forestiers pour les constructions navales aux XVe et XVIe siècles*, in *Le navire et l'économie maritime du Nord de l'Europe au moyen âge*, Travaux du 3e Colloque international d'histoire maritime, Paris, 1960, p. 5-40.

H. AMMANN, *Wirtschaftsbeziehungen zwischen Oberdeutschland und Polen im Mittelalter*, in *L'artisanat et la vie urbaine en Pologne médiévale*, Warsaw, 1962, p. 337-345.

B. LEPOWNA, *Gdansk im 10. bis 13. Jahrhundert*, in *Hanse in Europa*, Ausstellung des Kölnischen Stadtmuseum, Köln, 1973, p. 219-231.

P. SMOLAREK, *Gdansk, sein Handel und seine Schiffahrt vom 14. bis 17. Jahrhundert*, in *Hanse in Europa*, Ausstellung des Kölnischen Stadtmuseums, Köln, 1973, p. 233-249.

NORBERT ANGERMANN
Professor at Hamburg University

The Hanse and the Russian World

Trade between the Hanse and Russia began in the 12th century and lasted as long as the Hanse did, so its history extended over half a millennium. During that long time the Hanseatic merchants acted as an intermediary between Russia and the West and for a very long time dominated the scene undividedly.

NOVGOROD

In 1165, merchants from that Hanse, which was formed in the Baltic, got a foothold in trading relations with Novgorod, whereas those relations had long been the prerogative of the Scandinavians from Gotland. Novgorod, connected by rivers to the Baltic and Southern Russia, was the political and economic centre of a gigantic domain. The very favourable situation of that town meant that in the Middle Ages it remained the principal relay for Hanseatic communications with Russia.

Trade The Hanseatics came to Novgorod and its region with cloth, salt, herrings, silver, non-ferrous metals, amber, glassware, spices and wine. They also sold arms, although they were forbidden to do so.
Finished products of Dutch or German origin played a large part in that assortment, whilst the Hanse merchants bought almost solely raw materials: wax and furs. That is explained by natural reasons but also by the backwardness of Russia. Furs were often a tribute delivered to Novgorod by the tribes subject to its authority. Wax came, for the most part, from mid-Russia.
Business between the Russians and the Hanse was founded on barter. To avoid conflict, the Hanse forbade credit in either direction.
The Germans succeeded in excluding non-Hanseatic merchants from commercial traffic with Novgorod, whilst the town, for its part, ensured the monopoly of relations with its Western visitors.
The golden age of the Hanseatic business house in Novgorod was situated in the 14th century and first half of the 15th. At that time the city on the Volchov received up to 200 German merchants at the same time; the Peterhof and the Gotenhof could not accommodate them all and some of them lodged with the inhabitants. Besides those from Lubeck and Livonia, there were always numerous Westphalians among the guests of the business house.
In the second half of the 15th century, however, trade with Novgorod wilted and the Prince of Moscow, Ivan III, who had annexed the town in 1478, closed the Hanseatic business house in 1494 and had the last occupiers imprisoned.
Various theories have been put forward, none of them absolutely convincing, to explain that step. According to some recent interpretations, Ivan III wanted to exert pressure on the Hanse, either to prevent it from supporting Sweden,

277-278. *Corn that pays* and *Corn that does not pay*.
Corn trading on the banks of the Vistula, Torun.
Anonymous painting, late 18th century.
Torun, Town Hall Museum.

with which country he was at war, or to improve the situation of Russian trade in Livonia. What is certain is that closing the Hanse business house precipitated a movement which had already begun: the commercial decline of Novgorod to the benefit of German towns in Livonia, in particular Reval (Tallin) and Dorpat (Tartu) which were increasingly frequented by Russian merchants.

Cultural relations

Despite denominational differences, and although the Germans lived in their palisade-surrounded business house, trade in Novgorod itself and the frequentation of Hanseatic towns in Livonia by merchants from that city encouraged cultural relations.

In the second half of the 14th century and the early 15th, for example, Novgorod saw the erection of churches with richly decorated facades which revealed Roman and Gothic influences and contrasted strongly with the rather primitive architecture of local churches. From Roman art they borrowed, but simplified, the apse technique; from Gothic art: the window and portal arches.

Without contact with the Hanse, the Western influences found in mediaeval art in Novgorod, in gold and silver ware, sculpture, embroidery and painting, would be incomprehensible. In 1433 German architects assisted Russian masters in erecting the archbishop's palace and other buildings.

Then there were two Germans in the service of the Archbishop of Novgorod at the end of the 15th century: the doctor and theologian Nicolas Bülow and the printer Bartholomew Gothan. Several works were translated into Russian at the archiepiscopal court with the participation of Gothan.

If the Hanse, in its mediating role between East and West, was marked by Western influences – those of Bruges in particular – here it was the Hanse itself which left its mark.

279. Russian trapper.
Part of the stalls, Lubeck cathedral, 1450-1478.
Lubeck, St. Annen Museum.

PSKOV

After Novgorod, it was Pskov which was the second biggest trading centre in Russia. Its importance really began after the Hanseatic business house in Novgorod was closed down in 1494. The town, situated inland, was mainly frequented by Hanseatic merchants from neigbouring Livonia, those of Dorpat in particular where the inhabitants of Pskov had shown remarkable activity towards the end of the Middle Ages. To understand that, it suffices to know that when war between Livonia and Russia was declared in 1501 no fewer than 150 Pskovians were interned in Dorpat.

With the same causes producing the same effects, Hanse trade with Pskov was, on the whole, identical with what it was with Novgorod, but as the Pskov region produced no salt of its own until about 1500, salt imports played an even bigger part.

Although relations between Pskov and Livonia were often marked by political tension and even armed combat, cultural relations developed. In a part of Pskov the discovery was made quite recently of a church some of the portals and recesses of which reveal Gothic influence without a shadow of doubt.

Similarly, in the 1470's a group of Pskov architects went to Livonia to improve their knowledge. That partly explains why churches in Moscow and its surroundings built between 1475 and 1489 are not devoid of Gothic elements.

THE DVINA

In the second half of the 12th century, Holy Empire merchants sailing from Gotland did not content themselves with navigating as far as Novgorod; they continued to the Gulf of Riga and, by the Dvina, reached the territories of the ancient Russian principality of Polotsk.

Vitebsk, Smolensk, Riga and Polotsk

By Polotsk, the merchants of what was not yet quite the Hanse gained Vitebsk and then left the Dvina to continue to Smolensk on the Dniepr. In the 13th century, distant Smolensk was in the heart of Hanseatic trade in those regions. At that time, numerous merchants came from towns situated between Groningen and Riga, as is shown by a census figuring in the trade treaty with Smolensk in 1229. Subsequently, trade was concentrated in two points: Riga on the mouth of the Duna, and Polotsk. The Polotsk business house which existed until the 16th century virtually depended on Riga.

Wax

A feature of Hanseatic trade with the Dvina regions was the importance of wax, which played a larger part in imports from Russia than furs, which were more difficult to obtain in these regions, especially good quality ones, than in the neighbourhood of Novgorod. It was also in the Dvina regions that timber imports began in the 15th century, with the Hanse obtaining it from merchants and from the Polotsk Boyars. Another particularity of trade with the Dvina was the extension of credit, explained by the fact that the Riga merchants were able, despite Hanseatic interdictions, to impose that measure so indispensable for the development of their business with Russia.

THE UKRAINE

At the end of the 13th century, Prussian merchants, in particular those of Torun, traded with Volhynia and Lvov (Lemberg). The latter also had contact with Cracow.
It should be mentioned, however, that the goods which the Hanse obtained in Lvov were, for the most part, Eastern products in transit, passing through Italian, German or Armenian merchants installed in Lvov.
At the beginning of the Renaissance, Danzig became the principal trading partner in the Ukraine, where the nobility successfully specialized in cereal deliveries.

DEALING WITH PARTNERS

TRAFFIC WITH THE WEST IN THE 16th CENTURY

Until the 16th century, trade between Russia and the West mainly went through Livonia and the Hanse, whose roles as intermediaries were laid down in the treaty of 1514 – the last of its kind between the Hanse and Russia. Incidentally, the signing of that treaty signified the reopening of the Hanseatic business house in Novgorod, but business there did not pick up in a lasting manner. To the competition by the towns of Livonia and Pskov was added that of Ivangorod – the first Russian port on the Baltic, created around the end of the 15th century – and Novgorod lost its commercial importance.

In 1533 the English, soon followed by the Dutch, opened up the Northern route to the White Sea via the Barents Sea and Cape Skagen. Whilst this Northern route was developing, the English and Dutch were also trading with Narva, which progressively became the Russian outlet on the Baltic as from 1558, when Ivan the Terrible occupied the town. The Hanse lost its status as a privileged partner.

All the same, Czar Fiodor I Ivanovitch, who reigned from 1584 to 1598, granted the Hanse new privileges, and trade between Hamburg, Lubeck and Russia still remained considerable in the 13th century.

Due to special privileges, the Lubeck merchants frequented markets in Pskov and Novgorod, where they had subsidiaries. In addition they bought Russian goods in the Baltic ports. The Hamburgers and, to a lesser extent, the Bremen merchants, traded more with Archangel by the Northern route.

So, for a very long time, only the Hanse was able to ensure for relations between the Russian and Slavonic Eastern world and the Western world the diversity which belonged to them.

The Hanse supplied the East not only with luxury products but also with goods of primary necessity such as salt and raw materials – non-ferrous metals, precious metals – indispensable for local craftsmanship. Furthermore, by offering them outlets, the Hanse stimulated Russian production – such as flax and hemp, exports of which continued to increase as from the end of the Middle Ages. For Russia, which was not very open towards the West, the activities of the Hanse were particularly important.

In the sphere of trade with Russia, the balance was very positive. Inversely, by furnishing products so important in the Middle Ages as furs or wax, Russia conferred on the Hanse and its economic system an importance which was far from being inconsiderable.

280. Russian trappers.
Part of the stalls of the *Novgorodfahrer* in St. Nicholas' church in Stralsund.
Second half of the 14th century.

On their return they displayed their products to a (German) merchant from the Peterhof. The merchant examined the furs brought by the hunter, whilst a man observed the meeting and stood by the manifestly latticed door leading to the business house, in fact surrounded by a palisade capable of serving for long sieges. The dealing seemed to be stamped with mistrust, if not uneasiness; the merchant risked himself outside of the business house, but protected; the business house itself contrasted with the 'natural' surroundings by its closed, fortified structure.

Until the beginning of the 15th century, commercial traffic was in barter form. Ware gegen Ware.

Novgorod was the centre for furs collected in the forest where trappers penetrated further and further to the north and east. The whole of North Russia, as far as Siberia, constituted the hinterland of Novgorod. The assortment was large: fox, lynx, bears, rabbits, squirrels, martens, ermines, otters, polecats, sables, musquash, beavers.

The Russians delivered the skins in lots (as here) or in sacks. The Hanseatics transported them in barrels, a thousand to two thousand per cask. Sometimes more than 200,000 *skins per boat.*

BIBLIOGRAPHY

P. JOHANSEN, *Der hansischen Russhandel insbesondere nach Novgorod, in kritischer Betrachtung*, in *Die deutsche Hanse als Mittler zwischen Ost und West*, Köln, 1963.
R. DELORT, *Vocabulaire et grand commerce: mots russes en Occident aux XIVe et XVe siècles*, in *Economies et sociétés du moyen âge. Mélanges E. Perroy*, Paris, 1973, p. 700-709.
P. JOHANSEN, H. VON ZUR MÜHLEN, *Deutsch und undeutsch im mittelalterlichen und Frühenzeitlichen Reval*, Köln und Wien, 1973.
E. TIBERG, *Moskou, Livland und die Hanse. 1487-1547*, in *Hansische Geschichtsblätter*, 93, 1975, p. 13-70.

KLAUS FRIEDLAND
Professor at Kiel University

Mapping the Hanse

Many maps today visualize the Hanse trade network in the North Sea and the Baltic. It is interesting to utilize them for their information and to analyse them from a methodological point of view. All these maps are certainly of value and have the advantage of speaking more clearly than the developments – sometimes dull – which they replace. Nevertheless, a map represents only the basic data. It cannot show up everything it is important to know in order to understand a maritime economy system; further explanations are sometimes necessary, the connections, the ports and – on looking more closely – the intensity of commercial activities.

281. Part of a stained glass window.
Lubeck, St.-Annen-Museum.

282. Road transport.
Part of an engraving devoted to the *Allégorie du commerce*, by Jost Amann. Circa 1585, Brussels, Royal Library, the Print-room.

THE COUNTRIES

Let us begin with the countries connected by the Hanse economic system – relations, in the last instance, between producers and consumers, even if there are middlemen, firms for finishing the unfinished or semi-finished product, brokers, wholesalers, distributors and consumers themselves, often served direct by the Hanse traders.

In this very general sense – producer and consumer relations – the following countries were put in touch: England and Scotland, France, Portugal and Spain, the Low Countries, including the Lower Rhine territories, Lower Germany, Denmark, Poland, the possessions of the Teutonic Order, Russia, Finland, Sweden, Norway and, more to the North, the Orkneys, Shetlands, the Faroe Islands and Iceland.

MARITIME TRADING LINKS

Maps show the sea routes or, more exactly, the ports of departure and arrival in sea trade. The lines traced do not precisely represent the trading routes. They are a sort of bird's-eye view or schematic reconstitution of trade relations uniting two towns or two regions.

The routes that seamen actually took often passed too close to the coasts and varied too much with the season and meteorology for it to be possible to represent them. On the other hand a diagram has the big advantage of showing the axes, the real lines of force of the system in question. Some sea routes were not opened up by the Hanseatics, others continued to be utilized by their trading partners. Really characteristic of the Hanse are the two systems for exchanging Western goods for Eastern ones and domestic products for Scandinavian ones, as well as the combination of these two systems in Norway, England and the Low Countries. Whilst the East-West connection is quite clear (Novgorod – Reval – Visby – Lubeck – Hamburg – Bruges – and, from there, Biscay), the North-South connection is less clear and rather recalls – the comparison has already been used – the rungs of a long ladder: from Visby to Stockholm, from Rostock to Oslo, from Lubeck to Bergen, from Hamburg to Iceland, from Cologne to Bruges or London.

THE PORTS

The map also shows that the East-West axis ports were situated on the lower course or mouth of the major rivers in Central Europe; that is true of Bruges, but also of many other ports on the lower course of the Rhine frequented by the Hanse, but which are sometimes omitted on maps. That is true of Hamburg and the big really Hanseatic ports such as Bremen (overlooked on maps) and especially Lubeck, linked with the Elbe upstream of Hamburg since the end of the 14th century and, from there, with the very important Luneburg salt-works. That applies to Rostock, Stettin (not regularly shown on maps), Danzig and Riga.

THE INTENSITY OF COMMERCIAL TRAFFIC

Most Hanseatic trade maps show where trade was the busiest. This intensity appears very clearly on maps where a line representing the East-West traffic, starting from the Gulf of Finland, winds round the island of Gotland, runs along the Swedish coast and gets thicker as far as Lubeck, like a river joined by its tributaries, from Riga, Stockholm, Visby and the continental towns, then, keeping the same thickness, continues via Hamburg to the West, to divide into several arms watering the big markets of the Low Countries and England.

Other maps develop the chronology, enabling the intensification of Hanseatic commercial traffic to be understood. The maritime sectors in which that traffic was the densest were the Western regions of the Baltic and – to a lesser degree – the lower course of the Elbe and the mouth of the Rhine.

Two routes existed: the overland one and the sea one which passed round the Jutland peninsula by Øresund and the Skagerrak. Both were equally used. On analysis, however, it appears that goods traffic between Hamburg and Lubeck via Holstein was greater than that passing through the Skagerrak in that it was the goods which were more voluminous and costly (they were unloaded from the ship in Hamburg and were loaded on to another ship in Lubeck) which travelled overland, generally to the East, to avoid them being exposed to the hazards of carriage by sea. On the other hand, in the case of more usual goods such as Bourgneuf bay-salt going to the East, wood, cereals or ash (for manufacturing dyes), the risk did not appear excessive, whereas the cost of a double trans-shipment was, comparatively, too dear.

INLAND COMMERCIAL TRAFFIC

Maps generally devote little space to inland trade. Yet the Hanse was also a very extensive inland trading system with a well ramified road network which needs to be known if one is to understand the Hanseatic towns, their situations, relations and realities.

We have mentioned eight towns as being the ports of the Hanse maritime commercial system, but it would be necessary to add at least 180 names of towns sometimes just as big as those eight if one desired to make a complete list of the Hanseatic towns quoted by sources.

However, it was not rare that contemporaries, speaking of the Hanse, also had those eight coastal towns in mind. For instance the Chancellery of King Ferdinand – the brother of Charles V – confused the word 'Hanse' itself (meaning, as everyone knows, a 'band' or 'community' of travelling merchants) by calling it a community of *See- und Anseestädte*, i.e. of coastal towns or towns turned towards the coast. A typical misunderstanding and one which serves our purpose: the Hanse trading network also took in towns 'turned towards the coast', in other words, situated on the courses of the big North to West rivers, between their mouths and their last navigable point.

THE HUMAN ASPECTS

Not much can be read from maps in this respect!
In the 1220's, armed conflict between France and England had made it indispensable to protect persons and goods in maritime commercial traffic. In that field Hanseatic trade benefited by favourable conditions: it possessed a specialized and skilled body of men and had set up a system of legal provisions protecting the interests of the shipowner (his ship) and of the merchant (the cargo) and, in so far as was possible, safety on board.

There was always one merchant (sometimes more) on board who took charge of sales in the port of arrival; he bought the return freight and supervised trans-shipment. All these operations sometimes lasted several weeks. He then returned with the ship and its crew. A common destination and shared dangers forged a community which customs of the time fully expressed: during the crossing the merchants helped the seamen, whilst on arrival the latter returned the compliment. Incidentally, they received part of their wages in the form of a specified volume of available freight, which they could put aside and sell.

These maritime trade rules were anterior to the Hanse and existed on the Atlantic and the North Sea, from Norway to Spain. The Hanse kept part of them and sometimes adapted some of them to the new situations resulting from the extension of the Hanseatic system.

Traditions were respected when merchants made the voyage with the cargo and took charge of its sale on arrival at their destination. That was the case in the Baltic and in a number of places which were scarcely accustomed to sea trade, when the Hanse began. It continued in the same way until the Renaissance, in Hanse trade with the Shetlands and Iceland.

What changed, on the other hand, both in law and in custom, was what obviously had to change: the type and quantity of freight, the dates on which it was forbidden to put to sea in winter because of the danger of storms in northern waters, the prevention of too risky or inopportune escapades, interdiction to overload ships, at least on deck. It was also necessary to guarantee equal chances as regards the quantity of goods offered and the date of their arrival on the markets. These were wise precautions on the part of the Hanseatic community to thwart the sometimes unscrupulous plans of certain merchants shamelessly exploiting the new possibilities of the Eastern market.

Contributions by the Hanse in the field of maritime law also concern the recovery of goods lost at sea due to a shipwreck, and guarantees offered the rightful claimant to such goods. The inhabitants along the Baltic coast often still claimed the 'wreckage right' which rendered them masters of the persons and goods of a ship that ran aground on their coast. That ancient custom was deeply foreign to the trading spirit founded on civilized commercial traffic. The jurisdiction of the towns, the rights of the burghers in all the big ports in which the Hanse had interests, and the principal business houses quickly defended persons in these matters. The contribution made by the Hanse itself lay in the protection of rights to goods.

In so far as companies watched over the buying, selling and shipment of cargo by foreign business houses, the merchants were no longer obliged to make the voyage themselves. They could manage their affairs from their own country and have themselves represented abroad, in most cases by a young employee, the *Kaufgeselle* or 'trade companion', who was at the same time a member of the business house guild.

Such was the basic form of the 'firm'. We know the origin of many of them with remarkable accuracy; inevitably a structure of this type, with its ramifications, subsidiaries, accounts, short or long term payments, deliveries, etc. involved a lot of paper work. The oldest commercial papers which have reached us date from the end of the 13th century and give us the date on which the 'firm' was founded.

At the centre of the preoccupations of the Hanse, at least within the context of its maritime commercial law, one does not find man – in the sense of an individual who produces, consumes, buys or sells – but property, and more precisely the property of the Hanseatic merchant. Sometimes it seems more important to guarantee the goods than to protect the ship or its crew. The fight against foreign competition – i.e. against legitimate foreign interests – was at the heart of many a Hanse economic-political operation. Some of the more audacious plans were never put into practice, e.g. the one to impose certain routes or certain ports on non-Hanseatic merchants, or the one to classify goods in two categories: those which could be freely traded and those reserved for the Hanse (the *Stapelgüter* of the 15th century). To succeed, a trader had to be able to choose his partners freely, explore production possibilities and satisfy consumer requirements.

When the Hanseatic system was immobilized, in the 16th century, the Hanse merchants had just explored new trading centres westward of the former ones. The great historical merit of the Hanse was to have been the link between Central Europe and the Baltic at the beginning of the Middle Ages and to have opened the way to Renaissance Western Europe.

BIBLIOGRAPHY

F. BRUNS, H. WECZERKA, *Hansische Handelsstrassen, Atlas, Text, Register.* Köln und Weimar, 1962-1968, 3 vol. *(Hansischen Geschichtsquellen,* N.F., 13).

P. JOHANSEN, *Umrisse und Aufgaben der hansischen Siedlungsgeschichte und Kartografie,* in *Hansische Geschichtsblätter,* 73, 1955.

H. KELLENBENZ, *Les escales hanséatiques,* in *Les grandes escales.* Recueil de la Société Jean Bodin, 32, I, 1874, p. 365-399.

A. FRIIS, *La valeur documentaire des comptes du péage du Sund. La période 1571 à 1618,* in *Les sources de l'histoire maritime.* Actes du 4ᵉ Colloque international d'histoire maritime, Paris, 1962, p. 365-379.

G. KISCH, *La carte. Image des civilisations,* Paris, 1980.

H. RICHTER, *Olaus Magnus Carta Marina, 1539,* Lund, 1967.

D. ELLMERS, *Frühmittelalterliche Handelsschiffahrt in Mittel- und Nordeuropa,* Neumünster, 1972.

G. ASSAERT, *Westeuropese scheepvaart in de middeleeuwen,* Bussum, 1976.

A daily Environment: The Town

Constructors of Urban Realities

It is in and by the town that the Hanseatics express their way of life, their concept of the world and society.
Unconsciously no doubt, but actually, they reproduce the monastic matrix there, dividing an empty, central quadrilateral in half and setting up there what relates to the world and to God: Salvation (the church) and municipal and business matters (the Town Hall and the market), providing the town in this way with what, in a monastery, corresponds to the chancel, the chapter and the cloisters. The town is really the daily framework of Hanseatic projects, just as the abbey is of monastic projects.
The Hanseatics are also, knowingly, the promoters and constructors of urban realities. They invest and mark the shores of the Baltic, from Lubeck to Reval, with imprints inspired by the Flemish. The gates of Bruges are found again in Lubeck, a measure of its monumental entrances. The boldly shaped naves of the Flemish patricians are adopted by the master builders of Lubeck, Luneburg and Stralsund. To furnish the interiors of these brick vessels and accumulate there things to appease even the keenest imaginations, the Hanseatics went to Bruges and then to Antwerp where, in the 15th and 16th centuries, an essential part of Western urban patrimony was founded. Flemish forms and structures of benevolence and liberality were also copied: the Holy Ghost hospital in Lubeck is based on the Bijloke in Ghent.
Daily framework of the merchant project, the town itself is the first importation, foremost among all those which the Hanseatics conveyed from the West for generations.
The town soon became its town, modelled in its image, and with means which in the 15th and 16th centuries were amazing.

ALBERT D'HAENENS

Lubeck

Lubeck, aller Stede schone,
van riker Ere dragest du die Krone.

Lubeck, in the Baltic, the medieval capital of foreign trade, the capital of the Hanse.
An island surrounded by the Trave and the Wakenitz. Two parallel streets joining two hills. Side streets (Grube) which slope steeply down to the Trave, and in their centre, on a third height: the market.
A clear plan, the rational mind of pioneer merchants and colonists.
Lubeck was definitively founded in 1159. To the bold, enterprising men he had sent for from Saxony, his native land, Henry the Lion granted plots of land of equal size on very favourable terms, as well as privileges which conferred on them the management and administration of the community.
In 1181, when Henry the Lion was overthrown, the town became imperial; Frederic Barberousse confirmed its liberty.
On the death of Barberousse it came under the domination of Holstein and then of Denmark (1201). In 1125/26 it became imperial again and a free city, which it remained until 1937.

283. The Trave and the cathedral.

284. Lubeck seen from the East. Circa 1660.
Wall painting surmounting the woodwork (1552) of the Chancellery of the Town Hall.

Lubeck took over the leadership of the Baltic region in the second half of the 14th century (the first Hansetag dates from 1356), and so became the second biggest town in Germany, after Cologne.
It was then that the urban landscape acquired a structure and profile which have virtually not been changed since.
The cathedral, the four parish churches, three convents, Town Hall and the Holy Ghost hospital date back to that time.
Brick archiecture: monumental manifestations of the tension between the episcopal feudality and urban bourgeoisie.

The surrounding wall   Lubeck was particularly well protected by the Trave and the Wakenitz. However, after the battle of Nornehöved (1227) which freed it from Danish dependence, it marked its liberation by erecting a surrounding wall and four gates. Three of the gates allowed traffic to pass: to the north, the Castle gate (*Burgtor*); to the west, the Holstein gate (*Holstentor*); to the south-east, the Windmills gate (*Mühlentor*). The *Hüxtor*, to the east, was but a simple passage through the wall.

In the 16th century, embankments were made with earth and round billets at the more exposed parts of the port, particularly on the left bank of the Trave.

In 1595 the Italian J. Pasqualini the Younger built a polygonal bastion opposite the *Marlesgrube*, on the other bank of the Trave.

In 1604 Jean van Rijswijck, of Antwerp, undertook to build a modern, bastion-fortified surrounding wall. His project took a good fifty years to be carried out (till 1660/70) and the original plan had to be modified several times, in particular by Jean de Valkenborgh around 1613 and by Jean de Bruxelles around 1640.

In the 18th century they began demolishing the medieval walls, systematically razing them to the ground and laying out parks and gardens. The moats were left, however, and part of a rampart grafted on to the *Holstentor*.

285. The Holstein Gate (*Holstentor*), like the Notre-Dame church, a symbol of the town.

Built between 1469 and 1478. The city owner of the work, Heinrich Helmstede, designed it on the model of the gates of Flemish towns, Bruges in particular. It served as an urban fortification and emblem. Three superposed rows of windows and arcades over the whole width of the building. Richly ornamented terra cotta friezes. Alternate rows of red and black bricks.

286. Plan of the Holsten Gate.

287. Gate to the city. 1552.
Part of the Panorama of Lubeck by Elias Diebel.
Lubeck, St-Annen-Museum.

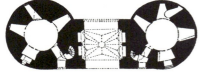

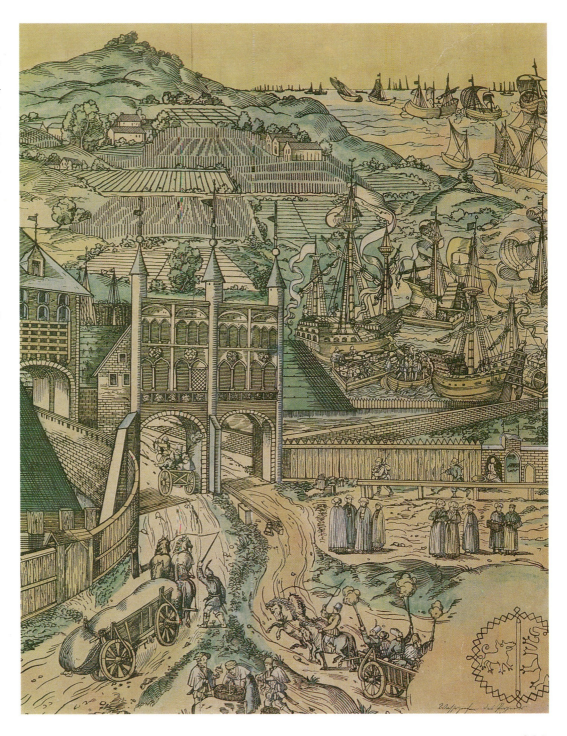

CONSTRUCTORS OF URBAN REALITIES

The cathedral   On rising ground at the southern end of the historic town: the cathedral. It is the oldest church in the town, the first monumental construction in brick in the colonies of North-Eastern medieval Germany.
The present sanctuary was built on the site of an original edifice (1163). It was Henry the Lion who laid the first brick in 1173.
It was modelled on Brunswick and Ratzeburg cathedrals, also undertaken by Henry the Lion, but Lubeck cathedral was of brick. In 1265 they began transforming the nave, for the Bishop and his chapter did their utmost, without really succeeding, to surpass the architectural feats initiated by the burghers and merchants in Notre-Dame church on the market place.

289. Clock by A. Polleke. 1627-1628. Dial decorated by M. Dax.
Gable sculptured by M. Sommer.

290. Pulpit by Hans Flemming. 1568.
This is probably the sculptor who designed the state staircase of the Town Hall.

291. Bronze fonts. 1455. By Lorenz Grove, of Hamburg.

292. Altar of the Virgin. 1506.
Made by a disciple of H. von der Heide.
The Annunciation is presented in allegorical terms: Saint Michael, disguised as a hunter, pursues the Unicorn, in a hortus conclusus. The painted volets represent scenes from the Maternity of the Virgin.

288. The oldest brick cathedral in Germany. It was completed in 1247.

293. *The bearing of the Cross.*
Anterior side of the left-hand outer volet of the Triptych of the Crucifixion, by Hans Memling. 1491.
This triptych was ordered by the brothers Heinrich and Adolf Greverade, of Lubeck, for the chapel erected by them in the Marienkirche in 1493.
Lubeck, St.-Annen-Museum.

Two large superposed areas. In the lower one, in which the figures are on the same scale as those of the central panel: Christ bearing the Cross, surrounded by his companions; the group had just passed through the Jerusalem gate.
The upper area contains the synoptic representation of episodes of the Passion prior to Calvary: Christ in the Garden of Olives, the arrest of Christ (with the kiss of Judas), the soldiers marching through town, the denial of Peter, the flagellation, the crowning with thorns, Ecce Homo, Pilate washing his hands.
The kneeling donor, left, has been identified by Weale (1901) with Heinrich Greverade.

CONSTRUCTORS OF URBAN REALITIES

The market-place and the Town Hall

The market-place showed the methodical planning of its founders.
In the heart of the city, at its culminating point: an empty quadrilateral. Its north part was reserved for Notre-Dame and its cemetery. The other, to the south, was for trade, exchange and the market. So the church and the urban authorities shared this central space equally between them.

Notre-Dame already existed at the end of the 12th century; it was made of wood, like most of the town's constructions.

The first Town Hall, also of wood, was situated in the north-west corner, between the cemetery and the market.

Around 1230, after the status of a free city had been obtained (1226), a new Town Hall was built in the north-west corner, between the cemetery and the main street (*Breite Strasse*). From what remains at cellar and foundation level, there were three long constructions whose facades gave on to the cemetery and the market. After 1250 the three gables were incorporated into one sole facade. In front of that they built at two levels, with the city court being on the ground floor. At the same time the long central construction disappeared, to be replaced by an inner courtyard. Between 1298 and 1308 the East wing was enlarged by a building called the *Lange Haus*. There was a big reception room on the first floor, whilst under the ground floor arcades the gold- and silversmiths had their shops (until 1868).

294. Lubeck market, circa 1580.
Anonymous engraving.
Lubeck, St.-Annen-Museum.

Around 1340-1350, when Lubeck was established as the leading city of the Hanse, the old Town Hall was rebuilt, with the exception of the cellars and the facade giving on to the market. On the first floor of the East wing was the *Hansesaal*, where meetings of the League towns were held.

The Town Hall was also installed there, whereas the West wing housed the 'halles', and a second monumental facade was built; it served as a model for Rostock, Stralsund and Torun Town Halls.

In 1345, Nikolaus Peck, the master builder of the town, strengthened the south wall, which consisted of two false ogival openings. He built a central tower and, in order to avoid the effect of gusts of wind, had two ovals pierced in the wall. The former Town Hall is hidden behind this monumental screen.

Its history reflects the progressive diversification of the political and administrative tasks of the urban council. It also shows, in space and brick, the leadership of Lubeck in the Hanseatic world.

So Lubeck Town Hall became not only the central headquarters of the Hanse but also a symbol and emblem. It structured the spatial and architectural imagination of those concerned with managing the urban realities of the Baltic region.

295–296. Lubeck Town Hall.

After that of Torun, the biggest and perhaps the most remarkable of the Town Halls built in the Middle Ages. The lay-out of the whole building dates back to 1200.

The Kriegstubenbau *(war rooms wing) was added to the* Danzelhus *wing in 1442. The facade of the* Kriegstubenbau, *with window-shaped openings, hides the roof of the building. The buttresses are round, capped by spear-shaped arrows.*

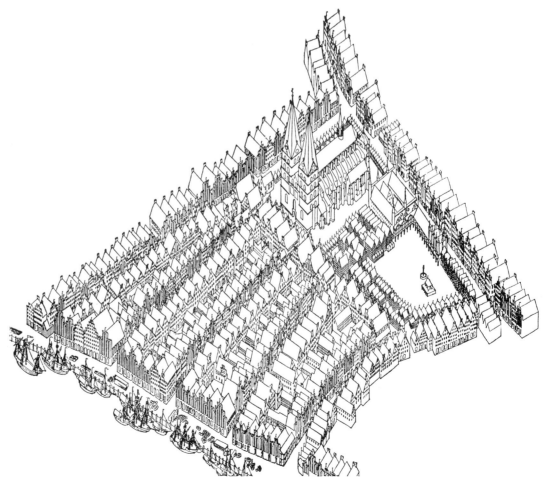

CONSTRUCTORS OF URBAN REALITIES

288

297. State staircase. Flemish Renaissance. Sculptured in 1570-1571 by Hans Flemming. It leads to the 'new room' (*Neuen Gemach* or war rooms), built in 1442-1444.

298. Sculptured door of the *grosse Kommissionsstube*. 1612-1615.
Sculpted by Tonnies Evers le Jeune.

Following pages:

299. Jürgen Wullenwever (circa 1488-1507). Lubeck, Town Hall.

Burgomaster of Lubeck. He championed a grandiose foreign policy scheme: to take advantage of Danish dynastic quarrels in order to establish Lubeck domination over the Sund and so close the Baltic to the Dutch. But it came to naught.
An ardent partisan of the Reformation, and fundamentally hostile to the Lubeck patriciate. On September 24, 1537 he was beheaded and his corpse was quartered.

300. Thomas von Wickede (deceased 1527). Lubeck, Town Hall.

Of a family hailing from Westphalia. The name appears in Lubeck in the 13th century. A member of the Town Council from 1506 to 1527. Burgomaster from 1511. His father and his brother also had seats on the Council.

CONSTRUCTORS OF URBAN REALITIES

Notre-Dame church

The *Marienkirche* was the church of the town and its council (*Kirche des Rats*). With the Town Hall, it constituted an impressive architectural complex – evidence, in monumental terms, of the power and wealth of municipal power.

It was the city burghers, the founders of the town and the Lubeck merchants who financed its construction and furnished it with a richness that was irremediably mutilated by bombardment in 1942.

The sanctuary lost a lot of its aspect – that of a typically communal church – through sudden changes in the plan during construction in the 1260's.

Originally built of wood (1163), it was, in a second phase around 1200, designed on the basilical plan and of brick, along the lines of the cathedral but of larger and more gracefully shaped dimensions. It was not yet finished when, around 1250, preference was given to the hall-church plan which better expressed the personality of the local bourgeoisie who wished it to be different from the style and structure of the cathedral: more modern, even bold and avant-garde. If it had been completed, Notre-Dame of Lubeck would have been the biggest German sanctuary of its type.

But in the early 1260's the idea was suddenly changed again, when the chancel was being erected. This time a Gothic formula was opted for, with an ambulatory. No doubt this was under the influence of similar things seen in the Flemish commercial towns with which Lubeck was in close, warm relations.

The chancel of Notre-Dame became the model for Gothic cathedrals in the Baltic region.

Between 1315 and 1330, Hartwich the master builder raised the central nave, bringing it into line with the chancel. In 1351, the western towers were built to finish off the work and the church had acquired its definitive form. Several official, urban and corporative functions were held there.

The *Bergenfahrer* had their chapel there, for instance. The public letter-

301. The spires of Notre-Dame, mid-14th century.

Concurrent symbols of the cathedral and of episcopal power.

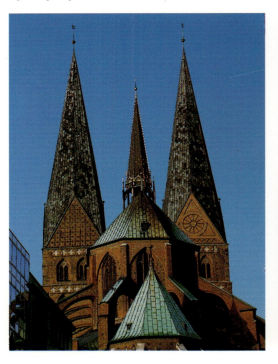

writers who used to draft deeds for merchants sat in the *St-Annen-* or *Briefkapelle*. On the first floor of the *Bürgemeisterkapelle* was the *Trese*, i.e. the charters and treasury of the council. The ground floor was sometimes used as a burgomasters' meeting place.

The *Marienkirche* was also the *Rumeshalle*, the Pantheon of the patriciate and bourgeoisie. Its votive furniture was impressive in its beauty and richness, but the bombardment in 1942 eliminated everything that was wood or paint, in particular the triptych by Adriaan Isenbrant of Bruges (1518) and the retable of the Trinity (1518), another product of a Flemish studio.

304. Cast iron font by H. Apengeter, 1337.

An inscription spread over two registers states the completion of the nave and mentions its architect.

302. Notre-Dame church is the biggest religious edifice in Northern Germany.

The 3-nave chancel was built between 1260 and 1290. Shortly afterwards, around 1304, another Clerk of the Works built the Briefkapelle *and the two western towers, the spires of which date from 1350.*
The initial project provided for a church hall. But that was abandoned and the central nave was raised to give light to it by a clerestory. The transformation of the planned church hall into a basilica is the work of Hartwich, Clerk of the Works from 1310 to 1330.
The vault paintings date from the Middle Ages. The decoration of the vertical structure goes back to each phase of the construction.
Gothic style, free from heaviness.

303. Part of the retable of the Virgin, circa 1495, the work of Christian Swarte. Intended for the *Bürgemeisterkapelle*.

305. Saint-Jacques' Tower. The copper spire was designed by K. Walter in 1657.

306. Part of font, by the founder Klaus Grude who also cast the tabernacle in Notre-Dame church (1466).

On the sides of the font: the twelve apostles supported by three kneeling angels.

307. The navy chaplain (*Schiffer-Prediger*) and vicar of St. Jacques', Sweder Hoyer. 1566.
Votive painting offered by Hoyer's mother.

The chaplain, on board a warship, is reading the Bible to the crew. Sweder Hoyer died in 1565, a victim of an epidemic, while Lubeck was at war with Sweden.

308. The retable of the Brömse family. End of 15th century.
The central part and two of the side volets.

The central part is a sandstone relief representing the Crucifixion. It is the work of a Westphalian sculptor, Heinrich Brabender who, between 1498 and 1500, sculptured the four reliefs of scenes from the Passion which are to be found in the chevet of Notre-Dame church.
Two of the side volets represent members of the family of Burgomaster Heinrich Brömse.

CONSTRUCTORS OF URBAN REALITIES

The Holy Ghost Hospital

Bertram Morneweg had made a fortune in Riga. He thought of his companions, their misfortunes, their hard life, the risks they constantly took, without which it was not possible to make big profits. He therefore decided to allocate a large part of his profits to the foundation of a hospital where old, sick or destitute seamen would be taken in and looked after.

A hospital, dedicated to the Holy Ghost, was therfore built on the corner of the *Pferdemarkt* and the *Marlesgrube* in 1227. The town took it over and, in the 1260's, transferred it to the Koberg. Designed on the model of the Bijlike in Ghent, it was completed around 1285.

Like the Town Hall and Notre-Dame church, the *Heiligen-Geist-Hospital* expressed with strength and beauty the dynamism and spirit of the city founders. Here the feeling of solidarity is implanted in urban space in a remarkable manner. Unique in Germany, as a significant, well-preserved medieval complex providing non-ecclesiastical public assistance, it is of the highest interest in western urban history, being comparable to the Bijloke in Ghent and St. Jean's hospital in Bruges.

The foundation, private at first, was not long in benefiting by the total backing of the council, which saw in it one of the important sectors – that of public assistance – where it could fit in with the traditional monopoly of the Church, and more particularly of the cathedral and its chapter. The council endowed it with property, income and masterpieces of all kinds.

309. The jube of the Holy Ghost Hospital chapel.

It is fixed to the wall which separates the chapel from the Langes Haus.
*Under the jube: the two doors to the Great Hall (*Langes Haus*); frescoes representing the Crucifixion, the Dormition of the Virgin, the crowning and the Holy Trinity. From the end of the 13th and the second half of the 14th century.*
On the balustrade: frieze painted with scenes taken from the legend of St. Elisabeth of Hungary. Anonymous work, first half of the 15th century.

310. The jube and stained glass windows of the chapel.

On the jube wall: candelabra or chandeliers from the second half of the 17th century (1650-1697).

311. West wall of the Great Hall (*Langes Haus*).

On the wall separating the chapel from the Great Hall, on the Hall side: calvary painted around the middle of the 15th century.

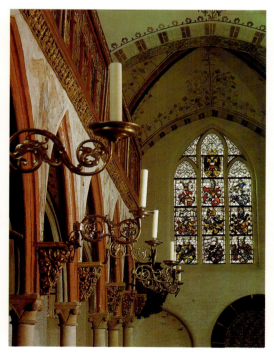
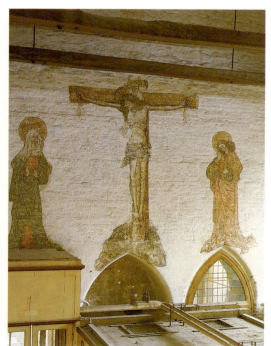

312. Part of one of the frescoes ornamenting the north wall of the church of the Holy Ghost hospital.
Christ is surrounded by the tetramorph and medallions representing the founders (in particular Morneweg, on the left) and presidents of the hospital.
First third of the 14th century.

This fresco is both religious and diplomatic.

313. Retable of the Virgin. Circa 1520.

*It is on one of the three chapel altars.
Central panel: Mary protecting some of the city's social groups.
Left-hand side volet: a Jesse tree.
Right-hand side volet: Whitsun.*

314. Construction of the Koberg hospital was no doubt completed in 1286.

With the Town Hall, it is the most important Lubeck urban construction dating back to the time of the founders.
It is also a significant, well-preserved example of a Middle Ages charitable institution. Like the Town Hall, the west facade gables are flanked by turrets resembling minarets or spearheads.

315. Plan of the Holy Ghost Hospital.
After G. Dehio, *Handbuch der Deutschen Kunstdenkmäler, Hamburg, Schleswig-Holstein*, 1971, p. 969.

316. Attempted reconstitution of the original complex, which dates from 1285-1290. Central perspective of the interior of the church and the *Langes Haus*.
After *Archäologie in Lubeck*, Lubeck, 1980, p. 71.

317. The chapel of the Holy Ghost Hospital.

Entering the Holy Ghost Hospital means first going into the chapel which runs the whole width of the hospital frontage. It has three naves but only two bays.
Width: 14 m. Height: 12.5 m.
The central nave is crowned by a star-shaped vault (1495).

The 5-bay jube closes the east side of the chapel.
The frescoes at the end, on the north wall, date from the first half of the 14th century. Here, the Saviour on the throne, surrounded by benefactors of the hospital.
On the left, on the adjoining wall which is not visible: Christ and the Virgin (Solomon's throne).

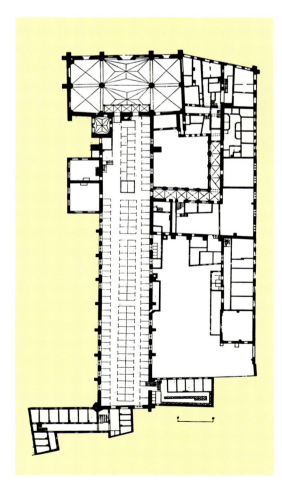

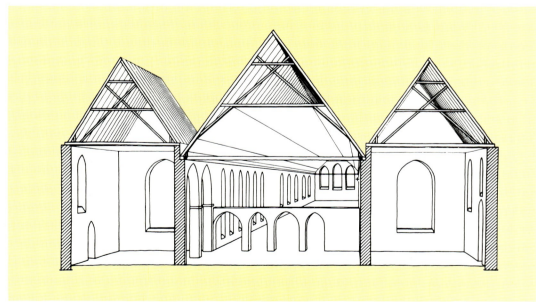

CONSTRUCTORS OF URBAN REALITIES

LUBECK

The Captains' Guild House

There were about seventy confraternities in Lubeck at the beginning of the 16th century. They grouped merchants, craftsmen, sailors and workers involved in Lubeck's port and trading activities. They, too, actively developed the spirit of mutual aid and assistance, and did so with zeal stimulated by emulation and rivalry. They were concerned, therefore, with founding altars and chapels, making donations to them, giving them valuable objects, installing votive elements, practising benevolence and, of course, founding trade-guild houses.

The *Schiffergesellschaft* was one of those strong solidarity associations. Its house has been preserved intact.

318-320. The captains' guild house (*Schiffergesellschaft*).

The confraternity of captains, placed under the patronage of St. Anne, and the Confraternity of St. Nicholas, founded a house of refuge 'for poor seamen' here in 1535.

There were similar houses in other towns, generally called Schütting, *but the captains' guild house in Lubeck has been preserved in its original state.*

Renaissance facade, restored in industrial brick in 1880. The rococo door dates from 1768 (D.J. Boy). The two limestone signs are from 1745. On the right, the entrance to the house of the mercantile agent of the guild. A frieze with proverbs. On the sides: God the Father and Moses.

In the middle: a three-master (13th century), surmounted by the date of foundation of the house (1535).

On the top of the gable, a 17th century weathercock.

The house rests on the next one, above the street, by means of flying buttresses.

In 1535 the *Schiffergesellschaft* grouped the confraternities of St. Nicholas and St. Anne, which were merged after the Reformation.

The *St-Nikolaus-Bruderschaft* was formed on December 26th 1400 to come to the assistance of sea-going persons, merchants and sailors, alive or dead. Prayers were offered, especially, for men of the sea who had perished without having been able to be fortified with the rites of the Church, Confession and the last Sacrament. The confraternity was presided over by four *Olderlude*, two captains and two merchants. Members undertook to say a daily *Pater* and *Ave Maria* for the salvation of the souls of the living and the dead. The confraternity's assets mostly came from legacies in wills.

In 1497 the *St-Annen-Bruderschaft* had founded a chapel at St. James'. Little is known about it but it would seem that it mainly grouped those connected with shipbuilding.

In 1530 the Reformation imposed the dissolution of confraternities. Luther energetically and radically opposed any pious works and indulgences. Bugenhagen, the Reformer who operated in Northern Germany, decided to have finances from pious foundations and confraternities paid into a central account for the poor, *Haupt-Armenkasten*, but that simply ended up by changing religious confraternities into purely laic trade associations.

321. The captains' guild house. After an engraving by Vincent Lerche (1837-1892), at the end of the 19th century.

322. The Eagle (*Adler*), the flag-ship of Lubeck.
Painting of the second half of the 16th century.

323. The Great Hall (*Dielenhalle*) of the guild house.

In the place of the usual Diele, *a large hall the ceiling of which is supported by roughly squared wooden pillars.*
Today it is used as a restaurant. But its arrangement is still as it was originally: big oak benches with their ends sculptured with the coats of arms of the merchants of Bergen, Reval and Riga; rough tables made of ship's planks; woodwork, beams.
The objects are all historical: scale models of ships; Bungen *or drum-shaped lanterns; brass chandeliers.*
The frescoes on the walls should be noted: they concern biblical subjects! The seamen occupied the hall in companies, in Gelagen, *clearly separated. The* Ältermann *kept to the raised rows, the grandfather-chairs (*Beichstuhl*).*

324. Brass ewer and basin. 17th century.

325. Sculpture of a bench. First half of the 17th century.

326. *Hohn- und Spottafel*. 1580.
Two coats of arms.
In the sculptured fronton: the Saviour.

327. Brass chandelier. 1685.

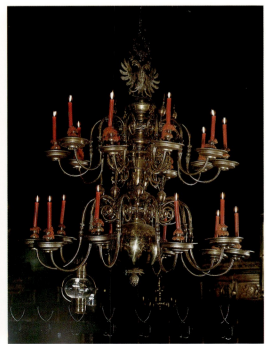

328. Virgin in mandorla. Early 16th century.
329. St. James. Early 16th century.
330. People's sculptures. 1535.

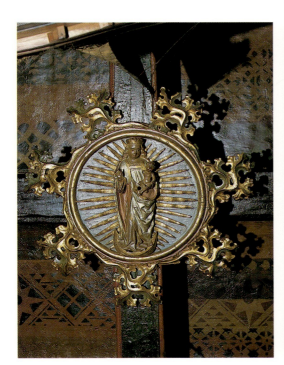

332-333. Salt granaries along the Obertrave. 16th-18th centuries.

In the 16th century these granaries replaced the herringfishers' houses, which had been bought by salt merchants. Later, they were changed into corn granaries and timber warehouses.
The first granary from the left is 1754.
Salt from Luneburg, brought by the Stecknitz boatmen, was stored here for subsequent exportation to the Scandinavian countries.

334. Quays on the Trave at Lubeck.

Houses   Forms and structures of Lubeck houses were closely linked with the original elements dating back to the time when the town was founded. Land was strictly and correctly divided into lengthwise lots. This meant narrow frontages, essentially vertical, and houses which were close up against one another. Fires in 1251 and 1276 led to brick being used as a construction material.

On the ground floor, porches were different but all were high, the doors being topped with imposts. They gave on to a very large entrance hall, a ground floor (*Diele*) which served both as a workshop and as a residence. This was based on the big rooms that were characteristic of farms in Lower Saxony. The *Diele* was lighted by daylight entering through high windows situated on the courtyard side. Its ceiling was generally supported by a richly decorated pillar. There was a room with a glazed window and a fireplace. A gallery gave access to an intermediate floor, made up of *Hangelkammer*. It was furnished with large cupboards, *Schapps* and wooden panelling.

The upper floors were used as a loft and store-house. The stepped gables of the Middle Ages remained general until the 18th century. During the Baroque period, gables began to be covered with rough coats of plaster, and stepped gables were replaced by more flexible forms. During the Renaissance, false Gothic windows were replaced by false round windows such as those that can be seen in the Captains' Guild House.

In the 17th and 18th centuries the merchants, wanting more comfort, converted the intermediate floor with which they had contented themselves until then into a real first floor with large windows, but the entrance hall and the wing giving on to the garden retained their medieval features.

335-339. Medieval facades in Lubeck.

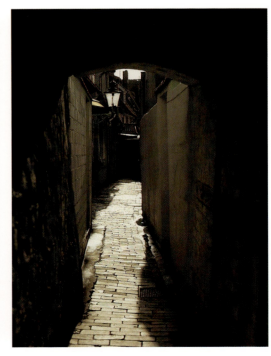

BIBLIOGRAPHY

L. VON WINTERFELD, *Gründung, Markt- und Ratsbildung deutscher Fernhandelsstädte. Untersuchungen zur Frage des Gründerkonsortiums, vornehmlich am Beispiel Lübecks*, in *Westfalen, Hanse Ostseeraum*, Münster, 1955.

B. AM ENDE, *Studien zur Verfassungsgeschichte Lübecks im 12. und 13. Jh.*, Lübeck, 1975.

M. ZMYSLONY, *Die Bruderschaften in Lübeck bis zur Reformation*, Kiel, 1977.

W.-D., HAUSCHILD, *Kirchengeschichte Lübecks. Christentum und Bürgertum in neun Jahrhunderten*, Lübeck, 1981.

W. SPAATZ, *Bernt Nokte und sein Kreis*, Berlin, 1939.

A. VON BRANDT, *Geist und Politik in der lübeckschen Geschichte*, Lübeck, 1954.

ALBERT D'HAENENS

Luneburg

340. Luneburg Town Hall.
On the 9-metre wide double archway on one side of the Gerichtslaube *there is a statuette of Saint Ursula, the patron saint of Luneburg, sculptured by Hinrik Reymers in 1506.*

341. One of two pictures painted circa 1607 by Daniel Frese for the Council Chamber (*Ratsstube*).
Luneburg, Rathaus.

In the foreground: the allegories of the city and its government.
In the background: panorama of Luneburg.
Here and there: patricians.

In the Middle Ages, Luneburg was the Hanse, at least as from 1300.
In 1363 it joined the league of 'welfe' towns, with Brunswick, Hanover, Goslar, Einbeck, Hameln and Helmstedt. In 1371 it joined the Hanse in its own right and played an important part therein. In precedences at the 1418 *Hansetag* it came immediately after Lubeck and Hamburg, and from 1412 to 1619, thirty-six meetings of ths Hanseatic League were held within in its walls.

Its most flourishing period was the second half of the 15th and the first third of the 16th centuries. It was then that its Town Hall was enlarged by the Banqueting Hall, the Chancellery, the Archives room, the *Körkammer*, St. John's church was endowed with its magnificent High Altar, and the *Nikolaikirche* was built to the north of the city between 1407 and 1440. The city was also embellished by some of the finest patrician brick residences.

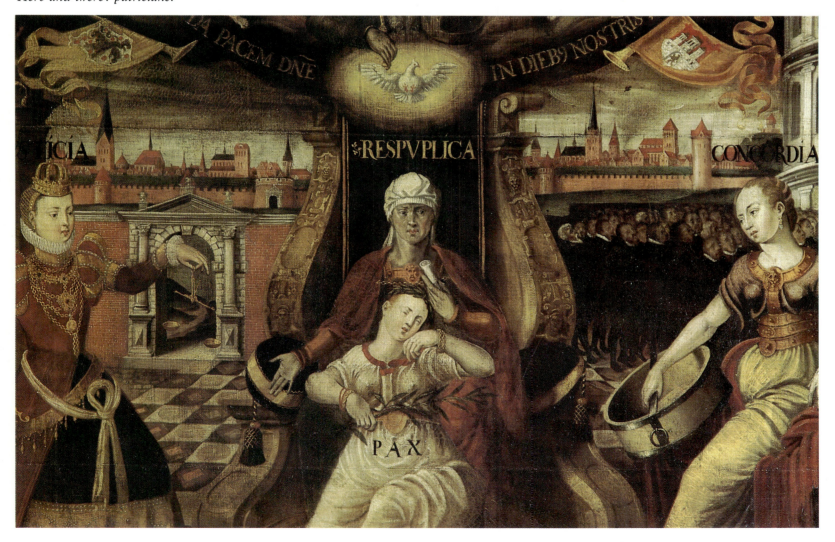

311

CONSTRUCTORS OF URBAN REALITIES

342. Up to the first third of the 14th century, generations of salt carriers had to trans-ship their cargoes to get them to Lubeck.
To overcome that inconvenience and increase the flow of supplies to Lubeck, a waterway was made in stages in the 14th century linking Luneburg and Lubeck. The *Strecknitzfahrt* was completed in 1398.

But Luneburg in ths Middle Ages was also salt: *De Sült dat is Lüneborg*. In Northern Europe it was the capital of salt, one of the principal cargoes in major international trade.
The salt content in the water of the salt-works situated south-west of ths city was close on 26 per cent, whereas that of sea water was 4 to 5 per cent.
The salt-works was already operating in the 10th century: a diploma of Otton I in 956 allocated the tax (*es salinis*) to St. Michael's abbey. In 1205 the various sources were brought together in one sole undertaking, *communis salta*. Until 1231 there were 48 salt-works (*Siederhäuser*), each with four boilers (*Pfannen*). In 1276 there were 54, employing more than five hundred workers and producing about 20,000 tons a year.

At the end of operations of all sorts – exchanges, sales, donations, engagements – which concerned not only the real estate but also the boilers, quarter shares were arrived at, and even 1/24th of boilers. Through transactions in the early 14th century, 53 boilers and a half, and in 1360, 61 boilers and a half, were the property of ecclesiastical communities. Hence the name of *Prelates* which was eventually generally given to the salt-works lords and those who had unearned incomes.
The burghers were interested far more in salt-working than in property: the *Sülfmeister* was the real master of the salt market. So they dominated the city council, they were the real holders of urban power. To enter their select circle which largely favoured endogamy, or the Town Hall which managed the city, it was necessary to be connected with the salt-works and operate with salt in one way or another.

343. Pumping shop at Luneburg salt-works, 1639.
Silk and silver thread embroidery. Diameter: 22 cm.
Luneburg, Museum für das Fürstentum Luneburg.

Bottom: the coat of arms (a sheaf and the initials S.G.) of the Garbers, one of the families operating the salt-works.
*Six workmen (*Sodeskumpane*) working a new pump system (*Solepumpe*).*
It was Georg IV Töbing, Sotmeister *from 1568 to 1571, who developed this system in the summer of 1569.*
Born in 1527, Georg IV Töbing studied at Wittenberg with Luther and Melanchton. Then he made a study trip to the Southern Low Countries. He spent some time in Louvain and its university. He brought back a globe probably made by Gérard Mercator and at present kept in Luneburg museum.

344. Boiler tub (*Siedepfanne*). End of 18th century.
Lead. About 100 cm × 12 cm.
Luneburg, Museum für das Fürstentum Luneburg.

It was in this recipient, the only one still preserved, that the salt water concentrate was brought to boiling point.
*Each workshop (*Siedehaus*) had four of them.*

345. A pickling brine (*Sole*) pumping station at Luneburg salt-works. 1595.
Drawing taken from the *Bilderchronik der Stadt* Luneburg of 1595.
It is a copy of one of the four pictures that decorated the administrators' room (*Küntje*), on the first floor of the house of the Source (*Brunnenhaus*) at Luneburg salt-works.
It reads: *Abconterfei wie für alten Zeiten die Sale auff der alten Sültzen aus dem Sode von den Soedess Cumpanen is gezogen worden.*
Luneburg, Museum für des Fürstentum Luneburg.

*We see the pickling brine being pumped. It is discharged into a conduit (*Rinne*) which carries it to the various workshops (*Siedehäuser*). A burgher wearing a hat and ruff, no doubt the manager (*Obersegger*), enters the number of discharges in a register.*

346. The *Kalkröse* at Luneburg Kalkberg. 1592.
Painting on canvas. Perhaps by Daniel Frese.
Luneburg. Museum für das Fürstentum Luneburg.

However, the salt-works was not the only centre of industrial activity in Luneburg, there was also the Kaklberg plaster quarry, which ended up by having rights over almost the whole of the hill (about two million cubic metres) at the foot of which it carried out its activities.

A 1592 painting, which may well have been the work of Daniel Frese, the brilliant and prolific decorator of the Town Hall, provides a remarkable description of technical information and life.

Several towers mark the horizon of the quarry: the New Tower (left), the deposits control tower, the white tower and the spire of St. Lambert's.

In several places, workmen are seen clearing blocks. The latter were broken up into small pieces and then carried in carts and wheelbarrows to the foot of an enormous millstone, the base of which consisted of faggots. Using wicker baskets, women passed the broken stones along to two workmen who placed them at the top of the cone, around a chimney stack. When firing was finished, plaster was obtained which went into mortar and stucco.

Luneburg was undoubtedly an industrial capital in the Middle Ages, as it was in the 16th century. It was not by chance that several paintings and drawings dating from the end of the 16th century were preserved. They provide evidence, rare for that time and of exceptional documentary value, in the matter of industrial archeology. They bear witness to the imaginative quality of the people of Luneburg, the equivalent of which was not found elsewhere in the West before the 19th industrial century.

CONSTRUCTORS OF URBAN REALITIES

347. Baroque facade, 1706.

In 1706 the town instructed its Stadtbaumeister, Georg Schults, to replace the Renaissance facade of the Town Hall by a Baroque frontage.
The Gothic base, with its arcades, subsisted. The five turrets were replaced by pillars surmounted by allegorical figures. A Mansart style roof and a belfry rounded off the work.

348. Isometric reconstitution of the Rathaus evolution phases.
After Urs Boeck and Fritz von Osterhausen.

1. *First Town Hall, circa 1230.*
2. *The Holy Ghost hospital: 1254 (?).*
3. *Chapel of the Town Hall zum Heiligen Geist (circa 1287).*
4. *Cloth-hall, circa 1300.*
5. *New Town Hall (novum consistorium) Later, court-room.*
6. *Wine cellar (Ratsweinkeller): 1328.*
7. *Weight (Ratswaage): 1367.*
8. *Enlargement of the Ratskapelle (1402-1414).*
8. *Market justice (Niedergericht): 1389.*
9. *Room connecting the 13th and 14th century Town Halls: 1408-1411.*
10. *Marienplatz rooms (Kammereigebäude) 1478-1481.*
11. *The Neues Rathaus: 1564-1567.*
12. *The Syndic's house: 16th century.*
13. *Liaison between the Kammereigebäude and the Neues Rathaus.*
14. *Huldigungssaal – und Traubensaal: 1702-1706.*
15. *City archives (Stadtarchiv): 1899.*

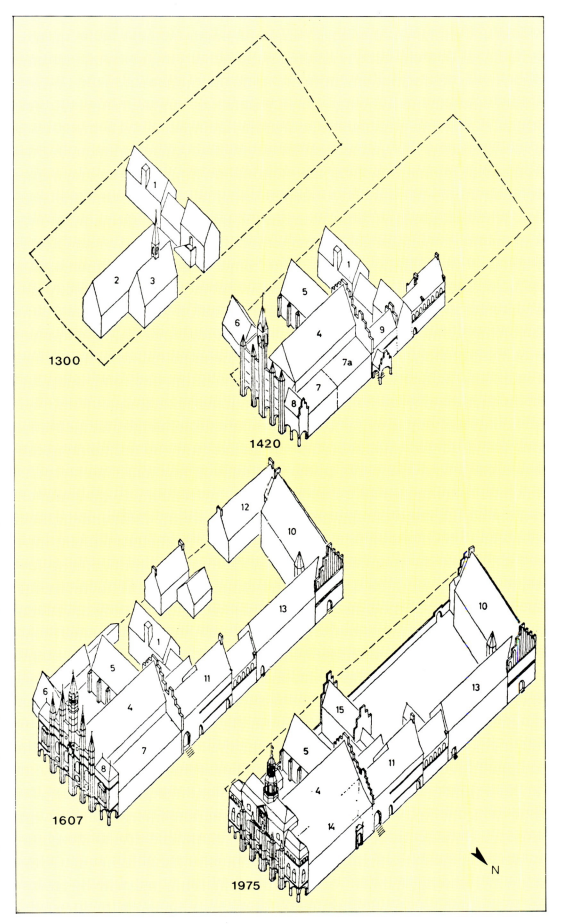

CONSTRUCTORS OF URBAN REALITIES

The Town Hall   It was probably Henry the Lion who gave Luneburg its municipal regulations after the destruction of Bardowick (1189).

The city council was made up of twenty-four members (*consules*). Until 1294 it had to accept the right of oversight of the ducal magistrate (*Vogt*), but after that date the *Rate*, the emanation of the powerful burgher families, either owners or operators of the salt-works, was able to devote itself entirely to consolidating the interests of the city. Power was now in its hands. It was from the narrow, select patriciate of the *Sülfmeister* that burgomasters and members of the council were selected.

349. At the bottom of the grand staircase leading to the *Fürstensaal*: the figures of Law and Peace.

On its left, access to the former cloth-hall (Gewandhaus), above which is the Fürstensaal. And, by a Gothic doorway, to the court-room (Gerichtslaube).
It was Daniel Frese, of Luneburg, who in 1606 painted the pictures at the top of the stairs.

350. The Gothic door on the left of the grand staircase beside the one leading to the cloth-hall. It opens on to the court-room, the *Gerichtslaube*.

351. One of the fireplaces and perforated partition-wall of the *Fürstensaal*.

352. One of the five chandeliers of the *Fürstensaal*.

They are by Heinrich Reymers. 1500-1502. Wrought iron, stag antlers and wooden statuette (here, St. George).
Ceiling decoration painted by Daniel Frese (1607): 150 portraits of Roman and German emperors.

353. Ceilings and walls painted by Daniel Frese. Shortly after 1600.

Gallery of the members of the House of Brunswick-Luneburg.
Two views of Luneburg: one taken from the north, the other from the west.

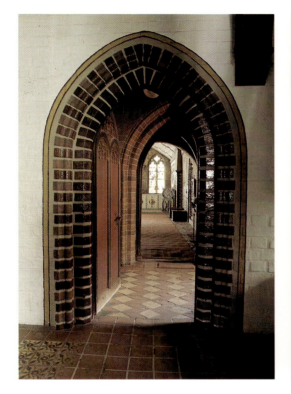

354. The southern side of the *Gerichtslaube*.

355. Cradle decoration. 1529.

356-357. Heating.

A system of ceramic piping, already mentioned in 1386/87, brought in hot air from the stove in the cellar to the feet of the members of the Council. The lid of the hot-air vent was taken off and the vent covered by the person's cloak or gown.

358. The northern side.

The courtroom (*Gerichtslaube*) was built between 1330 and 1350.
A hundred years later, a stained glass window that was unique of its kind was placed in the south wall; it was the most refined and grandiose to be found in any secular building in the western Middle Ages.
Nine figures of princes represented the exercise of earthly justice: David, Judas Maccabaeus, Joshua, Godefroid de Bouillon, Charlemagne, Arthur, Julius Caesar, Alexander and Hector.
The north wall consisted of a double asymmetrical arcade, above which figured, in counterpoint to the windows, a 1495 fresco representing Christ the day of the Last Judgment.

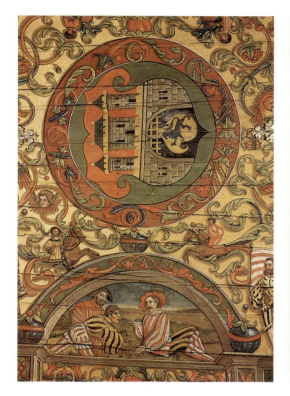

The cradle-ceiling of the courtroom (*Gerichtslaube*) (4 × 20 m) was made of wood.
It was decorated (1529) with scenes attributed to Marten Jaster and patterned on engravings (Burgkmair, Baldung, Gien and Schaüffelein) illustrating a 1523 edition of Livy's *Roman History*.
From then on, *Auctoritas*, the authority on the basis of which justice was exercised, was no longer founded on biblical, testamentary references or religious history but, in the spirit of the Renaissance and Humanism, on examples of Roman Antiquity.

Cupboards were built into the walls for the archives.
Between the windows there were three cupboards (*Schenkeschieven*) dating from 1487, 1474 and 1521, the last being sculptured by Heinrick Reymers. These pieces of furniture, among the finest accomplishments of medieval craftsmanship, contained the silver table-service that was brought out on special occasions.

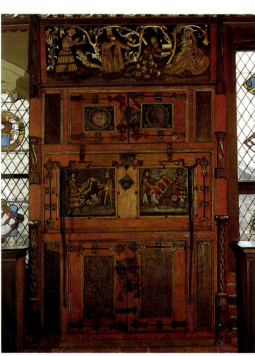

The main Council Chamber (*Grosse Ratsstube*) was preceded by the chamber of the Councillor's civil servants (*Dienergemach*).

The *Grosse Ratsstube* was decorated and furnished in some twenty years (between 1566 and 1584) by four master craftsmen. The Council's joiner, Gert Suttmeier, designed the panels, the doors and the *Ratsstuhl*. The allegorical paintings were by Daniel Frese. The painted, coffered ceiling was by Peter up dem Borne, the sculptures by Albert von Soest.

The subject matters originate from the Reformation and Humanism. They were intended to inspire the Councillors in the exercise of their duties and their office.

366. Self-portrait (?) of Albert von Soest (1566-1584), the woodwork sculptor of the Council Chamber.

367. Entrance door of the *Grosse Ratsstube*.

368-372. Parts of sculptures by Albert von Soest for the *Grosse Ratsstube* of Luneburg Town Hall. The sculptor is seen therein.

373-374. The crane (*alter Kran*).
Mentioned for the first time in 1346, rebuilt in 1482, changed in 1537 and renewed in 1797.
Wheel diameter: 5 m.
Height: 12 m.
Jib length: 10 m.
It was still in use on August 13, 1840, to hoist to the ground one of the first English locomotives for Germany.

375. The crane and the *Kaufhaus*.
Facade, 1741-1745, by the city architect, Haeseler.

376-378. The port of Luneburg and its surroundings.

CONSTRUCTORS OF URBAN REALITIES

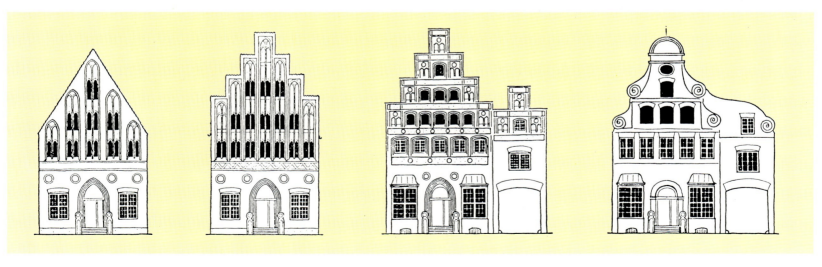

Houses

The earliest mention of a brick-works in Luneburg dates from 1282, the time when they began building brick houses. Before then they had been made of *Fachwerkbau*, in which stones, which were abundant in the region, were used. So at the end of the 13th century the town took on a different aspect. True, it had just begun to commit itself avowedly to trading with Lubeck. In future, bricks were to be used systematically not only for public buildings but also for the facades of private constructions. Here, as elsewhere in Northern Germany, the traditional type so widespread in Lower Saxony dominated. On the ground floor was a vast hall, the *Diele*, which was initially without dividing walls. Serving as a workshop, business house and living room, it was made up of two unequal parts; the hearth and chimney were situated in the middle of the narrow part.

On the first floor was the *Lucht*, which originally served as a store-room. From the 16th century, living rooms were made of it.

There was also a store-room above the *Lucht*, under the roof. The goods to be stored were hauled up the outside with a pulley attached to the gable-end.

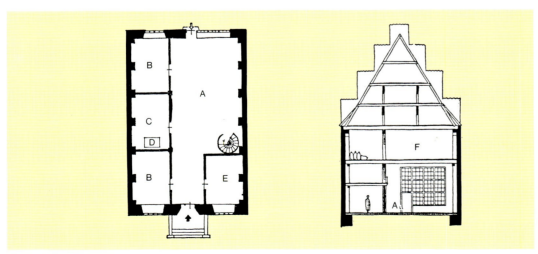

Plan of a citizen's house at Luneburg.
A: *Diele*; B: room; C: kitchen; D: hearth; E: front room; F: *Lucht*.

CONSTRUCTORS OF URBAN REALITIES

St. John's church   Of Luneburg's three medieval churches, the one dedicated to St. John was undoubtedly the most imposing, with its five naves and a tower that was more than 100 metres high.
It was a hall-church. In the Middle Ages it had 39 altars and was served by a hundred priests.

387. Votive painting, 16th century.

386. Luminary with Virgin in mandorla. Circa 1490.

387. Interior of St. John's Church. In the foreground, a luminary which originally lighted the chancel. 1667.

It was begun in 1289-1308 on the site of a sanctuary which dated from 1174. It was modelled on Magdeburg, Schleswig and Verden cathedrals and the *Marienkirche* in Lubeck, and was completed about 1400.
In 1457-1463 a tribune for the city council (*Ratslektor*) was erected above the vestry.

388. Font by Master Ulricus. Circa 1325.

CONSTRUCTORS OF URBAN REALITIES

Lune abbey   Originally a hermitage (1140) and then a chapter for canonesses (circa 1170), Lune adopted Benedictine rule in the 13th century.
In 1372 it experienced a crisis, after which it was moved nearer to the town (1373).
The community then entered a period of prosperity corresponding to that of the town, which was now a member of the Hanseatic League.
Its red brick buildings, and its rich furniture which is still in place, provide an astonishing idea of what a nun's convent was like in the 15th and 16th centuries, both in symbiosis and on the fringe of the Hanse.
For several generations, Luneburg patricians and merchants heaped kindness upon this community of women among whom were more than one of their daughters.

390-391. Vestibule. Early 15th century. Baroque staircase. Early 18th century.

389. Cloister wing. 1372-1412.

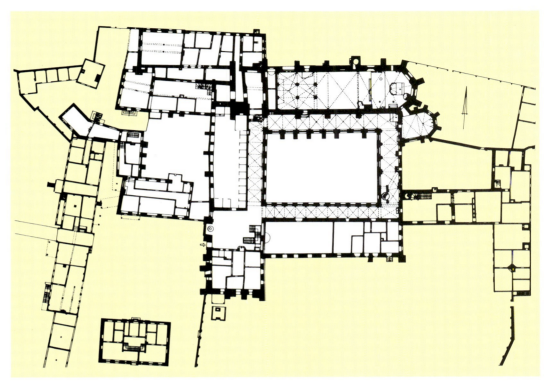

392. Plan of Lune abbey.

393. Gothic fountain in the vestibule. Early 15th century.

394. Parts of 17th century stained glass in a cloister window.

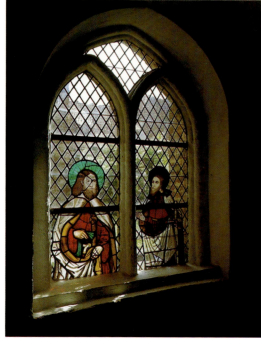

395. The nuns' chancel.
Early 16th century altar.
Baroque organ, 1645.
Pulpit, 1608.

396. Choir screen.
In the foreground: bell ropes.

397-398. Wooden tabernacle. First half of 15th century.

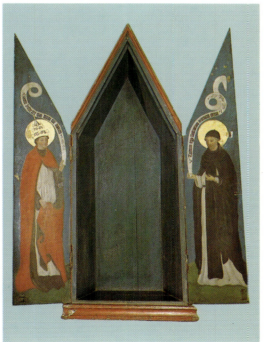

ALBERT D'HAENENS

Bremen

399. The *Schütting, Gewerbehaus* or *Kauffmans Haus*.

The Schütting was built in 1619-1620 by Johann Nacke (deceased 1620) for the cloth merchants' guild. It was a semi-detached house with two entraces.
It was in 1862 that this door was transferred to the place where it stands today and the smaller of the two doors was removed. The portal sculptures are by Nacke's successor, Ernst Krossmann.

400. The market square.
On the left, the *Schütting*.
Engraving. 17th century.
Paris, National Library.

It was Ansgar (deceased 845), a missionary trained in Torhout, in maritime Flanders, who founded an archbishop's palace in Bremen, replacing the Hamburg one destroyed by Vikings in 845. Rimbert (deceased 888), another cleric from the Torhout seminary which trained the Northern evangelists, reports it in his *Vita Ansgarii*, a biographical text that abounds in information about the Baltic and Scandinavia in the 9th century.

So Bremen became a centre for the christianization of the North and the Viking regions.

Its cathedral was at the origin of the town's evolution. Ramparts were built and on them were grafted a suburb and a market; the population organized itself into an urban community around 1167.

The port was situated on the southern side of the market, along one of the arms of the Weser.

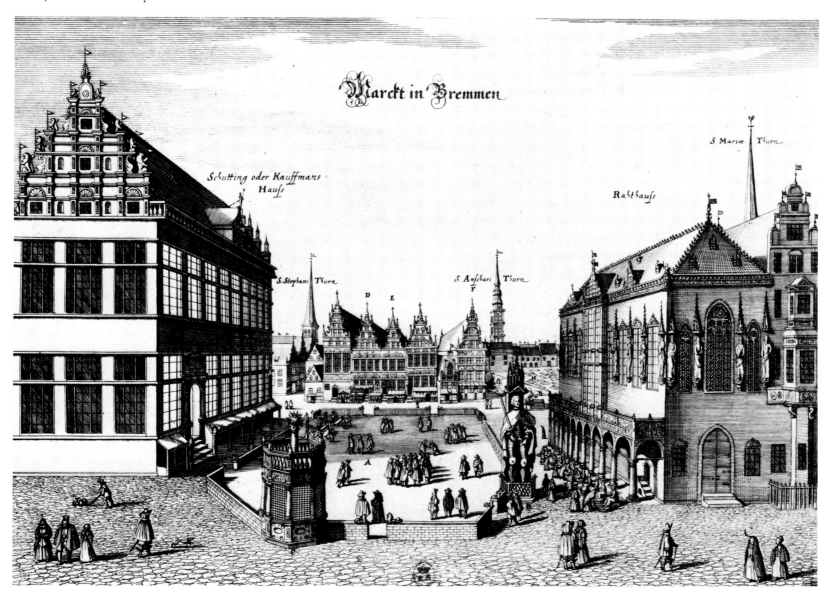

CONSTRUCTORS OF URBAN REALITIES

Bremen and the Hanse

"Situated outside of the group, in an area that was poor in Hanseatic towns... the big archiepiscopal city which was to be known in modern times as a *Hanseatic free town*, appeared to be singularly intractable.

"It was excluded from the community three times: in 1285, 1427 and 1563. The first time, it seems, was for more than seventy years, a unique case.

"The prosperity of Bremen was in fact founded less on the carriage of goods between East and West than on active relations from the 11th century onwards with Norway, England and the Northern Low Countries, as well as with the Weser hinterland, Saxony and part of Westphalia." [Philippe Dollinger]

402. Roland, on the Market. 1404.
It is the oldest and biggest Roland (more than 5 m tall).

The Market-place

On the market-place stood the Town Hall, the Merchants' House (*Schütting*) which was called *Mercatores Imperii*, the tower of Notre-Dame... and a Roland.

"In front of the *Rathaus*, he stands guard as solemnly as Roland of Verona at the cathedral door, or as the Roland at the door of Chartres cathedral. The Bremen Roland, by his strength, guarantees the freedom and the right to justice which Charlemagne, according to tradition, had been good enough to grant the town. In his legend Charlemagne is not only the warrior emperor, he is also the legislator, the source of right. It is he who organizes the minting of sterling money, decides weights and measures and guarantees... a series of basic liberties...

"In the entourage of Charles, the guardian of right... is Roland who, on every occasion, appears as the 'destre bras', the depositary of the thoughts and wishes of the sovereign, he who bears the glaive of the emperor, the symbol of justice, right and power." [Jacques Stiennon and Rita Lejeune]

403. Wedding procession on the market place. Circa 1620.
Anonymous painting. Bremen Landesmuseum.

CONSTRUCTORS OF URBAN REALITIES

The Town Hall   The *Rathaus* is mentioned in 1229 as *Domus teatralis*, and in 1251 as *domus consulum*. Master John, who rebuilt it in 1405-1410, is represented in the north corner of the edifice. Lüder von Bentheim (deceased 1613) gave it its present aspect in 1595.
To the north, the *Neues Rathaus* was built from 1909 to 1913 on the site where, on the immunity of the cathedral Archbishop Giselbert had built a *palatium* in place of a former construction that was destroyed by fire during the 1275 riots.

404. The Town Hall. 1405-1410.

405. Untere Rathaushalle. 1405-1410.
It is the original trading hall on the ground floor of the Town Hall.

Two storeys, glazed brick, alternately red and black.
Facade richly decorated with sculptures.
On the ground floor, eleven archways on the market side. In the roof, three frontons, with the middle one corresponding to the *Güldenkammer*. Between the windows: statues of the Emperor and the Palatine Princes. A balustrade completes the picture.
Two halls on the ground floor: the *Untere Rathaushalle*, which was the merchant hall until the 19th century, and the *Obere Rathaushalle*, the city banqueting hall.

406. Reliefs on the facade of the Town Hall. Early 17th century.
Inspired by engravings of the time (Goltzius in particular), they represent themes of Antiquity and a number of allegories (wisdom or the trading and intellectual virtues, for instance).

407-408. Wooden sculptures in the Town Hall. 17th century.

409-410. Sculptured and painted doors of the *Oberen Halle*. 17th century. They lead to various rooms.

BIBLIOGRAPHY

H. SCHWARZWÄLDER, *Geschichte der Freien Hansestadt Bremen*. vol. 1: *Von den Anfängen bis zur Franzosenzeit (1810)*, Bremen, 1975.

H. SCHWARZWÄLDER, *Bremens Aufnahme in die Hanse 1358 in neuer Sicht*, in Hansische Geschichtsblätter, 79, 1961, p. 58-79.

E. THIKÖTTER, *Die Zünfte Bremens in Mittelalter*, Bremen, 1930.

R. STEIN, *Das Bürgerhaus in Bremen*, Tübingen, 1970.

W. LÜHRS, *Der Domshof. Geschichte eines bremischen Platzes*, Bremen, 1979.

K.-P. KIEDEL, U. SCHNALL, *Die Hanse-Kogge von 1380. Geschichte, Fund, Bergung, Wiederaufbau und Konservierung*, Bremen, 1982 (Förderverein Deutsches Schiffhartsmuseum Bremerhaven).

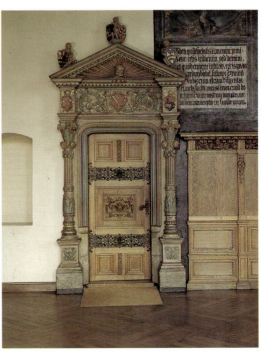

ALBERT D'HAENENS

Goslar

Goslar appeared as a member of the Hanse in 1267-1268.

The Harz copper and silver mines, and particularly those of Rammelberg, animated the urban economy, especially as from the late 13th century. In 1290 the town obtained autonomy and its guilds were directly associated with mining operations.

In 1330 Goslar codified its laws. In 1340 it was recognized by the Emperor as an imperial free town (Freie Reichsstadt). In 1359 it received the tithe of the mines in pledge.

About 1450 the discovery of new deposits revitalized the urban economy. The peak came about 1520: 26 pits, 19 mines, and a beer, the *Gose*, which was exported far afield. So the town fitted out its ramparts and gates luxuriously, whilst merchants and craftsmen installed imposing guild houses.

In 1552, however, Goslar had to assign the mine tithes to the Duke of Brunswick. From then on, recession threatened; it was, unfortunately, irremediable.

411. Founder, in the *Huldigungssaal*. Early 16th century.

412. The Town Hall.
Part of the painted decoration of the *Huldigungssaal* or *Ratsheerstube* of the Town Hall. Early 16th century.

The Market-place

In the centre of the *Markplatz* stood a 13th century fountain formed by two bronze basins surmounted by the imperial golden eagle. On the west side was the Town Hall, the ground floor of which served for merchants and the lower court of justice (*Niedergericht*). On the south side was the *Kaiserworth*, the house of the Drapers' Guild. Its facade, with a balcony forming a turret, was ornamented with the statues of eight emperors. On the corbels were sculptured designs patterned on the spirit of the Renaissance, and particularly Hercules and Abundance, surmounting a man of money (*Dukatenmännchen*). Here again the central urban space was shared equally between the church, dedicated to Cosmas and Damian, and the Town Hall and market.

413. The market square and Town Hall. 15th and 16th centuries.

414. The trading hall on the ground floor of the Town Hall.

415. The Kaiserworth, on the Marktplatz.

416. South facade of the Town Hall. The staircase (1537) leads to the Council Chamber (*Ratslaube*).

The Town Hall

The first Town Hall dated back to the 12th century, at which time Goslar acceded to urban status.

At the end of the century a meeting-room for the burghers was built on a vaulted ground floor (*lobium fori*, 1186) giving on to the market place and used by merchants.

In the middle of the 15th century that construction was replaced by the present 2-storey, 5-arched building.

On the ground floor, opening on to the market-place, were the merchant hall and the justice hall. The pillory (Pranger) and the Goslar ell were placed between the fourth and fifth arch, in front of a blind wall.

An outside staircase was added to the south facade in 1537 to give access to the first floor, to the *Senatorenzimmer*. Access to the vaulted cellars was close to that staircase.

The vaulted council chamber (Ratssaal) was on the first floor. A late 15th century fresco on the walls represents the Last Judgment.

417. The *Ratsherrenstube* or *Huldigungssaal*.
Wooden walls decorated with paintings. Early 16th century.

418-419. Painted panelled ceiling in the *Huldigungssaal*.

420. Founder and the Virgin, in the *Huldigungssaal*.
Early 16th century.

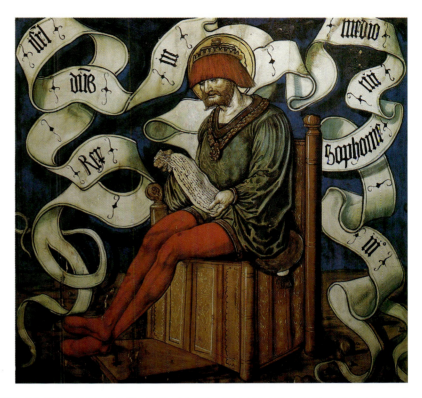

CONSTRUCTORS OF URBAN REALITIES

The walls and ceiling of the *Ratsherrenstube* or *Huldingungsaal*, built circa 1500, are decorated with early 16th century paintings on wood, of exceptional beauty and freshness. They illustrate the Incarnation of Christ, by persons dressed as Renaissance burghers.
There are four scenes on the ceiling of the Youth of Christ or the Life of the Virgin: the Annunciation, the Nativity, the Adoration of the Three Magi, and the Presentation at the Temple. They are surrounded by the four evangelists and the twelve prophets.
On the walls, decorated with blind archways sculptured in wood by Hans Smet and Heinrich Marborg, are twelve Sibylles alternating with eleven emperors, Justice, the Madonna and the Donor.

In the East wall there is a chapel dedicated to the Trinity (1505). It is reached by opening two panels. There are scenes from the Passion and the Death of Christ and the Last Judgment (on the ceiling).

421. The east wall of the Huldigungssaal.
Here, too, alternating Sibylles and emperors.

422. The Virgin, in the *Huldigungssaal* of Goslar Town Hall.

423. Christ, the Last Judgment.
Fresco decorating the ceiling of the *Huldigungsaal* chapel.
Early 16th century.
Goslar Town Hall.

Against an azure and clouds background, Christ invites humanity to join him: Venite. He is nimbed with the lily of purity and the glaive of justice.

424. In the east wall a door opens on to the chapel of the Trinity.

On the left: the man of sorrow.
On the right: Mater dolorosa.

CONSTRUCTORS OF URBAN REALITIES

The Alms-houses

In 1254 the lawyer Dietrich von Sulinge founded the *Grosse Heiliges Kreuz*, originally dedicated to Saint John the Baptist and called the *Grote Gasthus*. The urban bourgeoisie took the foundation in hand and invested it a rival to the alms-house founded at the same time by the Teutonic Order.

The St. Anne alms-house was set up in 1488-1494 by the Geismar family, who dedicated it to Anne and Gertrude. It is a typical example of a medieval alms-house, with two levels giving on to the chapel.

425. The hospital *Zum Grossen Hl. Kreuz*, founded in 1254.

426. St. Anne's chapel.

427. Vestibule of *St.-Annen-Stift*. End of 17th century.

On the right: chapel door.
On the left: staircase to first floor.

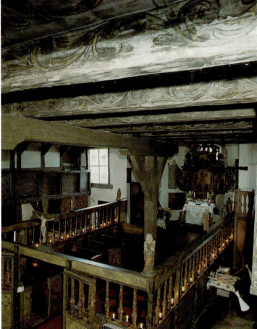

GOSLAR

351

ALBERT D'HAENENS

Stralsund

After Lubeck, Stralsund was the most important Hanseatic town on the Baltic. It already existed in the early 13th century and acquired the freedom of the city in 1234.

Its extension was rapid and impressive, for its situation on land and sea was particularly favourable. So by the end of the 13th century it had attained a structure which was to last till the 19th century.

After 1249, following aggression by Lubeck, and uneasy about such a go-ahead and enterprising rival, the town built ramparts round itself. It was destroyed by fire in 1271 and from then on endeavoured to build in brick. Stralsund successfully defended itself against the Danish invader in 1316. Its peak came in the second half of the 14th century. Its decline began around 1500.

Stralsund thrived on overseas trade. It exported farm produce, fish and beer. It imported Scandinavian ores, English and Flemish cloth and Russian furs. Its fleet consisted of more than three hundred ships in the second half of the 14th century, so it is not surprising that it was a big shipbuilding centre, especially as the wooded surroundings supplied it with abundant raw materials. The oldest of the town's books, which covers 1270 to 1310, mentions several *Botmaker*. Thirteen shipyards are mentioned in 1393, and twenty-one in 1428.

428. The port and the town.
Part of a pen-and-ink water colour. Anonymous. Mid-16th century.
Stralsund, Stadtarchiv.

429. Stralsund seen from the Baltic.

430. The old port.

431-432. The Town Hall. After 1440.

On the ground floor: the hall.
Above the windows on the first floor: the coats of arms of Hamburg, Lubeck, Wismar, Rostock, Stralsund and Greifswald.
Above the floors, a purely decorative facade with three registers surmounted by frontons, inspired by those of Lubeck Town Hall.

In the 14th and 15th centuries, Stralsund also imported Western works of art; its craftsmanship in that field did not develop until the late 15th century. It imported sculptured stalls and retables, statues, paintings, stained glass windows and tombstones from Flanders, Brabant, Bruges and Antwerp, mainly and first of all for its own churches with innumerable altars.
In 1564 one of its burgomasters, Franz Wessel, counted over two hundred, of which 56 were in Saint Nicolas' church, 44 in Notre-Dame and 30 in St. James'.
Still today, the main part of the rich furniture in St. Nicolas' is the product of those imports.

The Town Hall Stralsund *Rathaus* is one of the finest laic brick buildings in North Germany. It made a pair with St. Nicholas' church; here too both shared the central urban space.

On the first floor there was space for official state display; the ground floor was a commercial centre and hall. The original core, which dates back to the 13th century, consists of two bodies of parallel buildings aligned round a narrow inner courtyard. A passage between them leads to the west portal of St. Nicholas' church. The whole building is surmounted on the market-place side by a purely decorative facade placed after 1450. Lubeck Town Hall obviously served as a model.

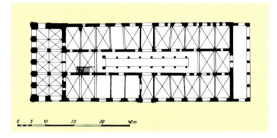

CONSTRUCTORS OF URBAN REALITIES

Saint Nicholas' church

433. St. Nicolas.
End of row decoration. Detail.
15th century.

434. The door to the Archives.
Second quarter of the 14th century. Detail.

435. Retable of the Bergenfahrer. Circa 1500.

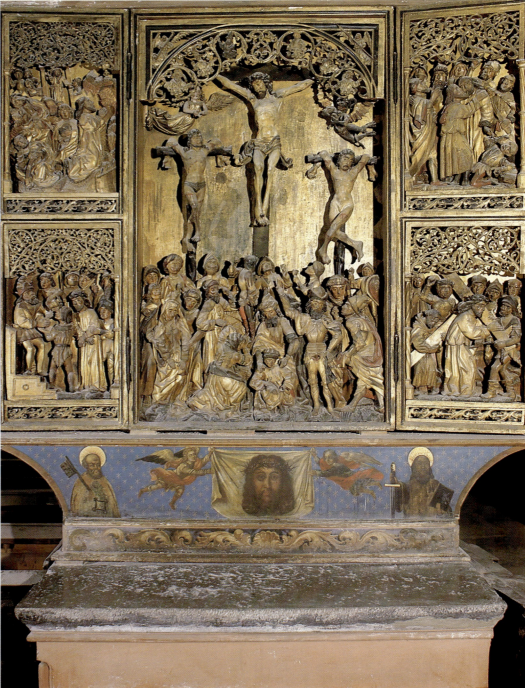

436. Plan and drawing of the St. Nicholas' after Günther Binding.

437. Epitaph by Heinrich Schwerin (deceased 1602). *Stadthauptmann*. Painted in 1591.

438. Tombstone of Burgomaster Albert Hovener (deceased 1357). Detail. Flemish studio.

439. Tombstone of Burgomaster Joachim Klokow (deceased 1601) and his wife.

The *Nikolaikirche* was the church of the *Rat*, which attended divine service, and held important meetings and negotiations there. It formed a monumental whole with the Town Hall, expressing the power and conscience of a young, go-ahead town. Initially, before 1260, St. Nicholas' was designed as a hall-church; then in 1270, on the model of a Gothic cathedral with an ambulatory, following the example of Lubeck, of which it was an original replica. St. Nicholas' was the church of the patricians. Like Notre-Dame in Lubeck, it was their pantheon, as is evidenced by the altars, the stalls (in particular those of the *Novgorodfahrer*, the Town Council, the gold and silver smiths and landowners), and the numerous votive monuments.

440–441. St. Catherine's.
West facade. First quarter of the 14th century.

Church of the Dominican convent that was founded in 1251. 73 m long, it is one of the most imposing Backsteingothik hall-churches. Built in the early 14th century, it formed part of one of the biggest Baltic conventual complexes; the community buildings date from the early 15th century.

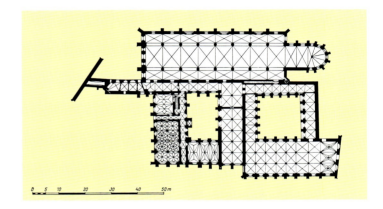

442–443. Notre-Dame. Second half of the 14th century.

The tower collapsed in 1382, no doubt because of the spongy soil. It crushed the nave and chancel.
Work on rebuilding the main western part in 1416. The spire was 150 m high but was burnt down in 1647. It was replaced by a Baroque structure in 1708.
It is one of the most imposing and original accomplishments in the Baltic in the late Middle Ages.
It was built at the expense of the Corporation of Cloth Merchants, which was at loggerheads with the patricians of the City Council. The church had to outdo the Nikolaikirche.

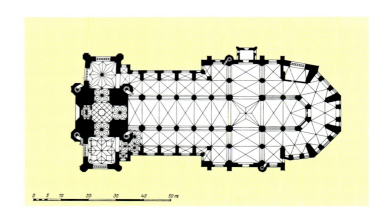

CONSTRUCTORS OF URBAN REALITIES

The Houses Most of the houses of the patricians and merchants were made of brick, especially after the fire of 1271.

The structure of these big residences hardly varied over the centuries, up to and including the Baroque period. The form of land apportionment and the continuance of functions contributed a lot thereto.

Everything turned around the *Hausbaum*, a large, slightly out of centre beam on which the first floor, loft and roof were hinged.

The ground floor was divided into two unequal parts.

The narrower part was occupied by the *Döns*, the front room of which gave

444–446. House in the Frankenstrasse, No. 28.
Facade, restored, 14th century. Vestibule (*Diele*) 1687.

on to the street, and a kitchen with a chimney (*Rauchfung*). The bedrooms and other rooms were on the first floor.

The *Diele* occupied a larger space and took in the two floors in height. It was the principal space, used for both family and business life.

The street door, in the middle of the frontage, gave directly on to the *Diele*, because of the slight decentring of the bearer beam.

Goods came in through the *Diele* and from there they were hoisted up to the loft, which was generally very spacious, by a pulley fastened to the roof. The impressive size of the gables gives an idea of the extent of the storage space.

447. Wulflamhaus, Markt No. 5, 15th century.

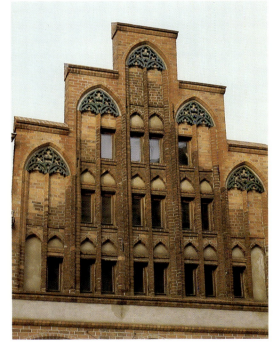

448-449. Houses on the old market place.

BIBLIOGRAPHY

H. EWE, *Stralsund*, Rostock, 1981.

H. TROST, *Stralsund*, Leipzig, 1973.

K. FRITZE, *Stralsunds Bevölkerung um 1400*, in *Greifswald-Stralsunder Jahrbuch*, 6, 1966, P. 15-28.

N. ZASKE, *Die gotischen Kirchen Stralsunds und ihre Kunstwerke. Kirchliche Kunstgeschichte von 1250 bis zu Gegenwart*, Berlin, 1964.

K. BLASKHE, *Nikolaikirchen und Stadtenstehung im pommerschen Raum*, in *Greifswald-Stralsunder Jahrbuch*, 9, 1970-1971, 21 p.

H. EWE, *Schätze einer Ostseerstadt. Sieben Jahrhunderte im Stralsunder* Staatarchiv, Weimar, 1974.

450. No. 40, Badenstrasse. Second half of the 15th century.

451. No. 21, Mühlenstrasse. Second half of the 15th century.

452. Part of a house built in 1750.

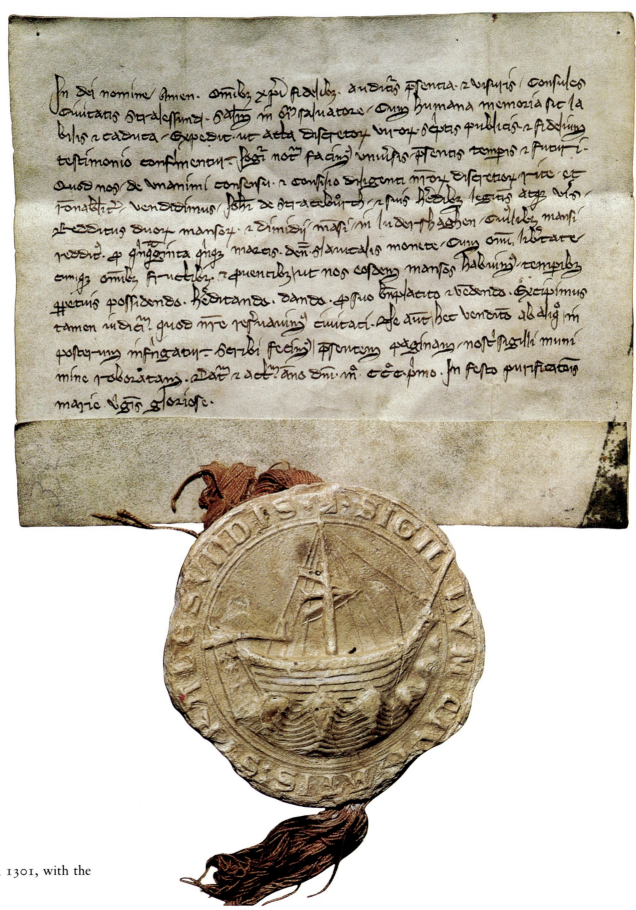

453. Charter of February 2, 1301, with the seal of Stralsund.
Stralsund, Stadtarchiv.

ALBERT D'HAENENS

Torun

It was the Teutonic Knights who undertook the rural and urban colonization of Prussia. They invited settlers from Silesia, from Central Germany, of which many of them were natives, and, later on, also from Northern Germany.

And so, on the right bank of the Vistula they founded Torun and Chelmo, under the protection of a castle. In 1233, Hermann de Salza granted the inhabitants of both towns a statute, on which other Prussian towns were subsequently patterned. The burghers obtained part of the income from legal proceedings, the urban right of Madgeburg and some administrative autonomy, but the Order remained master of the fortifications and insisted on very hard military service.

The Old Town – as opposed to the New Town founded in 1264 – was essentially commercial in nature. The New Town, aside from the river, was an artisanal, cloth and brewery centre. They had their own surrounding walls and institutions and were connected by a thoroughfare which ran W-E, parallel with the Vistula. Both were designed on an identical model: a regular chess-board plan; an empty quadrilateral in the centre, with the Town Hall and the town church on the sides.

In the 14th century, Torun was a member of the Hanse and, after Danzig, the most important Prussian town.

454. Corn granaries, Pickarystreet, at Torun.

The granary at left was built 1370; the one on the right date from the beginning of the 17th century.

455. Torun at the 17th century.
Part of an engraving.
Torun, Town Hall Museum.

CONSTRUCTORS OF URBAN REALITIES

The Teutonic Order

456. The ruins of the castle of the Teutonic Order.

In 1440 the burghers of Torun banded together against the Knights and headed a league of Prussian towns against the Order. They chased the latter out of their town in 1454. Only the ruins of the Teutonic castle remain; excavation and restoration work on them was begun in 1958.

The Knights had big commercial interests in Prussia.

As a rule, nuns could not give themselves to commercial traffic; canon law was explicit on that subject. But in 1257 the Teutonics obtained a privilege from Alexander IV which freed them from that interdict.

The Order did not limit itself to operating with corn from the quit-rents and tithes it received. It went out and bought corn with which to trade, and it claimed a priority right so as to be able to buy grain at a low price in the autumn. After it had dried out in its granaries, it was sold to the West in the Spring.

It disposed of 40,000 tonnes in this way in 1400.

TORUN

The Order, which had become a member of the Hanse, endeavoured to develop its role as an intermediatery between Eastern Europe anf Flanders. At the end of the 14th and beginning of the 15th centuries, it "comprised two big treasurerships, one at Mariemburg and one at Königsberg. Under them came representatives, generally remunerated annually, in Bruges, London, Scotland, Lubeck, Danzig and Riga, with full powers to take delivery of goods, sell them at the best price, buy goods and ship them. Liaison was ensured by clerks who accompanied the cargoes, bought for the account of the Order and were also authorized to undertake transactions for their own account." [Philippe Dollinger]

457. The Seamen's Gate (*Zeglarska*) in Torun.
First half of the 14th century.

CONSTRUCTORS OF URBAN REALITIES

The Town Hall

A brick belfry was built around 1250 in a detached position south-east of the Market-place. It was heightened in 1385.

The Town Hall and the booths were made of wood. From 1393 they were built of brick, around an inner courtyard.

Torun *Rathaus* was typical of those found in the East, in particular in Wroclaw, Danzig and Reval: big square buildings with an inner courtyard and a belfry. No doubt that was because in those regions the Town Hall served longer as a covered market and trading centre.

Until the 14th century, craftsmen, butchers and bakers, and not only merchants, displayed their wares in Torun Town Hall.

458. The Town Hall, which dates back to the late 14th century, looks more like a market hall or *Fondaco* than a Town Hall. It takes in a belfry, which was separate at first, begun in 1259.

459. Nicolas Copernic (1473-1543) and the belfry.

460-461. Jean, the King of Poland, gave permission for the first bridge to be built in Torun. 1496.

The seals of Torun archives are impressed upon wax substrates which contrast with those of the West by their abundance.

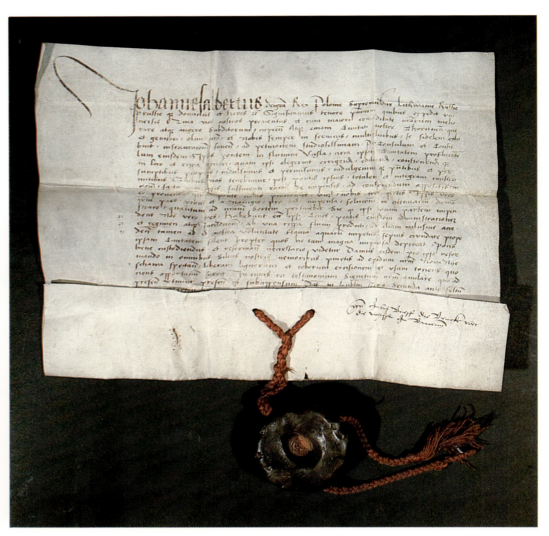

464. A Council session in Torun Town Hall.
Anonymous painting, circa 1615.
Torun, Town Hall Museum.

462-463. Wax writing-tablets. 15th century.

Torun archives house a rare and precious collection of wax tablets which bear accounts and city censuses.
Professor Karol Gorski, who has patiently studied them, has obtained from them information which is of exceptional interest for history and the historical demography of Torun.

CONSTRUCTORS OF URBAN REALITIES

St. John's The church of the Old Town was dedicated to St. John.
It was a hall-church the oldest part of which, the chancel, dated back to about 1250.
The naves, which date from 1260-1290, were heightened in 1468-1473.
Several of these altar retables were of Flemish origin, as were brass tomb plates. The only one that still subsists is that of Burgomaster Johann von Soest (deceased 1361) and his wife. It calls to mind those of the same period found in St. Peter's church in Lubeck and the *Nikolaikirche* in Stralsund.

465-466. St. Jean's church was begun in about 1250. Its tower goes back to 1407.

467. The retable of the main altar was made in Southern Germany around 1505.

It represents St. Wolfgang flanked by the apostles Bartholomew and Simon.
On the inner side volets: four Fathers of the Church.

468. Johann von Soest (deceased 1361), Burgomaster of Torun. Part of a tombstone of Flemish origin, on which he figures with his wife.

469. Votive painting to the memory of Nicolas Copernic, born in Torun in 1473.

ALBERT D'HAENENS

Danzig

470. The *Rathaus* began to be built in 1379.

In the foreground, the Neptune fountain. On the right, the tower of Notre-Dame, the city church. Far right: a bay of the Artushof which dates back to 1348 as the headquarters of the patrician Confraternity of St. George. Its facade, by Abraham van den Block, dates from 1616-1617; its structure, from 1477-1481. At the end of the 14th century it housed sea-going merchants. From the end of the 15th century, foreign merchants and ship-owners also.

In 1308 the Teutonic Order seized the Slav town which dated back to the end of the 10th century (997). It destroyed it and dispersed its population.
In 1340 it built a castle in the place of the original *castrum*.
In 1343, south of the Old Town, it built a New Town (*Rechtstadt*) the lay-out of which, centered around Notre-Dame church, differed appreciably from that of its neighbour.
In 1361 Danzig was a member of the Hanse. Integrated in the Polish State in 1466, it became Royal Prussia.
The town made great strides at the end of the 15th century.
The main part of its income and profits came from corn exports and Flemish and English cloth imports.
Its golden age coincided with the Renaissance. This is still evidenced by several remarkable edifices and works, painted and sculptured by Flemish and Italian masters for the town's patricians and merchant bourgeoisie.

471. The belfry is 82 m high. Its crowning, which dates from 1559-1561, is in Renaissance style. At the top: the gilded statue of Sigismond-Auguste, King of Poland.
On the quoin turret of the Gothic facade there is a sundial (1589); the writing states the futility of human life.

472. The east facade of the Town Hall dates from the end of the 15th century.

473. The Neptune fountain. Cast iron. By Hans Reichel of Augsburg 1620.

CONSTRUCTORS OF URBAN REALITIES

The port

From the 15th to the 17th centuries Danzig was the corn store of Europe. The Polish, Prussian and Pomeranian cereals which it exported to the West were the essential source of its wealth.

The accounts of the Sund clearly show that Danzig was by far the leading Baltic port in the 16th century, both for the number of ships and for the value of the goods. In 1481, eleven hundred ships left Danzig for Flanders.

In this traffic in the 16th century, Danzig ships played a fairly small part. It was mainly the Dutch who were active in this field, followed by Southern Germans, for the Danzig merchants acted almost solely as intermediaries.

474. This large crane was erected in 1443 on the quay of the Motlawa, on the boundary of the Rechstadt and the Neustadt.
With its two powerful hoists, it was used for the trans-shipment of provisions and for construction work.

475. The Merchants Gate.

476. Windmills.

477. Corn granaries on the banks of the Motlawa, 15th century.

Danzig ships' cargoes

Danzig also exported wax, Swedish iron and Hungarian copper which came in from Cracow via the Vistula. It produced beer for Finland and its shipyards were prosperous.

Another of its specialities was amber collected on the shores of the Samland peninsula. It was obligatorily delivered to the officials of the big Teutonic treasurership at Königsberg which had the sole shipment rights. They sent it to Lubeck, Bruges and Lvov, from whence it was taken to the Orient.

The mid-15th century cargo found in the harbour bay in 1969 is a concrete illustration of the typology of what was exported. Work on freeing it, together with the 'cogge', went on till 1975, and everything then went to the Navigation Museum in Danzig. It included copper ore, timber, cereals, wax, ash and pitch. The boat, to which the name of *copper boat* was given, is 25 metres long.

478-484. Remains of the cargo of the 'cogge' which sank in the port of Danzig in about 1460.
The boat went down as it was leaving the port, following a fire that broke out in the galley.
The barrels contained ash, wax and pitch. They bore three kinds of marks, referring to the contents, the owner and the consignee.
Zinc ore extracts.
Timber from Torun, also marked.

CONSTRUCTORS OF URBAN REALITIES

Bourgeois habitation   Most of the houses in Notre-Dame street (*Mariacka*) or the Long-Market, dated back to the second half of the 16th and early 17th centuries. The model and style of their design gave them real homogeneity. Flemish town-planning and architecture are remarkably recognizable.
Generally speaking, they were three-storey houses with three broadwise windows on the frontage.
In the rue Notre-Dame the pavement, three to four metres wide and bordered by railings, ran along the houses. From there one came down to the street by about ten steps.

485-486.   The Long Market in Danzig.

487-488. Notre-Dame street (*Mariacka*).

CONSTRUCTORS OF URBAN REALITIES

Notre-Dame church 105 m long and 27 m wide, with a 78 m tower, the *Rechtstadt* parish church is the biggest Gothic church in Poland. Its construction, in brick, was begun in 1343. When it was finished in 1502, it had become an immense Gothic building capable of taking more than 20,000 worshippers.
The most famous item in its furnishing is undoubtedly the triptych of the *Last Judgment* by Hans Memling.
Paul Benecke, who seized it in the Channel, whereas the painting was on its way to Italy, gave it to the church of his town. In the second half of the 15th century, this work by Memling was a continual source of inspiration for plastic artists impressed by its 'green light' (*das grüne Licht*).

489. Notre-Dame church.

490. Virgin and child. Early 15th century.

491. Votive painting of the Oehm family. Circa 1540.

CONSTRUCTORS OF URBAN REALITIES

492. The nave.

493-494. Side volets of the *Last Judgment* by Hans Memling.

Long-lasting Dynamism

The Flow of Surpluses to the East

In the north, in the 11th and 12th centuries, men worked out the connection between the availability of certain products and the potential profit that could follow from moving them over long distances and inserting them in contexts out of the usual range.

In this way they created distant markets on which, both outward and homeward, they unloaded surplus products, under conditions that were initially rough and demanding and in which they were personally involved.

The Hanseatic enterprise was not first of all an abstract project, but a combination of empiric, concrete and individual steps, the convergence of which progressively aroused the association and togetherness of those who exposed themselves by undertaking them. Merchants found themselves on the same routes, especially sea routes. On the same markets, the same procurement and disposal places, where they were all foreigners. In common they faced up to the risks and dangers of their travels; together they pursued promising profits.

By the very force of things they thus constituted the first form of grouping, at a stage in the evolution of European mentality and society when the latter were negotiating their way to the written word, to the urban model and to inter-regional relations.

As soon as the Western world attained its structural and institutional maturity these groups of men were taken up in relays by urban associations, but without thereby losing their original forms. The Hanse of the towns then appeared.

In actual fact, the Hanseatic undertaking came within the flow of surpluses from Europe to the East. As long as such surpluses existed, the Hanse showed in a remarkable manner the Western dynamization of margin and excess.

However, in the second half of the 15th century, Europe began to overflow towards the South and the West. Its surpluses now pushed it elsewhere than to the East. The Baltic world, around which the Hanseatic enterprise gravitated, was less and less prompted by dynamisms engendered by European surplus.

The internal strength of the Hanse then dried up, like that of other entities – abbeys and convents too – which had been raised up at the same time as the Hanse by the early surpluses.

The Hanse could then to nothing more than survive on its accumulated attainments, its own surpluses. [A. d'H.]

inter vigilias noctis assiduitate clangoris testatur. ullius autem animal ita odorem hominis sentit ut anser. unde ex clangore eius gallorum ascensus in capitolio deprehensus. unde talamus hic prudos homines et erga custodiam suam bene vigilantes significare potest. Anserum due sunt species domestice videlicet et campestres. Campestres in altum et ordinate volant. illos qui designant qui remoti a terrenis ordinem bene suum vivendo servant. Domestice vero in vicis simul habitant multociens conclamant se ipsos rostris lacerant. illos significant qui etsi convenit aviance loquacitati tamen et detracto in natantis in campestribus habet color enuritus i. in huis qui a seculo sunt remoti penitentie vitis habitus.

Est bestia in mare que dicitur serra pennas huius imitantes per cum viderit in mare navem nitentem elevat pennas suas

PHILIPPE DOLLINGER
Professor at Strasbourg University II

When the Hanse was strong

During its 500-year existence, from the 12th to the 17th century, the Hanse passed successively through three forms of organization, all of which were very loose.

From 1161 to 1299 it was an association of German merchants backed by their towns of origin. From 1299 to the middle of the 14th century it was a community of towns trading abroad and headed by the Hanseatic Diet (Hansetag). After 1356 and until final effacement in the 17th century, a league of a smaller number of towns subjected – in principle – to precise financial obligations.

Each of these three forms was affected more or less rapidly by decadence.

495. The original Hanseatic.
Drawing illustrating an English beast-fighter, end of the 13th century.
Oxford, Bodleian, Ms. Douce 88, fol. 129 recto.

At the beginning of the Hanse: rudimentary means men almost unprovided for, delivered to the sea and to all sorts of hallucinations, fears and agonies.

496. The Hanse, at the outset.

- ● *League of Westphalian towns.*
- ■ *League of Saxon towns and towns associated with that league.*
- ▲ *League of Wendish towns.*
- ▼ *Prussian towns, frequently associated.*
- ∗ *Livonian towns, frequently associated.*

LONG-LASTING DYNAMISM

497. Henry the Lion and his wife. Brunswick Cathedral.

In 1158-1159 Henry founded Lubeck on the Trave some twenty kilometres from where it flows into the Baltic; that was to avoid the risk of the town being destroyed by pirates. Henry played a big part in the German colonization of Eastern Europe. Saxons, Frisians, Westphalians, Rhinelanders, Dutch, Flemish and Franconians, attracted by the promise of receiving land and by the hope of quickly becoming rich, participated massively in that colonization.

The first wave of immigrants, to be followed in greater numbers in the middle of the 12th century, mainly moved towards Holstein and Brandenburg.

The founding of merchant towns everywhere accompanied occupation of land by peasants; it ensured the formation and expansion of the Hanse.

THE ORIGINAL VITALITY

The formation of the Hanse of merchants was the result of a number of factors. The most general was undoubtedly the German migration to the East and North (*Drang nach Osten*).

It intensified from the beginning of the 12th century, beyond the Elbe which at that time still marked the limit of Germanism.

That migration was due to the over-population of North West Germany, to the excessive parcelling out of peasant land into small holdings, to the shortage of provisions, and to the call of German and Slavonic colonizing seigniors. This migration was accentuated in the middle of the century under the impetus of conquering dynasts such as Adolphus, Count of Holstein, Albert the Bear and especially Henry the Lion, Duke of Saxony from 1142 to 1180.

The religious factor also played a not inconsiderable part. Despite missionaries' efforts, the Slavs on the right bank of the Elbe remained aggressively pagan, in particular the Wagrians of Holstein, the Obotrites of Mecklenburg and the Lieutics of Brandenburg. After the failure of the 1147 crusade, the German princes methodically undertook the conversion and conquest of the country between the Elbe and the Oder.

WHEN THE HANSE WAS STRONG

The strides made by German towns

The strides made by these towns, in which more and more merchants settled, contributed to a large extent to the formation of the Hanse. Cologne played a particularly important role in the urban process.

In the 10th century, a merchant quarter, mainly populated by Frisians, had grown up on the banks of the Rhine and had been given a right which was later partly adopted by the towns on the right bank. Among these the most influential were: Dortmund, whose right was applied to several Westphalian towns, Goslar whose role was similar for the Lower Saxony towns, Soest, whose right was later to be applied, with some modifications, by Lubeck.

Beyond the Elbe too, in Slav country, and contrary to what was formerly thought, the urban action had developed since the 10th century by the formation of a quarter inhabited by craftsmen and merchants, often foreigners, in a palisade-surrounded stronghold.

Such was Old Lubeck on the Trave, where Christian German merchants settled in the first third of the 12th century, but which was ruined by pirates in 1138.

Such, too, was Jumne, on Wollin island, where there were Scandinavian, Saxon and even Greek colonies.

There was also Stettin, the most populous town of the sector (about 5000 persons) where German merchants multiplied in the 12th century. It was the same in Danzig.

The go-ahead spirit of the German merchants

The basic cause of the formation of the Hanse is assuredly to be found in the go-ahead spirit of the German merchants.

In the North Sea, the Cologne merchants began going to England regularly in the 11th century. Before 1130 they obtained the right to stay in London, and then to acquire a warehouse on the banks of the Thames, the Guildhall. Henry II gave them his protection (1157), in particular for the sale of Rhine wine.

They also traded in Jutland, crossing the Holstein Isthmus to Schleswig, the big trading centre with the Scandinavians, which had replaced Hadeby (Haithabu) after its destruction by the Wends in the middle of the 11th century.

Bremen was trading actively with Norway, Denmark and Schleswig.

Trade in the Baltic, however, was mainly in the hands of peasant-seamen from the island of Gotland. They radiated in all directions; to Schleswig, to Saxony where Lothair III accorded them privileges in 1134, to Stettin and Truso, but especially to Novgorod, which they reached by sailing up the Neva and then the Volchov. In the 11th century they had founded a business house there, with a church dedicated to St. Olav. The articles which the Gotlanders brought back from Russia were principally furs and wax, which were much appreciated in the West. They took with them, inter alia, at least from the early 12th century, Flemish cloth and probably salt.

LONG-LASTING DYNAMISM

FROM 1161 TO 1249: THE HANSE MERCHANT

The German merchants aspired to penetrate the Baltic themselves, make closer contact with the Gotlanders and follow them into Russia to bring products back. To achieve that, the backing and protection of a powerful German prince was indispensable, as was a base on the Baltic Sea from which to start. Lubeck was founded as a result of these needs.

Lubeck: a new town for trade in the Baltic

The new town was first of all created by Count Adolphe II of Holstein, who called upon Westphalian and Dutch colonists. But the Duke of Saxony, Henry the Lion, obliged his vassal to surrender his rights, and it was he who carried out the definitive foundation of Lubeck in 1158-1159.

He pacified Holstein, attracted foreign merchants by privileges and concluded a standing peace with the Gotlanders, to whom he granted free access to Lubeck on a reciprocal basis. So German commercial expansion in the Baltic was ensured.

498. Plan of Lubeck in the Middle Ages.

1. Town Hall
2. Cathedral
3. St. Peter's
4. Notre-Dame
5. St. James'
6. Holy Ghost hospital
7. St. Giles'
8. St. James' convent
9. St. Catherine's
10. Burgtor
11. Dominican nuns' convent
12. Captains' guild house
13. Holstentor
14. Hüxtertor
15. Mühlentor

In Lubeck: German seasonal merchants for Gotland

Beginning in the spring of 1161, merchants from various West German towns assembled in Lubeck in order to go to Gotland.

Henry the Lion gave them an 'Elder' (*Oldermann*) as their leader (he was probably elected by them). He received from them an oath of obedience and mutual aid and was responsible for exercising justice over his companions and representing them vis-à-vis foreign authorities.

The Duke gave the association legal status, marked by a seal bearing the fleur-de-lis and the inscription: Universai mercatores imperii Romani Gotlandiam frequentantes, the community of Gotland seasonal merchants.

The association developed rapidly. In the 13th century it was headed by four Elders, elected respectively by the merchants of Lubeck, Visby, Soest and Dortmund. Progressively, merchants from the new towns founded by the Germans on the south coast of the Baltic – Wismar, Rostock, Stralsund, Danzig, Elbing and Riga – joined the association.

499. Seal of the association of Hanseatic merchants taking the Gotland route. 1291. After a moulding. Lubeck, Archiv der Hansestadt.
Inscription: SIGILL[UM] THEUTONICO[RUM] GUTLA[N] DIA[M] FREQUENNTANTIUM.

The lily symbolized royal protection.

*In Visby:
German merchants living in
Gotland*

500. Visby ramparts.

*Gotland island had been in contact with Russia, Germany and England since the Viking era.
In the 11th century its trading activities were concentrated in Visby, where a well-planned stone-built town grew up. The Germans constituted a colony there which was at the origin of Hanseatic movements.
At the end of the 13th century the town surrendered its trade leadership to Lubeck.
The Visby ramparts date from the 13th and 14th centuries: 3,400 metres of surrounding wall and 44 towers to protect 90 hectares.*

At the end of the 12th century, numerous merchants, rather than returning to their town each autumn, decided to settle in Gotland, where they founded the German town of Visby, bordering on a Scandinavian conurbation. They had their own seal, bearing the inscription: Sigillum Theutonicorum in Gutlandia Manentium.

Visby prospered extremely quickly, to such an extent that at one time it threatened Lubeck influence in the Baltic

A few years after they had come to Gotland, an increasing number of association members accompanied Scandinavians to Novgorod. Initially housed in the Gotlanders' establishment, they soon founded their own business house, the Peterhof, with a church dedicated to St. Peter.

Also, after the foundation of Riga (1201), German merchants, sailing up the Duna, opened a privilege-endowed business house in Smolensk. Contrary to the Peterhof, this house soon declined and it was abandoned before the end of the 13th century. Lastly, German merchants participated in the foundation of Stockholm (1251), but without obtaining privileged status there.

WHEN THE HANSE WAS STRONG

Initially: regional town leagues German merchants in the North Sea

The association of merchants frequenting Gotland also traded in the North Sea.

At an unknown date a privileged business house, the 'German quay' (Tyskebrygge) was set up in Bergen, Norway. Its main purpose was the carriage of Norwegian dried cod to Lubeck.

In England, merchants from the East perhaps settled at Boston first of all. In London they came up against the ill-will of the Cologne merchants who, not very keen on receiving people they regarded as intruders, refused them entry to the Guildhall. However, Henry III accorded the association merchants his protection and tax exemption (1237).

Finally, in 1282, none too easily, the Cologne merchants and the 'Esterlins' came to an understanding and united in a 'German Hanse' without merging completely, but all residing within the privileged establishment of the Stalhof (Steelyard) around the house of the Cologne merchants.

It was fairly late, only in the middle of the 13th century, that the Germans established themselves in Bruges, which was to become their most flourishing business house. There they obtained various privileges from the Countess of Flanders. One of those (1252) was awarded to "the Roman empire merchants frequenting Gotland".

Contrary to the other business houses, they possessed no bounded and privileged place for transacting their business; the merchants stayed in hotels or in houses which they rented.

Organized business houses but an inorganic structure

In one century the Hanse merchants had achieved a lot, extending Hanse activity to all the shores of the northern seas of Europe and beyond.

Yet from the institutional point of view the association was on the wane in the second half of the 13th century. The tasks incumbent upon it by far exceeded the possibilities of a modest group of seasonal merchants as it had originally been constituted. Furthermore, from that time onwards, towns represented the real power capable of backing up the interests of their merchants abroad, and they took offence at the independence which the Association of merchants frequenting Gotland sometimes showed.

Lubeck in particular frowned upon the Hanse. The town first of all decided that the court of appeal of the Novgorod business house would be transferred from Visby to Lubeck; it then suppressed the association seal (1299). Hence the association no longer had any legal existence or institutional infrastructure. Only the business houses kept their organization based thereon, one or more elected Elders having authority and jurisdiction over the merchants who stayed there temporarily.

Actually, the Hanse subsisted, as the community of interests was sufficient to ensure solidarity between its members. It kept going for another half-century with that inorganic structure.

FROM 1356 TO THE MIDDLE OF THE 16th CENTURY: THE HANSE OF THE TOWNS

However, about the middle of the 14th century this simple and very loose solidarity proved insufficient. New competitors made their appearance: the Southern Germans and the Dutch, who threatened the commercial preponderance of the Hanseatics, especially to the west. In addition, the business house merchants saw their privileges increasingly violated and contested.

Lastly, the German towns became uneasy about the excessive autonomy of their business houses which, negotiating with foreign authorities for their interests, were liable to involve them in international complications. The only solution was to take charge of their merchants abroad and give them increased support.

Initially: leagues of regional towns

This solution was facilitated by the solidarity which had developed between towns in the course of a century: the creation of leagues of regional towns. The oldest was the Wendish league, so called because the towns of which it was constituted were principally situated in the former Slav regions of Holstein and Mecklenburg.

In 1230 Hamburg and Lubeck entered into an alliance. They were joined by Kiel, Wismar, Rostock, Stralsund and Luneburg. The Wendish league, constituted in 1265, was to play a considerable role in Hanse history.

Other similar leagues were formed at that time or later: that of the Westphalian towns, headed by Dortmund; the Saxon towns under Brunswick, the Prussian towns between the Vistula and Niemen; the Livonian towns with Riga and Reval; the Zuiderzee.

It should be noted, however, that these leagues were not Hanseatic in origin. Formed for the protection of their merchants, they were mainly concerned with maintaining their legal status and defending themselves against the designs of their lords. It would be inexact to think that the Hanse of the towns stemmed from a regional league merger.

The Hanse of the towns manifested its existence for the first time in 1356, following difficulties encountered by the German business houses in Bruges, which were in conflict with the town and the Count of Flanders.

Uneasy about their trade with Flanders being compromised, a large number of towns – unfortunately we do not know which ones – sent their delegates to Lubeck to discuss the steps to be taken. That was the first general Hanseatic Diet (Hansetag). It did nothing more than to decide to send ambassadors abroad, instructed to have the submission of business houses to the community of towns recognized – which was easily obtained everywhere – and to negotiate with local authorities to smooth out pending difficulties, which was more laborious and always precarious. Other general meetings of the same kind were subsequently held at irregular intervals.

What the Hanse was

Which were the towns making up the Hanse? It is not easy to answer that question, for no exhaustive list was ever drawn up.
Merchants who benefited by privileges abroad, particularly in the four big business houses, and who turned them to account, were Hanseatic. In most cases the dates of their admission and those of their withdrawal, when they ceased to make use of their trading privileges are unknown. Actually, the question of membership was seldom examined and then only in the event of a contestation, generally for marginal towns such as those of the Low Countries or for very small towns. In the latter case the neighbouring towns, in the 15th century, took counsel together to decide.

A league of more or less 200 towns So one can only attempt to make a detailed account of the towns which were at any given time, and sometimes for only a few years, members of the Hanse. One arrives at a total of approximately 200 between the 14th and 16th centuries, the highest figure seeming to have been reached around the middle of the 15th century. They range from the Lower Meuse and the Zuiderzee to the Gulf of Finland with Reval (Tallinn) and Dorpat (Tartu). North of a line Cologne – Erfurt – Francfort-on-Oder – Dorpat. Plus Cracow and Breslau. This shows that while maritime towns played a determinant role, most towns were situated inland, sometimes several hundred kilometres from the sea. They were unequally distributed: very dense in Westphalia (more than 80); scattered in the east. Nearly all were situated on the territory of the Empire and the Teutonic Order, with the exception of Cracow and a few Swedish towns such as Stockholm and Kalmar which, in any case, withdrew from the community at the end of the 14th century.

About 70 active members In a few rare texts of that time, reference was made to 72 or 77 towns in the Hanse, which is far from 200. This difference is explained by the fact that the community comprised two categories of members. There were active members – they could actually have been around 70 towns – convened directly or indirectly to general meetings of the Hanse and participating in the expenses of delegations. Then there were passive members, whose merchants benefited by commercial privileges abroad but were never convened to diets and did not bear the cost thereof.

A territorial prince The Hanse had just one territorial prince among its members: the grand master of the Teutonic Order.
That exception stemmed from the considerable part played by the Order, after its installation in Prussia (1230), in the colonisation of the country and the expansion of Prussian towns, which remained very much under the sway of the grand master.
Whilst the adhesion of this illustrious personage undoubtedly conferred increased prestige on the Hanse, the latter was embarrassed time and again by the singular policy conducted by the Teutonic Order.

Hanseatic institutions

The General Meeting or Hansetag

The General Meeting of Hanseatic towns (Hansetag), which was generally held in Lubeck, was the directing body of the Hanse. It regulated, normally without appeal, all matters concerning the community: ratification of treaties and trading privileges, negotiations with foreign princes and towns; the sending of ambassadors, peace, war or blockade, financial and military measures, economic regulations, debarring or admission of towns, arbitration in disputes.

Despite the importance of its role, the diet did not meet as often as one would have thought. There were only 27 meetings between 1356 and 1400, i.e. about one every other year; 19 from 1400 to 1480: one every four years. The rareness of the meetings in the 15th century is partly explained by the growing role of Lubeck Council. From the start, it expedited current matters between General Meetings, and in 1418 the Diet officially invited Lubeck and the Wendish towns to settle problems concerning the community, even if they had to justify themselves before the Diet. But, more especially, it cost a lot of money to send a delegation, particularly for the more distant towns, and so they resigned themselves to doing so only when they felt that the agenda really concerned them. Consequently generally only ten to twenty delegations attended the Hansetag, for some 70 towns. The highest attendance was 39 delegations in 1447, scarcely half the active strength.

After the items on the agenda had been dealt with, the decisions adopted by a majority vote were drafted in ordinance form and stamped with the seal of the town where the meeting had taken place. Each delegate received a copy and, on returning to his country, made other copies to be sent to the towns in his sector. The whole of these ordinances constituted, in a way, the legislative compendium of the Hanse.

Meetings of 'thirds'

The reluctance of towns the most distant from Lubeck to take upon themselves the high cost of sending delegations to the General Diet, explains the institution of 'third' meetings (derdendeel).

The Hanse towns divided themselves into three groups, mentioned for the first time in the statutes of the Bruges business house in 1347.

The most influential third was the Lubeck-Saxon one, headed by Lubeck; apart from the Wendish and Saxon towns, it included the Pomeranians and the Brandenburgers. The second third was Westphalian-Prussian, with Dortmund at its head; it had the singular feature of bringing together townships that were geographically separated, Westphalians and Rhinelanders on the one hand, eastern and western Prussia on the other. This particularity undoubtedly followed less from a community of interests than from a desire to counterbalance the powerful Lubeck third. Lastly, the Gotland-Livonian third, under Visby and then under Riga, was the weakest; it grouped the Swedish and Livonian towns.

The meetings of the 'thirds' obviously had more limited competence than the general Diet. Actually, they were basically concerned with trade relations between their sector and Flanders.

Some big towns were irritated at not being recognized as head towns of thirds, so a change was made at the end of the 15th century. The thirds were replaced by four quarters: the Rhineland-Westphalian quarter, owing allegiance to Cologne; the Saxon quarter, under Brunswick; the Lubeck quarter; and the Prussian-Livonian quarter under Danzig.

The leagues and urban councils   Besides the 'thirds', the regional leagues, which were not specifically Hanseatic and which included towns that were not members of the community, also played a part in its organization, the more so in that they grouped towns on a smaller territory, sometimes having the same lord. The Wendish league and the Prussian one in particular actively undertook to have *Hansetag* decisions applied.

At the base of Hanseatic organization was the Council of each member town. That Council, too, was not specifically Hanseatic. Its role was to act in concert with other towns to provide for a regional Diet, ensure correspondence with those towns and with Lubeck, form the delegation to be sent to the General Meeting; and have the ordinance applied to the Diets.

In short, it can be said that the Hanse worked at three levels: at the bottom, the urban Councils; above them the Diets of the regional leagues or thirds; and at the top the *Hansetag*, earnestly backed up by the Lubeck Council.

The Hanse of the towns, a body acting in concert   The Hanse of the towns was in reality a body that was almost unsubstantial. None of its members was fully independent – not even prosperous cities which enjoyed Empire town status, such as Lubeck, Dortmund and Goslar. Almost all of them were more or less closely under the sway of laic or ecclesiastical princes.

Contrary to the Gotland merchants Association, it did not have its own seal and therefore had no legal status. It had no civil servants, no regular income, no fleet and no army. It was a community existing only in concert.

This inorganic structure could not always cope with acute crises.

In the 15th century, Lubeck endeavoured on several occasions to change the community into a league called Tohospesate, with precise financial and military obligations. But this was never more than of limited duration and efficiency; the Hanse could not go beyond the stage of a community exclusively pledged to trading activities.

Effective means of pressure   Nevertheless, the Hanse did not lack means of exerting pressure on its members if they refused to bow to the general will or tried to overthrow the patrician regime by violence.

After negotiations and arbitrations the Hansetag sometimes went so far as to expel a rebel town.

If negotiations with foreign States or towns proved unsuccessful, the Hanse used various tactics. Against Norway it barred the Danish straits to prevent shipments of cereals. Against Russia and England it decreed the cessation of traffic, forbidding its merchants to go to the business houses – sometimes for several years.

Lastly, in extreme cases, the Hanse reluctantly went to war, against Denmark especially, but also against Sweden, England, France and even Castille, with unequal results.

LONG-LASTING DYNAMISM

AFTER 1556 TO THE 17th CENTURY: A LEAGUE OF HANSEATIC TOWNS

In the middle of the 16th century, following many setbacks in all fields, the Hanse appeared to be close to its end. Solidarity between its members had slackened, each town tending to bother solely about its own interests. Yet a remarkable revitalization took place at that time.

The general Diet of 1554

The general Diet of 1554, grouping delegates from 63 towns, imposed on them an annual financial contribution proportional to the assumed wealth of each.

Three years later, another Diet drafted statutes with ten articles, providing in particular for joint armed intervention against violators of the peace; those statutes remained in force up to the Thirty Years War.

At last a Hanseatic League was achieved, with precise commitments; something which previous efforts had tried in vain to do.

The Syndic of the Hanse in 1556

A second salutary measure was the appointment in 1556 of a 'Syndic of the Hanse', a high *salaried* official – for the first time – in the person of Heinrich Sudermann of Cologne, a Doctor of Laws.

In charge of juridical and diplomatic matters, he devoted himself unstintingly for thirty-five years, ploughing the seas, smoothing out difficulties between towns, and reanimating Hanseatic solidarity. His great thought was to restore the trade of the Low Countries' league, by setting up a traditional business house in Antwerp, with a vast place of residence where German merchants would be subject to strict discipline during their stay in a court endowed with privileges.

But its construction had hardly been completed when the revolt by the Low Countries against Spain caused the business house to be deserted and ruined Sudermann's efforts.

An irremediable decline

The decline of the Hanse was irremediable.

Despite some success, such as the development of trade with Spain at the beginning of the 17th century, the towns concerned themselves only their own interests, to the detriment of the general interest.

This, incidentally, enabled some of them who were able to adapt to the new conditions, such as Hamburg and Danzig, to progress by leaps and bounds. The institutional decline of the Hanse did not involve the decline of all its members. The Thirty Years War delivered the knock-out blow. The Hanseatic towns, under the influence of enemy powers, were incapable of adopting a common policy.

In 1629 the General Meeting of the Hanse asked the towns of Lubeck, Hamburg and Bremen to take charge of the interests of the entire community, which meant its liquidation.

The last Hansetag, meeting in 1699 with delegates from nine towns present, came to nothing. All that now remaind was the modest league of 'free, Hanseatic towns' of Lubeck, Hamburg and Bremen, formed in 1630, which at least had the merit of lasting until the 20th century.

501. The Peace of Stralsund. May 24, 1370.
Stralsund, Ratsarchiv.

"The Peace of Stralsund marked the advent in Northern Europe of a new power which replaced the inert imperial authority in this sector.
This power was not even sovereign, since the towns of which it was composed remained juridically subject to multiple princely dominations.
The only foundation was the will to defend trade interests, by arms if necessary.
A strange happening, unique in the Europe of those times." [Ph. Dollinger].

BIBLIOGRAPHY

PH. DOLLINGER, *La Hanse (XIIe-XVIIe siècles)*, Paris, 1964. 3rd German ed.: *Die Hanse*, Stuttgart, 1981.
D. ZIMMERLING, *Die Hanse*, Düsseldorf und Wien, 1976.
J. SCHILDHAUER, K. FRITZE, W. STARK, *Die Hanse*, 2nd ed., Berlin, 1975.
K. PAGEL, *Die Hanse*, re-ed. by. F. Naab, Brunswick, 1983.
Hanse in Europa, Brucke zwischen den Märkten 12.-17 Jahrhundert. Katalogusstellung des Kölnischen Stadtmuseums, Köln, 1973.
E. DAENELL, *Die Blütezeit der deutschen Hanse. Hansische Geschichte von der zweiten Hälfte des XIV. bis zum letzten Viertel des XV. Jahrhunderts*, 2nd ed. Berlin, 1906, re-ed. 1972.
H. SPROEMBERG, *Die Hanse in europäischer Sicht*, in *Annales de la Société Royale d'Archéologie*, 50, 1961.
R. BOYER, P. JEANNIN, M. GRAVIER, *Mers du Nord et Baltique*, Paris, 1981.
Hanse und der Deutsche Orden. Katalog Ausstellung Staatliches Archivlager Göttingen, Göttingen, 1966.

404

HERMAN VAN DER WEE
Professor at the Katholieke Universiteit Leuven

The Slow Process of Disintegration

502. A meeting of Ratisbonne Council in 1536.
Miniature on parchment by Hans Mielich (1516-1573 for the title page of the Freiheitenbuch.
Ratisbonne Stadtarchiv, 1 Ab 2.

At the end of the room: the Last Judgment. The Constance Council in 1420 recommended the Last Judgment to be present in the Council's rooms so that each member of the Council had it before his eyes when taking the floor.

503. Statues of Germanic kings and emperors placed on the facade of the cloth merchants guild house on Goslar Market Place. 17th century.

The power of the Hanse was essentially connected with the medieval structures of a prosperous urban economy. Within this specific context, a system of regional solidarity was a factor of power, of purposeful economic and political action. During the 14th century the German Hanse expanded into a highly influential and powerful European organization.

However, as soon as the structure of the urban economy was affected by the mergence of the modern state, the Hanse also came under pressure.

From the 15th century onwards, the first signs of this development were already visible. Europe at that time was hard hit by the depression. The towns, which up to then had financed the princes in their struggles against the feudal lords and had in return acquired independent privileges, now appealed to the State to protect them against the threat of crisis. The price to be paid was a gradual process of subjection to princely authority, a process of assimilation into the more modern structure of the national State.

In this new, institutional context, the interurban solidarity of the Hanse gradually lost its meaning and relevance.

LONG-LASTING DYNAMISM

The international tensions

A second weakening factor lay in the very success of the Hanse. During the 14th century, the German Hanse had developed into a gigantic association of hundreds of towns. But the greater the number of members, the greater was the risk of disunity and division. It was, in fact, from this time onwards that rivalries and disputes between the Hanse towns increased.

Thus the Hanseatic League was weakened not only by the threat from outside, but no less by the confrontations within the association itself.

A secular decline

The decline of the Hanse was not a sudden phenomenon, but was dragged out over centuries.

This was above all attributable to the efficiency and flexibility of the Hanse system. The formula of interurban solidarity was flexible enough to overcome many successive tensions, conflicts and defeats. Even when members fell away because of political circumstances or mutual disputes, there was always a solid nucleus of towns able to rescue and maintain the idea of mutual solidarity. The decline was also held back by the geographical situation of the Hanseatic territory. North-eastern Europe was a vast region where the modern idea of the State penetrated more slowly than in the rest of the world; thus the medieval urban economy was maintained there for longer.

Finally, there were also important economic circumstances which were responsible for the remarkable capacity for resistance of the German Hanse. The European crisis of the 14th-15th centuries was followed by a spectacular economic expansion which lasted until far into the 17th century. North-eastern Europe was closely involved in this expansion. During this period, the Baltic became the granary for Western and Southern Europe. The Hanse still

504. Stralsund.
After a mid-17th century engraving.

505-506. Women of the Lubeck upper middle class, 17th century.
Lubeck, St-Annen-Museum.

The painting on the right is of Marguerite Brömse, née Köler (1626-1642). The one on the left was painted in 1650.

gave proof of so much vitality that it was able to integrate very actively in this expansion and even to show signs of institutional renewal. But the decisive breakthrough of the mercantile idea of State in the Scandinavian, North German and Russian region during the 17th century also meant the end of the Hanse.

The first phase of weakening extended over the whole of the 15th century and a good part of the 16th century.

It began with the serious political crisis experienced by Lubeck at the beginning of the 15th century. The town was even excluded for a time from the Empire. Thus for several years the Hanse was without effective leadership; a strong policy was impossible.

At the end of this crisis, the leadership was fully restored to Lubeck and this was solemnly recognized. But at the same time the dominant role of the patricians in the administration of the town was consolidated. For the future, a conservative policy was to be characteristic of the administration of Lubeck itself and in consequence for that of the Hanse as a whole.

This appeared to exclude the adaptation of the Hanse system to the changing structures of the New Era.

A second internal factor of weakening was the disastrous defeat of the Teutonic Knights against the King of Poland at Tannenberg on July 15th 1410. The strongest member of the German Hanse saw its hegemony over Prussia completely broken. Even if the defeat did not bring any immediate commercial catastrophe in the region, the emancipation of the Prussian towns also intensified the contradictions between the various groups of towns. The Prussian towns now had their own commercial interests which they defended forcefully against the Baltic towns: a new cause of numerous conflicts and mutual disputes.

The secession of powerful Cologne in 1471, as a consequence of the war with England, was a clear indication that the solidarity between the Northern European towns and those of the Rhineland no longer functioned automatically. The Treaty of Utrecht in 1474 restored unity, but the scars remained.

The dawn of nationalisms

From the beginning of the 15th century, weakening factors could also be observed on the periphery. The influence of the emergent national states was already clearly perceptible here.

In the towns where the Hanseatics had established a head office, namely in Bruges, London, Bergen (Norway) and Novgorod, there was growing resistance to the monopoly of the Hanse in trading with northern Europe. In Novgorod, the Russians began regularly to ignore the privileges of the Hanseatics. In 1478, Ivan III even took over the town and attempted to displace the trade to Moscow. This put paid to the prosperity of the *Peterhof* at Novgorod. In Bergen (Norway) the supremacy of the Hanseatics was undermined by the actions of the Danish king who favoured the Dutch to the detriment of the Baltic merchants. Relations with England were seriously disturbed by the Anglo-Hanseatic war of the sixties. At this time the crowd even destroyed part of the *Stalhof*, while the King proceeded to arrest the German merchants and to confiscate their goods. By far the most important of the Hanseatics' central offices was in Bruges, but even here they came into conflict with the growing power of the unitary Burgundian State.

The crisis culminated in the Anglo-Burgundian wars of the thirties and fifties. The Hanseatics thought they had prevailed when they announced the blockade of Bruges and moved their office from the town. But the ultimate result of the conflicts was the weakening of the Hanseatic position in the Low Countries and the more rapid decline of the Bruges office. More and more, the centre of gravity for trade between the Low Countries and Northern Europe was shifted to the large annual fairs in Brabant, and in particular to Antwerp. Moreover, trading between the Low Countries and Northern Europe passed increasingly into Dutch hands. Measures taken by the Hanseatics aimed at concentrating trade with Northern Europe permanently in the Bruges office, by compulsory warehousing at Bruges, proved powerless to contain these new trends.

The end of the offices

The weakening of the Hanse was not limited to the 15th century but continued into the beginning of the 16th century, a time in which the European economy and trade were in full upswing. The decline of the main offices changed into a phase of final decay.

In 1494, Ivan III had the Germans in Novgorod arrested, and closed the *Peterhof* for a period of 20 years. No renewal was caused by its reopening in 1514. In the meantime, Russian trade had shifted to the Finnish and Livonian towns, particularly to Narva and later to Archangel.

Nor was the office at Bergen in Norway able to retain its former splendour:

the number of houses on the 'Tyskebryggen' had fallen from about 300 in 1400 to about 160 in 1520.

Still more dramatic was the decline of the Bruges office. During the Flemish War at the end of the 15th century, the office was already moved temporarily to Antwerp, and after 1520 the *Bruges office* was moved to Antwerp for good. In 1539 it still consisted of three active members; only one remained by 1549. There was no Hanseatic merchant who took any notice of the prescriptions for compulsory warehousing, and nobody paid contributions to the office any longer. In fact, the London office was the only one able to maintain a strong trading position.

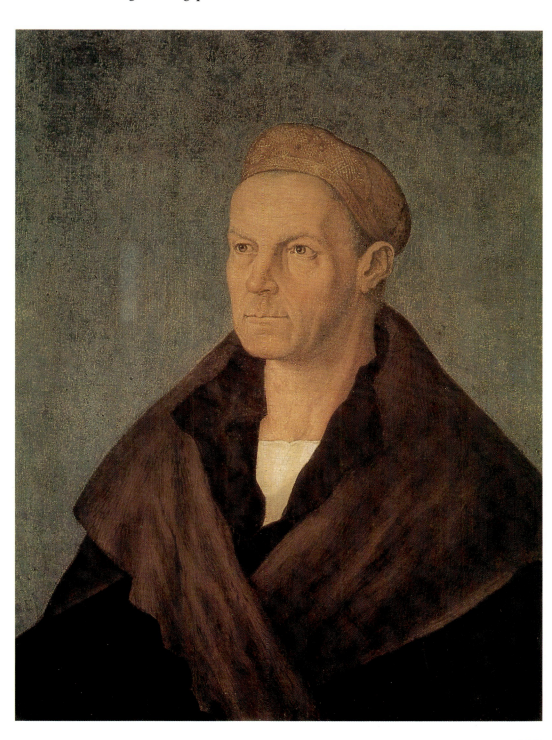

507. Jacob II Fugger.
Portrait painted by Albert Dürer. 1520.
It was a charcoal sketch which Dürer drew during the Augsburg Diet (Berlin, Kupferstichkabinet) which was the original of this portrait.
Augsburg, Staatsgalerie.

Jacob II is shown as an emperor; Dürer emphasizes the imperial look of the face and clothes.
Jakob first took Holy Orders, but then went into business with his father and sons. He opened up the international dimension of the family business and created trusts. It was he who built a housing estate (Fuggerei) in Augsburg.
The emperor ennobled him and gave him a seat on his council.

LONG-LASTING DYNAMISM

The Reformation: a supplementary factor for tension

During the 16th century, new circumstances contributed to the slow process of disintegration. The reformation introduced a new field of tension into the Hanseatic area. Some towns were converted to Protestantism, others remained Catholic. These changes were not exclusively connected with religious questions, but were deeply tinged by social and political considerations. In the towns where the Reformation was successfully introduced, the action of craftsmen and merchants was preponderant. In most of the Catholic towns, the old patrician groups retained their power. And there can be no doubt that the internal contradictions between the different Hanse towns were exacerbated by this development.

The Danish, Dutch and South German expansion

The success of the Reformation in Lubeck now brought the merchant Jurgen Wullenwever to power.

Wullenwever profited from the defeat of the patricians to set up a political and military action by the Hanse aimed at breaking Danish power and Dutch competition once and for all. The campaign ended in an ignominious defeat for the Hanse.

The Treaty of Spiers in 1544 officially recognized the Dutch right to free passage in the Sound, and thus consolidated the commercial supremacy of the Dutch over the Baltic Sea.

The Hanse was also forced to recognize the power of the Southern German merchants, as well as that of the Dutch. In particular the Fuggers became dangerous competitors for the Hanseatics: they brought their Hungarian copper via Danzig to Western Europe, thus threatening the traditional copper trade from Sweden which was under Hanseatic control. Here too, the Hanse had to give way.

A revitalization in the second half of the 16th century

Although the decline of the Hanse was evident and general in the 15th century and the beginning of the 16th, the system appeared to have unlimited powers of resistance.

The interurban solidarity contained so many elements of organizational flexibility that difficulties and tensions could finally be assimilated and did not lead to complete disintegration.

What was more, during the second half of the 16th century certain circumstances allowed the economic power of the Hanseatics to be re-established. And there was still sufficient vitality in the Hanseatic system to give a new and powerful impulse to the world trading of the Hanse.

The circumstances were twofold. The economic expansion of the 16th century had brought with it a new demographic growth in Southern and Western Europe and this, together with the increase in metallic currency, caused food prices to rise considerably. The regions round the Baltic Sea were the granary of Europe par excellence. Although the Dutch gained the greatest advantage from these new commercial possibilities, the Hanseatic trade was without any doubt also favoured to a great extent. When, from the last third of the 16th century onwards, the further maritime expansion of the Dutch was hampered by the Eighty Years' War, particularly in their trading to the Southern Low countries the Iberian peninsula and the Mediterranean, it was once again the Hanseatics who came in to fill some of the gaps.

508. Jakob Fugger in his business house. Circa 1520.
Drawing from Schwarz'sches Trachtenbuch.
Brunswick, Herzog Anton Ulrich-Museum.

Mr. Schwarz, the accountant, is seated at a table, ready to write in a register. Two other registers are on the table.
J. Fugger, standing, indicates the names of towns with which he has business relations.

Finally, the fall of Antwerp in 1585 and the increasing commercial isolation of the Southern Low Countries opened up new prospects of expansion for the Hanse. Cologne, and particularly Hamburg, attracted many merchants and considerable capital from the Southern Low Countries and thus took over much of the industrial, commercial and financial activity that had formerly been confined to the Southern Low Countries. Between 1586 and 1621 an average of 1104 ships sailed westwards each year from Danzig, mostly laden with grain. In Lubeck at the end of the 16th century there were sometimes more than 2000 ships at the quay.

An attempt at reorganization The recovery of the Hanseatic world trade led to attempts radically to reorganize the traditional Hanse system and adapt it to the newly changed circumstances.

Projects were advanced for encapsulating the Hanse in the modern structure of the national State, but they did not meet with sufficient support. Other proposals were for a league between all the towns of the German Empire, but this suggestion did not meet with success either.

More important was the constitution in 1557 of a league with precise

financial obligations and concrete statutes, which were adopted by 63 towns at that year's *Hansetag*. The league held on until the Thirty Years' War.

In 1556 a *syndicus* was appointed for the Hanse. The aim was to have permanently available a chargé d'affaires, a specialist in legal matters, who could prepare the *Hansetag* and look after current affairs in the meantime. This turned out to be a very fortunate decision, all the more so since the first choice fell on an extremely competent person. Dr. Heinrich Sudermann of Cologne was, until his death in 1591, the true soul of the Hanseatic community. With boundless energy and great intelligence, he devoted his efforts to giving an institutional and political content to the economic renewals of the Hanse.

The Thirty Years' War (1618-1648): the coup de grace

Sudermann's successors, however, lacked the personality and drive of this first *syndicus*.

In the meantime, the Thirty Years' War broke out in the German region in 1618. This war was fatal to the continued existence of the Hanse. The Hanse management opted for neutrality in the conflict, but the particular interests of the different towns prevented such a policy of neutrality. Some towns associated themselves with one prince or another, others linked themselves with his adversary. Thus urban solidarity became devoid of any meaning. The national States completely dominated the scene.

After the re-establishment of peace in 1648, a fresh attempt was made to re-establish the Hanseatic community. In 1651, Lubeck convened a new *Hansetag*, but the result was disappointing. In 1669 there was another and final meeting, at which only 9 towns were present. The discussions were acrimonious. No concensus could be reached on any point. Not a single community decision was taken. The Hanseatic community was dead. Only the alliance between Bremen, Hamburg and Lubeck, concluded in the middle of the war in 1630, lasted till the 20th century. But it was devoid of any real content.

509. The crane in the port of Bruges. Part of a picture by Pierre Pourbus (Gouda 1523 - Bruges 1584) painted in 1551. Bruges, Groeninge Museum.
In the background of a portrait of Jan van Eyerverwe, we have a view of the Kraanplaats (Crane Square). Also visible are: the Weeghuis (the Weighing House), the wooden crane with the workmen resting, and some brothers from St. John's Hospital discussing the arrival of wine with storekeepers.

BIBLIOGRAPHY

K. FRIEDLAND, *Der Plan des Dr. Heinrich Sudermann zur Wiederherstellung der Hanse*, in *Jahrbuch des Kölnischen Geschichtsvereins*, 31-32, 1956-1957.
G.-F. VON PÖLNITZ, *Fugger und die Hanse*, Tübingen, 1953.
W. VONSTROMER, *Konkurrenten der Hanse*, in *Hanse in Europa. Ausstellung des Kölnischen Stadtmuseums*, Köln, 1973, p. 329-339.
J.-H.-A. BEUKEN, *De Hanse en Vlaanderen*, Maastricht, 1950.
H. KELLENBENZ, *Unternehmerkräfte im Hamburger Portugal-und Spanienhandel. 1590-1625*, 1954.
K. FRIEDLAND (dir.), *Stadt und Land in der Geschichte des Ostseeraums*, Lübeck, 1973.
P. JEANNIN, *Les marchands au XVIᵉ siècle*, Paris, 1957.
F. VOLLBEHR, *Die Holländer und die deutsche Hanse*, in *Pfingstblätter des Hansischen Geschichtsvereins*, 21, 1930.
R. HÄPKE, *Der Untergang des Hanse*, Bremen, 1923.

KONRAD FRITZE
Professor at Greifswald University

The Hanse and Marxist historiography

The Hanse represents a special phenomenon in European history in feudal times.
During the four centuries of its existence as the principal association of towns in medieval Europe, it exerted lasting economic, social, political and cultural influence on numerous regions close to the North Sea and the Baltic.
Even today quite definite traces of that influence are to be found in the countries bordering on the Baltic, particularly in the fields of material culture and language.
The importance of Hanseatic history and the great influence of the Hanse in European material reality and imaginary quantity prompted Marxist historiography to give some thought to this subject.

CONDITIONS LENDING THEMSELVES TO THE APPEARANCE OF THE HANSE

Some factors played a particular part in the genesis and development of the Hanse.
One consequence of the considerable strides made in production in North-West-Europe, in particular in textiles and metallurgy, was that an increasingly large number of export products became available on the markets. Another consequence was that there was an increased demand for raw materials and means of subsistence in productive spheres themselves.
It was precisely as an outlet for the industrial production of the West and as a supplier of raw materials and farm produce that the Baltic region became increasingly important.
The 12th century had seen rapid development in agriculture, sylviculture, fishing and the mining industries.
In the territories south of the Baltic, this evolution was greatly encouraged by German feudal expansion accompanied, in the 12th to 14th centuries, by intensive immigration from territories west of the Elbe and interior colonization which gave rise to a large number of new towns and villages.
But long term, these cooperative associations were not powerful enough effectively to defend the interests of North German merchants against local or foreign feudal potentates or against their competitors. Therefore the North German towns themselves began more and more directly to take in hand the interests of their merchants.
The passage from an association of merchants to a Hanse of towns began to take place in the second half of the 13th century. There had already existed regional alliances of towns for the purpose of defending the economic and political interests of the bourgeoisie on several territories. Lubeck had played a leading role in that field.

510. Luneburg Town Hall.
Stained glass window in the south wall of the Courtroom (Gerichtslaube). Made circa 1430.

It is not a cathedral or abbey stained glass window, but a large window in a secular room in a Hanseatic Town Hall. It shows nine great judges around Charlemagne.
Here, Charlemagne in the middle with, from left to right: Joshua, Godefroid de Bouillon, King Arthur and Julius Caesar.
On the two narrower stained glass windows on either side of the central one: King David and Judas Maccabaeus in the left-hand one, and Alexander and Hector in the other.
It was in this room that the city magistrates sat. Therefore care was taken to see that the values and models which should inspire them were brought to the notice of those responsible for watching over the correct use of the laws and rules presiding over the life of the urban community.
Reference are still clearly Judeo-Christian here. But on the 16th century walls decorated in the spirit of Humanism and the Renaissance. The Roman world and law were evoked: one of the manifest signs of the end of an era and an ideology – and of the end, too, of the Hanse.

THE NATURE AND CHARACTER OF THE HANSE

On the economic and historical nature of the Hanse, Marxist historians agreed: it was a specific form of organization of commercial capital in feudal society. On the other hand, its political and juridical nature is still the subject of controversy.

The Hanse, in the form it was, is generally considered as a league of towns. Certainly it had no federal constitution or common permanent executive power, but it had members who, as a community, enjoyed privileges that had been obtained and forms of functional organization, such as the Hanseatic and regional Diets, which were often capable of finding means of imposing a uniform policy and having it respected.

As a league of towns, the Hanse had a dual function. Outside, it caused the economic and political interests of its merchants to be respected; within the Hanseatic towns themselves it tried to protect the political domination of the upper classes of urban bourgeoisie against middle and working class opposition movements. The Hanse was quite definitively of a class nature.

THE CAUSES OF SUCCESS...

By the end of the 14th century the Hanse had succeeded in conquering a dominant trading position in the North Sea and the Baltic.

Foreign competitors had been virtually eliminated, trade routes had been developed and enlarged, foreign business houses were subject to the association's authority, the political and economic positions of the Hanseatic merchants were stabilized by a series of privileges.

With the strength of its enormous economic potential, the Hanse was capable of successfully opposing even the biggest feudal powers. Its victory over King Valdemar IV of Denmark – sealed by the peace of Stralsund in 1370 – marked the height of its economic and political power.

The principal causes of its success were its economic power and technical advance – which lasted for a very long time in the field of navigation – its favourable geographical situation and the solidity of the links in the association of towns.

... AND OF DECLINE

In the 15th century the Hanse began to stagnate; in the 16th century the signs of decline were increasingly clear.

Dutch competition was gradually taking the lead over the Hanse in the North Sea and the Baltic; the birth of centralized states reduced its margin of political manoeuvering; the German princes encroached increasingly often on the autonomy of Hanseatic towns.

But the decisive causes of the decline of the Hanse lay less with the appearance of new outside factors than with the internal evolution of the Hanse itself.

The Hanse did not rest on a stable productive basis but on a role as intermediary between foreign producers, i.e. on commission trade.

"The law pursuant to which the autonomous development of merchant capital is in the inverse ratio to the degree of development of capitalist production is best seen in the history of commission trade (...) where the principal profit is not achieved by the exportation of products from their own countries, but by their role as an intermediary in the exchange of products from communities that are but little developed commercially and even economically, and by the exploitation of both producer countries. Here merchant capital is pure, separated from the extremes, the spheres of production between which it acts as an intermediary. That is one of the principal sources of its formation. But this monopoly of commission trade declines at the same time as the trade itself; it becomes endangered commensurately with the progress made in the economic development of the nations it exploited on both sides and whose absence of development was the basis of its existence.

For commission trade, that appears not only as the decline of a particular branch of commerce but also as a decline in the preponderance of purely merchant races and their commercial wealth based on the commission trade."
(Karl Marx, Das Kapital)

HANSE INFLUENCE IN THE BALTIC COUNTRIES

It is especially in the Baltic countries that the Hanse has left deep-rooted traces — both positive and negative.

Quite apart from the fact that its long and often pitiless economic domination considerably retarded the autonomous development of the middle class in Baltic and Scandinavian countries, the specific structure of the commission trade it practised — essentially the exchange of Western industrial products against raw materials and provisions from the East — quite definitely contributed to the establishment and maintenance for centuries of imbalance between these two regions in the distribution of work.

But on the whole the positive influences of the Hanse prevail.

Because of the network of stable commercial communications it created between Eastern, Western and Northern Europe, the commercial traffic increasingly indispensable to each of the countries concerned developed, in terms of goods but also in terms of technology and culture.

Though the Hanseatic merchant was at first guided in all his actions by the profit motive, he nevertheless encouraged the cultural development of a number of countries, by spreading or consolidating new middle class standards of living and by developing architecture and the sacred and secular arts. Community in these spheres is manifest wherever Hanse influence was felt.

Van schickinge unde vorderige des nedderste gherichtes.

ALBERT D'HAENENS

The World of the Hanse Today

The world of the Hanse is one of the first extensions of the West, one of its original overflows.
In it, Europe lives through the first synthesis of its specific virtualities, the first transfer of its exported surpluses. It is marginal space turned into urban concentration, the surplus produced in international traffic. It is the secularized monastic model, municipal management mastered, the urban entity systematically organized, the practice of mutual information, the priority of negotiation.

A CULTURAL MEMORY

Consider what subsists of this world of the Hanse as vast Hanseatic memories. Space memories, its urban spaces. Geometrical arteries, lofty symbolic towers, brick walls, extensive granaries, symmetrical facades, voluminous warehouses, mechanical cranes.
Retables and paintings, portraits and votive monuments, benches and chests. Personal memories of Hanseatic interiors.
Law books and census returns. Bills of exchange and accounts books. Wax tablets. Written memories in Hanseatic archives.
Graphic memories: emblematic views for each town, and hundreds of erudite titles: historiographic memories.

511. Hamburg Town Hall: a court scene.
Van Schicking unde Vorderinge des Neddersten Gherichtes.
Miniature illustrating the *Law Book of the city of Hamburg*, 1497.
Hamburg, Staatsarchiv.
Under a painting representing the Last Judgment there are two councillors, the secretary and, on the right, eleven burghers acting as municipal magistrates.
Before the table of justice the accused is accompanied by two sergeants carrying the white staff, the symbol of public authority; on the left, the plaintiff, bareheaded, states his case.
In the foreground, groups are discussing; on the right, a little to the side, a straw-hatted peasant is clutching his purse.
Outside, people throng to follow the debates. In the background: the town church and houses round the market-place.

ENOUGH TO IMPLANT IN THE FUNDAMENTAL

These Hanseatic memories constitute an indispensable part in the accomplishment of European projects.

Founder projects, if they are to succeed, need mobilizer aims. Techn(olog)ical means cannot alone ensure their dynamism and visibility. They also need a soul. Without one there can be no fertile projects; it founds them and mobilizes those who propose to carry them out.
A prospective imaginary quantity, certainly, allowing a glimpse of what Europe will be when European projects have led to something. A retrospective imaginary quantity, too, which recalls to mind what Europe was in earlier times. The imaginary quantity does not feed solely on the projection of gaps to be filled, of pre-visions to be put into concrete form. It seeks at the same time an original, an initial coherence to be progressively diluted to an incoherent present.
The retrospective imaginary quantity – in the West it invested in historian practice – ties up again with the original times and places. It knows them

419

again and so identifies its past incoherences, to be left behind, and its original coherence, to be re-installed.

In these times worked upon by major changes and by the setting up of founder projects, those who constitute Europe aspire to another Europe, integrated and with more in common, aware of itself and its specificity, coherent as it was originally.
But Europe seems to have forgotten what it was initially, to be confused about its origins. Yet the latter are real, not mythical or whimsical but historical; they really happened. It is therefore important to remember them and know them again, thereby reviving affective and symbolic references which render projects more beloved, guarantee their coherence long term and implant them in a common origin.

What subsists of the Hanseatic world is one of the places in which Europe can link up with its origins. The Hanseatic town with its main square and symbolic towers is like Rome with its sanctuary, Gothic cathedral and monastic space; places where Europeans can get back to their fundamental origins.

The purpose of this book is to show how Hanseatic enterprise helped to construct the original Europe, to revive something in which the western project can be implanted.

Indices

INDEX OF PERSONS

Abond 127
Abraham 15
Adalbert, archbishop of Bremen 105
Adam, burgher of Gotland 184
Adam of Bremen 52, 141
Adolphus II of Holstein 59, 392, 394
Albert the Bear 392
Albrecht, burgher of Dortmund 184
Albrecht, solicitor of Riga 184
Alexander IV 366
Amman, Jost 67, 72, 121, 127, 136, 138, 147, 151, 273
Anne (Saint) 48, 76, 301, 302, 350
Ansgar 335
Apengeter, H. 293
Arembrecht, burgher of Dortmund 184
Armenians 269
Arthur, king 74, 318, 415

Badoire, Thierry 239
Baillet, Jean 239
Bardi (family) 127
Barrat, Jean 235
Batory, Stephen 264
Bayonne (natives of) 230
Ben, Hans 197
Benecke, Paul 143, 384
Bening, Simon 131
Berck, Elisabeth 241
Berck, Tideman 241
Bernek, burgher of Groningen 184
Bernhart, burgher of Riga 184
Bettenhauser, Jakob 220
Bisschop, Jan de 244, 246
Blanque, Jean de le 234
Blödange, Conrad 184
Blökel 100
Bodecker, Bonaventure 230
Bokel, Pierre 68
Bompuis, Th. de 236
Bonhors, Thildemen 232
Bornemann, Hans 15
Bourdon of Mons 236
Boy, D.J. 301
Brabender, Heinrich 294
Bremen (natives of) 66, 140, 175, 184, 212, 271
Bretons 230, 231, 233, 235
Breughel the Elder, Peter 164
Brinner, Kaspar 121
Brömse (family) 78, 294
Brömse, Heinrich 78, 294
Brömse, Marguerite (née Köler) 407
Brunswick-Luneburg, dukes of 34, 109, 316

Bruxelles, Jean de 283
Bruyn the Elder, Bartholomew 222
Bülow, Nicolas 268
Bueri, Gerard 129
Bugenhagen 102
Burgundians (dukes of Burgundy) 180, 181, 230, 236, 255
Buschener, Jan den 19, 37
Bussmann, Johann 83

Campin, Robert 21
Casimir the Great 262, 263
Castilians 235
Charlemagne 318, 337, 415
Charles V of France 230
Charles VI of France 230
Charles VIII of France 230
Charles V of Germany 210, 230, 275, 409
Charles of Orleans 189
Christ 24, 143, 295-298, 318, 348, 349, 386
Christus, Petrus 78
Cistercians 13, 389
Cloot, Cornelis 237
Coenen, Adriaan 168
Cologne (natives of) 109, 175, 189, 223, 224, 230, 237, 241, 256, 393, 397
Copernic, Nicolas 368, 373
Cranach the Elder, Lucas 127
Custos, Raphaele 256

Danes 133
Danzig (natives of) 143, 181, 189, 212, 235, 239, 263
Davidovitch, prince of Smolensk 66, 184
Dax, M. 284
Deliot, Hubert 239
Dethard, burgher of Gotland 184
Diebel, Elias 155, 283
Dreyer, Benedikt 173
Dümmon, burgher of Lubeck 184
Dürer, Albert 17, 141, 217, 409
Dutchmen 53, 66, 102, 129, 133, 180, 217, 227, 230, 231, 232, 234, 235, 245, 260, 271, 289, 376, 394, 398, 408, 410, 416

Edward I of England 241
Edward II of England 241
Edward III of England 241
Edward IV of England 243, 245
Elizabeth I of England 195, 245
Englishmen 127, 133, 169, 189, 210, 230, 236, 241-248, 271
Essarts, Pierre des 238
Esthonians 157, 181, 212, 239
Evers le Jeune, Tönnies 289

Fancillion, Robert 229
Ferdinand (emperor) 275

Fiodor I Ivanovitch (czar) 271
Flemings 121, 127, 143, 169, 180, 210, 229, 232, 234, 250, 260, 279, 283, 284, 293, 335, 375, 392
Flemming, Hans 284, 289
Fra Mauro 169, 249
François I of France 230
Franconians 392
Frederic Barberousse 281
Frederick II 224
Frenchmen 136, 169, 210, 229-239
Frese, Daniel 24, 34, 311, 313, 316, 322
Frese, Theophilus W. 37
Friedrich, burgher of Lubeck 184
Frisians 66, 184, 392, 393
Fuggers (family) 83, 121, 227, 246, 410
Fugger, Jacob II 409

Garbers (family) 313
Gascons 136
Geismar (family) 350
Gildemeister, Otto 37
Giselbert, archbishop of Bremen 338
Gisze, Georg 2, 70, 71, 241
Godounoff, Boris 185
Goltzius 339
Gossaert, Jean 119
Gothan, Bartholomew 268
Gotlanders 66, 107, 178, 179, 184, 185, 189, 393, 394, 396
Grassi, Cristoforo 255
Greeks 393
Greverade, Adolf 143, 285
Greverade, Heinrich 143, 285
Grove, Lorenz 285
Grude, Klaus 294
Guicciardini, L. 209, 210

Haeseler 46, 324
Hamburgers 109, 124, 125, 175, 212, 224, 225, 236, 239, 271
Hardenrath, Johann 75
Hartwich 292, 293
Heinssen, Hans 27, 84
Helmstede, Heinrich 283
Henri IV of France 230, 234
Henry the Goth of Soest 184
Henry the Lion 59, 107, 281, 284, 316, 392, 394
Henry II of England 223, 393
Henry III of England 66, 224, 397
Henry IV of England 243
Henry VII of England 244
Henry VIII of England 244, 247
Hogenberg, Franz 209
Holbein the Younger, Hans 2, 63, 71, 86, 90, 115, 166, 192, 195, 201, 241, 244, 246
Holstein (count) 107, 109

INDICES

Holzschuher, Heinrich 141
Holzschuher, Hieronimus 141
Hovener, Albert 357
Hoyer, Sweder 294

Ilier, burgher of Soest 184
Inghelbrecht, Jan 176
Isenbrant, Adriaan 293
Italians 121, 124, 127, 179, 180, 210, 225, 227, 249-257, 269, 375
Ivan III (czar) 187, 227, 267, 408
Ivan IV the Terrible (czar) 271

Jaster, Marten 28, 320
Jean, king of Poland 370

Kannengieser, Sybille 222
Kedin, Johannes 152
Kemmer, Hans 86
Kinot, Johann 184
Klokow, Joachim 357
Kraft, Adam 265
Kruse, Windel 86

Ladislaus the Short 261
Lautensack the Elder, Paul 73
Le Moisne 239
Lenzi, Domenico 253
Lerche, Vincent 302
Lettonians 66, 181, 184, 212, 235, 395
Lieutics 392
Livonians 178, 179, 181, 189, 230, 234, 268, 271
Lorichs, Melchior 167
Lothair III 393
Louis of Bavaria 224
Louis XI of France 230, 231
Lubeck (natives of) 66, 78, 83, 124, 125, 175, 181, 184, 197, 198, 212, 224, 225, 227, 230, 234, 236, 239, 256, 267, 271, 353, 395, 407
Luther 302, 313

Marborg, Heinrich 348
Marguerite de Constantinople, countess of Flanders 66, 175, 397
Mary (virgin) 34, 40, 56-61, 73, 77, 78, 100, 101, 143, 197, 205, 239, 259, 283-286, 292, 293, 294, 296, 297, 298, 305, 328, 348, 349, 357, 384, 385
Master John 338
Master of the Altor Halepagen 77
Master of the life of Mary 78, 219
Master W.A. 164
Maximilian of Austria 181
Medicis (family) 129, 143, 250
Melanchton 313
Member, burgher of Lubeck 184
Memling, Hans 40, 44, 129, 143, 219, 227, 285, 384, 386
Mercator, Gerard 232, 313
Metsijs, Jan 213
Middelborch, Cord 83
Mielich, Hans 405
Mildehöved, Marquardus 86
Mornewech, Reinekinus 124
Morneweg, Bertram 296, 297
Münster, Sebastian 151, 155
Müntzer, Dorothea 141
Mulich, merchant of Lubeck 225

Neudörfer the Elder, Johann 121
Nicholas, bishop of Riga 184
Nicholas (saint) 40, 41, 48, 76, 301, 302, 356
Normans 230, 232, 234, 238
Norwegians 197, 205
Nuremberg (natives of) 225, 227

Obotrites 392
Oehm (family) 385
Olaus Magnus 169
Olsens, J.W. 202
Olva, Jean 238
Osiander, Andrew 18
Otton I 312

Pape, Paschier de 83
Papebroeck, Daniel 208
Parler 19
Pasqualini the Younger, J. 283
Pasture, Roger de la 143
Peck, Nikolaus 287
Pencz, Georg 38
Peruzzi (family) 127
Philip the Fair of France 230
Philip the Handsome of France 181
Piast (dynasty) 260
Pointe, Arnoult de la 137
Poland (natives of) 141, 181
Polleke, A. 284
Pomerania (natives of) 202, 241
Portinari, Tommaso 129, 143, 250
Portuguese 169, 210
Poullier of Mons 236
Pourbus, Peter 83, 413
Praun, Stefan 73
Prussians 54, 178, 179, 181, 189, 230, 269

Rambach 101
Raponde, Dine 236
Regenbode, burgher of Gotland 184
Reichel, Hans 375
Reichenborn, J.J. 198
Reymers, Hinrick 34, 311, 316, 321
Rhinelanders 175, 219-227, 260, 392
Richard the Lion Heart 207
Richard II of England 230, 242

Rimbert 335
Rinck, Hermann III 222
Rinck, Johann 219
Rode, Hermen 38
Roede, Pierre de 68
Roland 19, 105, 336, 337
Rudolph II (emperor) 245
Ruge, Hans 36
Russians 68, 183-187, 267-271, 408

Sachs, Hans 244, 246
Sanderus, Antoine 179
Saxons 60, 124, 178, 189, 202, 239, 260, 281, 392, 393
Scandinavians 393, 396
Scarpagnino 256
Schilling the Younger, Diebold 105
Schultz, Georg 315
Schwerin, Heinrich 357
Sigismond (emperor) 238
Sigismond Augustus of Poland 264, 375
Slavs 94, 157, 158
Sluk, Albrecht, burgher of Riga 184
Smet, Hans 348
Sommer, M. 284
Sonnenschein, Hans 86
Southern Germans 210, 227, 230, 256, 376, 398, 410
Spaniards 169, 210, 233, 235
Spavento, Giorgio 256
Springintgut, Johann 86
Stalburg, Claus 83
Steiner, G.Fr. 74
Sudermann, Heinrich 212, 215, 402, 413
Sudeten 263
Suttmeier, Gert 322
Swarte, Christian 293
Swedes 133, 185, 264

Tani, Angelo di Jacopo 143
Teutonic Order 54, 56, 57, 131, 134, 160, 232, 233, 235, 237, 261, 262, 274, 350, 365, 367, 375, 399, 407
Thibaud, count of Champagne 230
Thiery, Loys 83
Töbing, Georg IV 313

Up dem Borne, Peter 322
Ursula (saint) 40, 227, 219, 311

Valkenborgh, Jean de 283
Van den Block, Abraham 375
Van den Bunen, François 238
Van der Borcht II, Pieter 210
Van der Goes, Hugo 250
Van Eyerverwe, Jan 413
Van Liere, Arnold 91
Vannarden, Gerhart 232
Van Rijswijck, Jean 283

Van Steene, Hinrick 68
Van Uden, Lucas 215
Veckinchusen (brothers) 125, 141, 225, 256
Veckinchusen, Hildebrandt 233, 235, 236, 238
Volker, burgher of Groningen 184
Volkin 184
von Bentheim, Lüder 37, 338
von Breydenbach, Bernard 160
von der Heide, H. 285
von Geldersen, Vicko 125
von Reesen, Bernhard 217
von Salza, Hermann 56, 365
von Soest, Albert 322
von Soest, Johann 372, 373
von Sulinge, Dietrich 350
von Utrecht, Jacob 88
von Wickede, Thomas 289

Wagenaer 169
Wagrians 392
Walter, burgher of Riga 184
Walter, K. 294
Warendrop, Heinrich 236
Wedich, Hermann 63
Wedigh, Hermann Hildebrandt 115
Weiditz, Hans 221
Welser (family) 83, 246
Wendish towns (natives of) 58, 59, 107, 178, 179, 181, 189, 202, 212, 230, 241, 395
Wessel, Franz 77, 354
Westfal, Elizabeth 78
Westphalians 41, 60, 175, 178, 184, 189, 202, 230, 241, 392, 394
Wolgemut, Michael 51
Wulflam, Bertram 361
Wullenwever, Jurgen 289, 410

Ypres, Johann d' 124

Zeisig, Heinrich 184

GEOGRAPHICAL NAMES

Aa (the) 57
Aarhus 52
Abbeville 236, 238
Aix-la-Chapelle 26, 77
Akkom 56
Alexandria 256
Alsace 137, 221, 225
Alster (the) 167
Amiens 239
Amsterdam 102, 163
Anatolia 2
Anklam 52, 58
Antwerp 16, 37, 45, 67, 75, 91, 93, 121, 140, 145, 147, 152, 163, 170, 181, 207-215, 217, 230, 239, 244, 246, 279, 283, 354, 402, 408, 409, 412
Archangel 271, 408
Ardenburg 180
Arras 187, 232, 238
Artois 187
Atlantic 276
Augsburg 137, 181, 195
Austria 207
Avignon 127, 225

Bâle 220
Balkans 263
Baltic (Space) 13, 15, 18, 41, 51, 52, 107, 123, 129, 132-136, 138, 139, 157, 162, 169, 180, 185, 189, 212, 217, 219, 224, 227, 234, 241, 242, 243, 245, 246, 249, 259-264, 267, 271, 273, 275, 276, 277, 279, 281, 289, 335, 353, 359, 389, 392, 395, 396, 406, 410, 415, 416, 417
Bapaume 230
Bardowick 107, 316
Barents Sea 271
Bayonne 236
Belt (the) 181
Bergen 47, 72, 127, 136, 140, 150, 160, 173, 180, 189, 191, 197-205, 234, 274, 303, 356, 397, 408, 409
Bergen-op-Zoom 140, 181
Berlin 105
Biscay 134, 180, 274
Biscay (Bay of) 242, 274
Black Sea 185, 259
Bohemia 263
Bordeaux 131, 235
Boston 241, 244, 397
Bourgneuf 234, 235, 236, 275
Brabant 181, 208, 223, 225, 354, 408
Brandenburg 135, 392, 400
Braunsberg 261
Bremen 19, 21, 32, 35, 37, 48, 66, 72, 77, 98, 105, 109, 111, 140, 141, 152, 158, 160, 161, 175, 184, 192, 197, 212, 213, 215, 227, 239, 271, 274, 335-341, 393, 402, 413, — *Roland* 19, 105, 336, 337 — *Town Hall* 19, 35, 111, 337, 338, 339, 341 — *Schütting* 37, 335, 337
Brest 236
British Isles 162
Brittany 232, 234
Brouage 212, 235
Bruges 40, 44, 68, 75, 78, 83, 121, 123, 124, 129, 131, 134, 139, 140, 143, 147, 173, 175-181, 189, 191, 207, 210, 217, 219, 227, 229, 230, 235, 236, 238, 239, 250, 256, 268, 274, 279, 283, 293, 296, 354, 367, 378, 397, 398, 400, 408, 409, 413
Brunswick 23, 113, 124, 137, 239, 284, 311, 392, 398, 401
Buda 225
Buxtehude 77
Byzantine (World) 185, 217

Cambrai 232, 239
Carpathians 263
Castille 180, 235, 401
Catalonia 180
Champagne (fairs) 134, 223, 224, 230, 237
Channel (the) 242
Chartres 337
Chelmno 365
Cherbourg 230
Coblentz 207
Cologne 2, 32, 48, 63, 75, 77, 97, 98, 101, 102, 103, 107, 109, 111, 115, 121, 122, 127, 133, 136, 175, 181, 189, 208, 215, 217, 219, 222, 223, 224, 225, 227, 230, 235, 241, 243, 247, 256, 274, 281, 393, 397, 399, 401, 408, 412
Comines 232
Compostelle 77
Copenhagen 52
Cracow 225, 233, 263, 269, 378, 399
Crimea 185
Culm 52

Damme 131, 161, 175
Danzig 2, 32, 37, 47, 48, 52, 54, 56, 61, 72, 90, 134, 135, 143, 149, 152, 154, 162, 164, 168, 169, 181, 189, 212, 215, 217, 222, 227, 232, 233, 234, 235, 236, 238, 261, 263, 274, 365, 367, 368, 375-386, 393, 397, 401, 402, 410, 412 — *Arthushof* 37, 72, 90, 375
Denmark 107, 112, 123, 125, 223, 274, 281, 393, 401, 408, 410, 416
Deventer 180, 229
Dieppe 230, 232
Dinant 139, 223
Dixmude 187

Dniepr (the) 185, 269
Dniestr (the) 185
Dordrecht 180, 237
Dorpat 52, 187, 235, 267, 399
Dortmund 23, 66, 184, 393, 398, 400, 401
Drausensee 56
Duisburg 239
Duna (the) 269
Dwina (the) 269

East (Byzantine) 217, 229, 236, 378
East (of the Elbe) 11, 13, 23, 38, 51, 52, 66, 132, 133, 134, 139, 145, 207, 224, 262, 263, 264, 268, 271, 336, 368, 389, 392, 397, 399, 417
Ecluse 131
Einbeck 137, 311
Einsiedeln 77
Elbe (the) 11, 13, 38, 52, 109, 134, 135, 162, 167, 168, 274, 275, 392, 393, 415
Elbing 52, 54, 57, 160, 161, 245, 261, 264, 395
Empire (Holy Roman) 179, 195, 245, 269, 399, 407, 412
England 66, 72, 77, 107, 109, 129, 135, 136, 140, 157, 170, 181, 189, 205, 217, 219, 222, 223, 224, 225, 230, 232, 236, 241-247, 259, 261, 274, 275, 276, 336, 353, 375, 393, 396, 397, 401, 408
Erfurt 399
Esthonia 157
Europe 7, 11, 127, 141, 224, 249, 252, 376, 389, 403, 405, 415, 419, 420
Europe (East) 132-136, 138, 139, 145, 229, 232, 367, 392, 417
Europe (mid-central) 53, 61, 132, 136, 138, 139, 232, 274, 277
Europe (North) 131, 133-136, 145, 173, 179, 185, 187, 207, 219, 221, 229, 238, 246, 312, 403, 408, 417
Europe (North-East) 107, 406
Europe (North-West) 53, 134, 135, 136, 138, 143, 145, 219, 392, 415
Europa (South) 109, 123, 136, 161, 208, 225, 227, 406, 410
Europe (South-East) 139
Europa (West) 53, 133, 139, 140, 161, 170, 230, 277, 406, 410, 417, 419, 420
Falsterbo 167, 234
Falun 139
Faroe (islands) 274
Fehmarn 150
Fellin 52
Finland 51, 52, 274, 378, 408
Finland (Gulf of) 162, 275, 399
Flanders 53, 66, 77, 78, 102, 121, 124, 127, 129, 134, 135, 140, 143; 150, 175, 180, 187, 223, 229, 232, 234, 236, 256, 260, 261, 267, 279, 292, 293, 335, 353, 357, 372, 373, 375, 376, 380, 393, 398, 400
Florence 180, 250, 253
France 77, 131, 169, 186, 210, 217, 221, 229, 232, 235, 238, 239, 241, 246, 274, 401
France (North) 134, 229, 232
France (South-West) 244, 246
Frankenburg 261
Frankfort-on-Main 83, 137, 181, 223, 224, 225, 227
Frankfort-on-Oder 141, 399
Friesland 157, 158, 392, 393
Frische'Haff 56

Garda (lake) 73
Gascony 235
Genoa 180, 225, 236, 249, 255, 256
Germany 107, 185, 207, 219, 225, 245, 255, 259, 260, 269, 271, 296, 394, 406
Germany (Central) 83, 121, 124, 139, 225, 365
Germany (East) 141
Germany (Lower) 53, 132, 139, 274
Germany (North) 30, 41, 107, 132, 137, 150, 179, 223, 224, 246, 293, 302, 327, 355, 365, 407, 415
Germany (North-West) 140, 392
Germany (South) 121, 217, 225, 227, 230, 246, 256, 373, 376, 398, 410
Ghent 124, 131, 140, 175, 279, 296
Goslar 48, 72, 84, 110, 137, 311, 343-351, 393, 401, 405
Gothard (mountain pass) 220
Gotland 52, 60, 66, 107, 170, 178, 179, 184, 185, 189, 267, 269, 275, 393, 394, 395, 396, 397, 400, 401
Gravelines 143
Greece 131, 393
Greifswald 52, 58, 225, 354
Groningen 66, 184, 269

Hedeby (Haithabu) 393
Hälsingborg 52
Halicz 261
Hamburg 15, 33, 43, 48, 52, 71, 72, 77, 83, 86, 94-98, 100-103, 107, 109, 112, 113, 114, 115, 121, 122, 124, 127, 147, 148, 149, 152, 162, 167, 170, 175, 180, 197, 208, 212, 213, 215, 217, 225, 227, 232, 234, 236, 238, 271, 274, 275, 311, 335, 354, 398, 402, 412, 413, 419
Hameln 311
Hanover 311
Harfleur 230
Harz 223
Heiligenthal 15
Helmstedt 311
Herford 124
Hildesheim 239

Holland 129, 139, 152, 169, 175, 181, 217, 225, 244, 245, 260, 336
Holstein 107, 109, 275, 281, 282, 392, 393, 394, 398
Honfleur 230
Hull 241
Hungary 131, 150, 262, 378, 410
Huy 127

Iceland 261, 274, 276
Ilmen (lake) 185
Ipswich 241
Italy 73, 121, 127, 129, 131, 134, 135, 205, 210, 217, 219, 220, 246, 249-257
Ivangorod 271

Jumne 393
Jutland 275, 393

Kalmar 52, 399
Kammin 52
Kampen 137, 230, 234, 235
Kiel 159, 398
Kiev 183, 185
Königsberg 52, 54, 134, 136, 181, 367, 378
Kolberg 53, 134
Korbach 222

Ladoga (lake) 185
Languedoc 236
Laon 239
La Rochelle 131, 230, 235
Leipzig 141, 227
Lendit 236, 237
Lens 232
Lierre 238
Lille 239
Linköping 52
Lisbon 236, 264
Lithuania 235, 263
Livonia 66, 150, 178, 179, 181, 230, 234, 235, 244, 261, 267, 268, 269, 271, 391, 398, 400, 408
Lofoten (islands) 133
Loire (the) 235
London 109, 123, 144, 145, 173, 180, 189, 191, 207, 217, 219, 224, 229, 236, 241, 242, 274, 367, 393, 397, 408, — *Stalhof* 2, 63, 70, 71, 78, 86, 90, 115, 144, 175, 180, 189-196, 223, 230, 241, 242, 243, 244, 246, 247, 397, 408, 409
Louvain 143, 313
Low Countries 102, 135, 152, 180, 207, 223, 246, 274, 275, 313, 336, 399, 402, 408, 410, 412
Lübeck 13, 17, 21, 23, 27, 33, 37, 38, 41, 47, 48, 51, 52, 54, 56, 57, 59, 60, 61, 66, 71, 72, 78, 83, 84, 86, 93, 96-103, 107,

109, 111, 112, 113, 124, 125, 127, 129, 134, 141, 143, 150, 152, 155, 157, 158, 159, 162, 173, 175, 178, 179, 180, 181, 184, 185, 197, 198, 205, 208, 212, 213, 215, 217, 219, 224, 225, 227, 229, 232, 234, 235, 238, 239, 245, 256, 261, 262, 264, 267, 268, 271, 274, 275, 279, 281-309, 311, 312, 327, 329, 353, 354, 357, 367, 372, 378, 393-398, 400, 401, 402, 407, 410, 412, 413, 415 — *House of the Captains* 37, 48, 301-305 — *St. Jacques' Church* 78, 294, 295 — *The Holy Ghost hospital* 93, 99, 100, 101, 296-299 — *Marienkirche* 143, 197, 239, 285, 292, 293, 296, 329, 357 — *Cathedral* 268, 284 — *Schütting* 173 — *Town Hall* 286-291, 296, 355
Lublin 261
Lucca 180
Lucerne 105
Lund 52
Lune (abbey) 330-333
Luneburg 15, 19, 24, 26, 27, 28, 31, 32, 33, 34, 36, 46, 48, 52, 71, 83, 86, 94, 95, 96, 102, 103, 107, 109, 111, 134, 150, 229, 231, 235, 274, 279, 307, 311-333, 398, 415 — *St. Nicholas* 15 — *Town Hall* 24, 26, 27, 28, 31, 32, 33, 34, 36, 109, 316-323, 415 — *St. John's Church* 83, 328 — *St-Michael's abbey* 312
Lvov (Lemberg) 269, 378
Lynn 241

Magdeburg 48, 97, 110, 124, 239, 329, 365
Mainz 221, 225
Malines 140
Malmö 52
Marienburg 235, 237, 367
Maubeuge 232
Mazovia 261, 263, 264
Mecklenburg 59, 135, 150, 202, 392, 398
Mediterranean regions 139, 221, 249, 255, 259, 410
Memel 52
Meuse (the) 127, 139, 399
Mezzogiorno 249
Milan 225
Moldavia 263
Mons 236
Montivilliers 233
Moscow 68, 187, 269, 408
Moselle 136, 221
Motlawa (the) 376
Munich 137
Münster 23, 30, 32, 66, 184

Nantes 235, 236
Narew (the) 263

Narva 52, 235, 239, 271, 408
Neuwerk 168
Neva 185, 393
Newcastle 241
Niederich 63
Niemen 398
Normandy 230, 232, 233
North Sea 7, 51, 107, 132, 133, 138, 157, 162, 168, 169, 189, 217, 219, 223, 225, 227, 232, 245, 255, 261, 273, 276, 393, 397, 415, 416
Norway 77, 133, 135, 140, 170, 197, 205, 217, 223, 244, 261, 274, 276, 336, 393, 397, 402, 408
Novgorod 68, 72, 78, 107, 133, 140, 167, 173, 175, 180, 183-187, 189, 191, 197, 205, 217, 219, 227, 261, 264, 267, 268, 269, 271, 274, 357, 393, 396, 397, 408
Nuremberg 18, 51, 65, 84, 99, 111, 121, 139, 141, 181, 225, 227, 265
Nyköping 52

Odense 52
Oder (the) 132, 168, 261, 392
Øresund 275
Oldesloe 109
Oleron 239
Onega (lake) 185
Orkneys (islands) 274
Orléans 131
Oslo 274
Oudenaarde 151

Paderborn 137
Paris 225, 231, 238, 239
Peene (the) 58
Pernau 52, 181, 232
Po (the) 249
Poitou 131, 235
Poland 57, 134, 135, 138, 141, 160, 232, 233, 259-265, 375, 376, 384
Polotsk 184, 235, 269
Pomerania 52, 59, 97, 150, 202, 260, 261, 262, 263, 264, 376, 400
Pomerania Minor 56
Poperinghe 187
Portugal 169, 210, 217, 219, 249, 274, 410
Posen 141
Pregolia (the) 54
Provence 230
Prussia 53, 54, 59, 74, 131, 134, 135, 150, 152, 160, 171, 178, 179, 189, 230, 235, 236, 263, 264, 269, 365, 366, 375, 376, 391, 398, 399, 400, 401, 407, 408
Pskov 268, 271

Raeren 139, 144
Rammelberg (the) 343

Ratisbonne 405
Ratzeburg 284
Ravensburg 227
Reims 230
Reval (Tallinn) 37, 48, 52, 72, 134, 180, 181, 187, 212, 217, 232, 235, 238, 239, 268, 274, 279, 303, 368, 398, 399
Rhine 131, 136, 139, 150, 157, 162, 167, 175, 207, 208, 219-227, 229, 241, 260, 274, 275, 392, 393, 400, 408
Riga 33, 48, 52, 66, 71, 72, 127, 134, 181, 184, 187, 212, 232, 235, 236, 269, 274, 275, 296, 303, 367, 395, 396, 398, 400
Rome 77, 127, 420
Roskilde 52
Rostock 32, 48, 52, 58, 59, 72, 181, 212, 213, 274, 287, 354, 395, 398
Rouen 229, 232, 233, 234, 236
Rügen 97
Russia 68, 123, 136, 138, 160, 184, 185, 223, 224, 229, 232, 244, 256, 261, 263, 267-271, 274, 353, 393, 394, 401, 407
Ruthenia 261

St. Bernard (mountain pass) 220
Saint-Denis 236
Saintes 235
Saint-Gall 235
Saint-Jean d'Angély 235
Saint-Omer 187, 232, 236, 237
Samland (peninsula) 378
Sandomir 261
Saremaa (island) 161
Saxony 48, 60, 107, 109, 134, 157, 178, 179, 189, 202, 260, 261, 281, 308, 327, 336, 391, 392, 393, 398, 400
Scandinavia 53, 133, 136, 139, 157, 158, 212, 224, 244, 246, 249, 267, 274, 335, 353, 393, 396, 407
Scandinavian peninsula 72, 150, 171, 223, 225, 227
Scheldt (the) 215
Schleswig 52, 60, 223, 329, 393
Schwerin (lake) 57
Schotland 68, 77, 180, 274, 367
Setubal 236
Shetlands (islands) 274, 276
Siberia 271
Siegburg 139
Siegerland 145, 223
Silesia 262, 263
Skagen (cape) 271
Skagerrak 275
Skanör 136, 234
Slovakia 139
Smolensk 184, 217, 269, 396
Soest 13, 66, 184, 239, 393, 395
Soissons 239
Solingen 236, 237

Southwark 192
Spain 72, 131, 166, 169, 180, 210, 217, 233, 235, 274, 276, 402, 410
Stade 109, 113, 195
Stecknitz (Canal) 134, 307, 312
Stendal 124
Stettin 52, 72, 152, 212, 235, 263, 274, 393
Stockholm 52, 72, 274, 396, 399
Stralsund 21, 23, 33, 38, 48, 52, 58, 68, 71, 77, 83, 97, 151, 152, 154, 159, 168, 181, 183, 212, 213, 263, 271, 279, 287, 353-363, 372, 398, 403, 406 — *St. Nicholas* 68, 83, 183, 271, 354, 355, 356, 357, 372
Strasburg 221, 223, 225
Sund (the) 135, 181, 234, 235, 289, 376, 410
Sweden 51, 52, 107, 141, 150, 178, 179, 262, 267, 274, 275, 378, 401, 410

Tczew 261
Thames (the) 189, 223, 393
Thuringia 225
Torhout 335
Toruń 23, 52, 54, 57, 68, 74, 233, 259, 264, 267, 269, 287, 365-373, 379 — *Arthushof* 74
Toulouse 230, 236
Tournai 137, 140, 186, 187
Transylvania 139
Trave (the) 59, 281, 282, 283, 307, 392, 393
Troyes 230
Truso 393
Turku 52

Ukraine 269
Ulm 225
Utrecht 180, 243

Valenciennes 232, 236, 239
Vendée 232
Venice 2, 53, 139, 180, 225, 249, 256, 257 — *Fondaco dei Tedeschi* 139, 255, 256
Verden 329
Verona 337
Visby 52, 53, 60, 61, 107, 185, 239, 274, 275, 395, 396, 397, 400
Vistula (the) (Weichsel) 56, 155, 261, 263, 264, 267, 365, 378, 398
Vitebsk 184, 269
Volga (the) 132
Volhynia 269
Volkach 25
Volkhov (the) 167, 183, 185, 268, 393
Vyborg 52

Wakenitz (the) 59, 281, 282
Wallonia 134
Warneton 187
Warsaw 261
Wattenmeer 175
Wenden 52
Wendish Towns 52, 58, 59, 107, 150, 178, 189, 230, 264, 391, 398, 400, 401
Wervick 187
Weser (the) 167, 335, 336
West 11, 13, 15, 38, 63, 66, 133, 134, 135, 139, 145, 207, 261, 262, 263, 264, 267, 268, 271, 279, 313, 336, 366, 370, 376, 389, 393, 415, 419, 420
Westminster 192
Westphalia 41, 48, 60, 123, 150, 175, 178, 179, 189, 202, 223, 230, 241, 256, 261, 289, 336, 391, 392, 393, 394, 398, 399, 400
White Sea 217, 271
Wismar 18, 32, 42, 43, 52, 57, 59, 159, 168, 171, 181, 354, 395, 398
Wittenberg 313
Wolin (island) 168, 393
Wroclaw 22, 141, 227, 236, 263, 368, 399

Yarmouth 241
Ypres 124, 140, 187, 229

Zealand 207, 232
Zuiderzee 175, 398, 399
Zurich 121
Zwin 175, 180, 181, 234

PHOTOGRAPHS

Centre de Recherches sur la Communication en Histoire, Université de Louvain. Louvain-la-Neuve (Jean-Jacques Rousseau) 1, 2, 12, 13, 16, 17, 18, 19, 20, 21, 22, 23, 24, 25, 26, 27, 28, 29, 30, 31, 32, 33, 34, 36, 38, 41, 45, 47, 48, 69, 76, 77, 81, 82, 83, 84, 86, 87, 88, 89, 90, 91, 92, 98, 99, 101, 102, 106, 107, 108, 124, 129, 130, 149, 153, 154, 155, 156, 171, 172, 173, 176, 177, 178, 180, 184, 199, 219, 272, 273, 277, 278, 279, 280, 281, 283, 284, 285, 287, 288, 289, 290, 291, 292, 293, 294, 297, 298, 299, 300, 301, 302, 303, 304, 305, 306, 307, 308, 309, 310, 311, 312, 313, 314, 317, 319, 320, 322, 323, 324, 325, 326, 327, 328, 329, 330, 331, 332, 333, 334, 335, 336, 337, 338, 339, 340, 341, 343, 344, 345, 346, 347, 349, 350, 351, 352, 353, 354, 355, 356, 357, 358, 359, 360, 361, 362, 366, 367, 368, 369, 370, 371, 372, 373, 374, 375, 376, 377, 378, 379, 380, 381, 383, 385, 386, 387, 388, 389, 390, 391, 393, 394, 395, 396, 397, 398, 399, 401, 402, 404, 405, 406, 407, 408, 409, 410, 411, 412, 413, 414, 415, 416, 417, 418, 419, 420, 421, 422, 423, 424, 425, 426, 427, 429, 433, 434, 435, 437, 438, 439, 440, 442, 444, 445, 446, 447, 448, 449, 450, 451, 452, 453, 454, 455, 456, 457, 458, 459, 460, 461, 462, 463, 464, 465, 466, 467, 468, 469, 470, 471, 472, 473, 474, 475, 476, 477, 478, 479, 480, 481, 482, 483, 484, 485, 486, 487, 488, 489, 490, 491, 492, 493, 494, 497, 499, 503, 505, 506, 510

Centre de Recherches sur la Communication en Histoire, Université de Louvain. Louvain-la-Neuve (Thomas David) 42, 62, 201, 202, 207, 208, 209, 210, 211, 212, 213, 214, 215, 216, 217, 218, 500

Foto Giacomelli, Venice 270

Karl-Heinz Jürgens, Cologne 10, 11, 42, 430, 432

Jean Vigne, Paris 97, 242, 274, 275

Amsterdam, Rijksmuseum, Prentenkabinet 162
Antwerp, Koninklijk Museum voor Schone Kunsten 228
Antwerp, Museum Plantin-Moretus 223, 224

– Nationaal Scheepvaartmuseum 95, 161, 225
– Prentenkabinet 143, 221, 222
– Stadsarchief 220
Arras, Bibliothèque Municipale 97, 242, 274, 275
Augsburg, Staatsgalerie 507
Bâle, Staatsarchiv 233
Bergen, Historiske Museum 200
– Det Hanseatiske Museum 207, 208, 209, 210, 211, 212, 213, 214
– Det Hanseatiske Museum Archiv 205, 206
Berlin, Archiv für Kunst und Geschichte 74, 158
– Museum für Islamische Kunst 250
– Staatliche Museen, Preussischer Kulturbesitz frontispice, 70, 71, 109, 115, 128
Bremen, Landesmuseum für Kunst und Geschichte 7, 9, 35, 105, 196, 403
– Ludwig Roselius-Sammlung 78
Bremerhaven, Deutsche Schiffahrtsmuseum 159
Bruges, Béguinage 174
– Groeningemuseum 39, 509
– St-Janshospitaal 43, 231, 238
– Stadsarchief 175, 176, 177, 178, 179
– Stadsbibliotheek 246
– Stedelijke Musea 85
Brunswick, Herzog Anton Ulrich-Museum 508
Brussels, Bibliothèque Royale Albert Ier 52, 67, 72, 111, 112, 114, 122, 125, 126, 134, 139, 140, 142, 144, 151, 282
– Institut Royal du Patrimoine Artistique, A.C.L. 182
– Musées Royaux des Beaux-Arts 3, 164
Cologne, Kölnisches Stadtmuseum 229, 232, 235, 236, 237
– Historisches Archiv 75
Dordrecht, Gemeentearchief 248
Dresde, Gemäldegalerie 230
Florence, Uffizi 263, 264
– Biblioteca Laurenziana 265
– Biblioteca Nazionale Centrale 262
Frankfort, Städelsches Kunstinstitut 165
Genua, Civico Museo Navale 268
Genève, Bibliothèque publique et universitaire 239
Gouda, Stedelijk Museum Het Catharina Gasthuis 147
Greifswald, Universitätsbibliothek 244
Hamburg, Kunsthalle 227
– Staatsarchiv 133, 135, 136, 152, 157, 160, 166, 511
– Staats- und Universitätsbibliothek 44
Kampen, Stadsarchief 123
Kansas City, William Rockhill Nelson Gallery of Art and Atkins Museum of Fine Arts 80
La Haye, Koninklijke Bibliotheek 167
Leningrad, Bibliothèque Saltychov-Shchedrin 190
Liège, Bibliothèque de l'Université 243, 247
Lille, Archives du Nord 230
London, British Museum 96, 103, 191, 192, 194, 257, 258, 259, 260, 266, 267
– London Museum 131, 132, 193
– Victoria and Albert Museum 195
Lubeck, Stadtarchiv 153, 154, 155, 156, 499
Luzern, Korporationsgemeinde der Stadt Luzern 104
München, Alte Pinakothek 79
– Bayerisches Staatsbibliothek 117
– Interfoto F. Raüm 321
– Staatliche Graphische Sammlungen 234
Münster, Stadtarchiv 226
New York, The Metropolitan Museum of Art 8, 63, 116
Novgorod, Musée historique 187, 188, 189
Nuremberg, Germanisches Nationalmuseum 4, 6, 50, 65, 73, 113, 150, 276
Oxford, Bodleian 66, 146, 495
Paris, Bibliothèque de l'Arsenal 64
– Bibliothèque Nationale 64, 94, 169, 269, 400
Ratisbonne, Stadtarchiv 502
Rouen, Bibliothèque Municipale 127, 245
Schwerin, Staatliches Museum 41
Stralsund, Stadtarchiv 141, 428, 453, 501, 504
– Eglise Saint-Nicolas 69, 83, 184, 280
Utrecht, Centraal Museum 93
Venice, Biblioteca Nazionale Marciana 261
– Museo Correr 271
Volkach, Stadtarchiv 14, 15
Washington, National Gallery 110
Wien, Graphische Sammlung Albertina 37
– Kunsthistorisches Museum 197

DIAGRAMS AND MAPS

Stéphane Lebbe. Louvain-la-Neuve 5, 54, 55, 56, 57, 58, 59, 60, 61, 120, 185, 186, 203, 253, 254, 255, 342, 384, 392, 496, 498

Kuratorium für Vergleichende Städtgeschichte. Münster University 51, 53, 504

PUBLISHED ON THE INITIATIVE OF THE BANQUE PARIBAS BELGIQUE IN ENGLISH,
GERMAN, FRENCH AND DUTCH IN SEPTEMBER 1984.
DESIGNED BY LOUIS VAN DEN EEDE.
TEXT COMPOSED IN SABON 12 BY PHOTOCOMPO CENTER, BRUSSELS.
PRINTED BY LANNOO, TIELT, ON PAPER BY KONINKLIJKE NEDERLANDSE PAPIERFABRIEKEN.
BLACK AND WHITE ILLUSTRATIONS AND COLOUR SEPARATIONS BY NEW LINE, ARRIGORRIAGA - BILBAO.
BINDING BY BRANDT, WEESP.